The Flocks of the Wamani

Llamas at dawn in their corral, Pallqa, Ayacucho.

The Flocks of the Wamani

A Study of Llama Herders on the Punas of Ayacucho, Peru

Kent V. Flannery
Joyce Marcus
Museum of Anthropology
University of Michigan
Ann Arbor, Michigan

Robert G. Reynolds
Department of Computer Science
Wayne State University
Detroit, Michigan

Academic Press, Inc.
Harcourt Brace Jovanovich, Publishers
San Diego   New York   Berkeley   Boston
London   Sydney   Tokyo   Toronto

ACADEMIC PRESS, INC.
San Diego, California 92101

United Kingdom Edition published by
ACADEMIC PRESS LIMITED
24-28 Oval Road, London NW1 7DX

Library of Congress Cataloging-in-Publication Data

Flannery, Kent V.
    The flocks of the Wamani : a study of llama herders on the punas
of Ayacucho, Peru / Kent V. Flannery, Joyce Marcus, Robert G.
Reynolds.
        p.   cm.
    Bibliography: p.
    Includes index.
    ISBN 0-12-259835-0 (alk. paper). ISBN 0-12-259836-9 (pbk. : alk.
paper)
    1. Wamani Indians—Domestic animals. 2. Llamas—Peru—Ayacucho
(Dept.) 3. Indians of South America—Peru—Ayacucho (Dept.)-
-Domestic animals. 4. Indians of South America—Peru—Ayacucho
(Dept.)Antiquities. 5. Ayacucho (Peru : Dept.)—Antiquities.
6. Peru—Antiquities.   I. Marcus, Joyce. II. Reynolds, Robert G.
(Robert Gene) III. Title.
F3430.1.W35F53   1989
636.2'96'0985292—dc19   88-7500
                                                           CIP

PRINTED IN THE UNITED STATES OF AMERICA
89 90 91 92   9 8 7 6 5 4 3 2 1

for our *llamkaccmasi*

RAMIRO MATOS

whose love of the puna, and all things Quechua,
has been an inspiration

Contents

Preface

One of the most hotly debated subjects of the last two decades is the underlying cause of human social behavior. Sociobiologists have insisted that its roots are to be found in evolutionary biology, arguing that much of human behavior stems from the pursuit of fitness in the reproductive sense. Many anthropologists have refused to assign so large a role to the genetic component, but they do see the causes of social behavior as functional. For some, human behavior represents a kind of ecological adaptation to the environment, while for others it reflects the application of practical reason to economic or sociopolitical problems. A large number of symbolic anthropologists reject both biology and practical reason, citing the arbitrary nature of many cultural institutions and the apparent failure of functional, ecological, and biological frameworks to explain them.

If ever there was a human group well suited to the testing of all these competing frameworks, it is the llama herders of Peru's Ayacucho highlands. These Quechua-speaking Indians occupy a bleak tundra environment above 4000 meters, noted for its stressful high altitude and relentless cold. Archaeological and ethnohistorical data indicate that herders have occupied the zone for thousands of years, long enough to have undergone both physical and cultural adaptation. With both their fertility and that of their llamas depressed by the extreme environment, they should provide raw material for anyone concerned with maximizing fitness. Yet the herders of Ayacucho also live in a world rich in arbitrary symbolism and filled with powerful supernaturals on whose whim the success of their herding depends. The possibilities for biological adaptation, practical reason, and arbitrary symbolic behavior are so great that rigorous testing and historical reconstruction are needed to evaluate their respective roles.

In this book, we examine five small communities on the puna, or treeless steppe, above Ayacucho, as they were between 1970 and 1972. Dynamic variables such as llama births; losses to rustlers, mange, and mountain lions; and deaths from senility were collected, then subjected to a series of computer models in which the effectiveness of various cultural strategies were evaluated. By simulating herd growth over periods of 100 years, we feel that we have shown the importance of certain ritual behavior in preventing herds from going to extinction.

Our ethnographic and statistical data are combined with ethnohistory and ethology to present a model for the evolution of llama herding from earliest times to the present. The behavior of domestic llamas is compared with that of their wild guanaco ancestors, and the social institutions of the late prehispanic Inca state are compared with those of today's herders. This long evolutionary perspective also helps to contrast the behavior of an animal with culture (the herder), an animal without it (the guanaco), and the domesticated descendant of the latter (the llama).

We consider the roles of Andean cosmology and religion, social organization, ecology, and camelid biology in trying to arrive at a balanced and plausible explanation for the herders' behavior. Our various quantitative models allow testing of possible explanations, rather than mere assertions, perhaps removing some of the objections leveled at functionalism. Finally, we are able to tie our model mathematically to the dual inheritance theory proposed in 1985 by Boyd and Richerson. This theory maintains that frameworks which take culture into account can provide better explanations for human behavior than sociobiology alone, without violating the presumption of a natural origin for culture.

The ethnographic research reported in this book, explicitly problem oriented rather than exhaustive, was done none too soon. Since 1980, Ayacucho has been the epicenter of a guerrilla war that has claimed thousands of lives and caused the abandonment of hundreds of small communities. Tragically, the fieldwork presented here could not be repeated today, since the estancias of Yanahuaccra, Toqtoqasa, Pallqa, Paltamachay, and El Balcón no longer exist. It is our hope that Andean scholars will be able to use our primary data, and that symbolic anthropologists, ecological anthropologists, and evolutionary biologists alike will find the theoretical conclusions provocative.

Acknowledgments

This is a research project that gestated for many years and has come to fruition only because of the help and cooperation of a great many friends. Richard S. MacNeish, director of the Ayacucho–Huanta Archaeological–Botanical Project, generously allowed Flannery to divide his time between the study of camelid bones and the study of living camelid herders. We also owe an enormous debt to Elías Vásquez F. of the Ayacucho Project, a superb hunter and native Quechua speaker, who opened the door to the puna herding communities reported on in this book.

Zoologist Elizabeth S. Wing and botanist Barbara Pickersgill of the Ayacucho Project both made the three-hour climb to Yanahuaccra and provided us with useful insights. Nate Rutter loaned us aerial photographs and enlarged our geological knowledge of the region. Dr. Saúl Fernández-Baca, a veterinarian specialized in camelid breeding and genetics, gave us advice on llama fertility and mortality. Animal ecologist William L. Franklin, a leading expert on the behavior of the wild Andean camelids, provided us with photographs of guanaco herds. And the constructive criticism of our colleague, anthropologist Sherry B. Ortner, greatly improved the manuscript.

Three young archaeologists, working on the hunting and early domestication of camelids near Junín, shared with us some of the data to appear in their future publications. We thank Katherine M. Moore and John W. Rick for data from the Panalauca project, and Jane C. Wheeler for data from Telarmachay.

Back in the United States, the Museum of Anthropology of the University of Michigan and the Computer Science Department of Wayne State University provided Reynolds with funds for the simulation of herd dynamics over hundreds of model "years." We thank Kay Clahassey and John Klausmeyer for their art work, and Kay Clahassey and Tim Pauketat for printing our photographs.

One of our main debts, of course, is to the people of Hatun Rumi, Toqtoqasa, Pallqa, Paltamachay, Toqto, and El Balcón, who opened up their homes and corrals and endured interminable questions. We thank them for their hospitality, their patience, their bowls of soup, and their hundreds of shot glasses of *cañazo*.

Finally, we come to the man to whom this book is dedicated. Both Flannery (in 1968) and Marcus (in 1980) first saw the Andes in a car driven by Ramiro Matos. Without his urging and his enthusiasm, neither would ever have worked there. Without the hours, and days, and months during which he sat with Marcus, describing to her in Quechua and Spanish what growing up in the indigenous village of Qaqa in Huancavelica had been like, this book would still be no more than a stack of field notes. It is one thing to collect a series of concepts in an American Indian language; it is quite another thing to have their underlying meaning revealed by someone who spent his entire youth thinking exclusively in that language. For Ramiro, there will never be a reality quite like that of the highlands where people speak Ayacucho Quechua. That is why, in a very real sense, this book is for him.

One

Introduction

High in the Andes of central Peru, on the cloud-covered rim of the Ayacucho Basin, lies a mountain tundra where frost can strike twelve months a year. It is a land above the tree line, steep and rolling, its Alpine meadows interspersed with peat moors and lichen-covered cliffs. Its colors are yellow-green and gray, but on those days when the fog and sleet pull back from the meadows, one can see snowcapped peaks shimmer in the distance against a cold blue sky.

The people who live permanently on this mountain tundra are among the toughest, hardiest, most stoic American Indians who ever confounded an anthropologist. Their thatched-roof cottages are surrounded by corrals of llamas and sheep, but they often lie far from the nearest human neighbor. Their simple meals are cooked over peat fires, and when the flames go out, the inside of the house is as cold as the outside. Their children play barefoot in the snow, and a good day is one in which women can wash clothes in a glacier-fed stream without being pelted with hail. Their men can walk 200 km behind a caravan of llamas and consider the trip a success if they return with bottles of liquor worth 50 cents a liter.

These herders all have cousins, uncles, aunts, and in-laws in the agricultural villages below the timberline. Those relatives and affines live in adobe houses with Spanish tile roofs, cook their meals over eucalyptus firewood, gather around propane lanterns at night, and grow fields of corn, beans, and potatoes. They regard the occupants of the tundra, or *puna*, as uncivilized mountain men—savages who engage in strange practices, violate incest taboos, and live lives of poverty and deprivation. But would the herders consider moving down to enjoy the comforts of town life? Never. Not unless forced to do so by circumstances beyond their control.

The llama herders of the Ayacucho puna speak a variety of Quechua, the language of the Inca. Their way of life, however, goes back much farther than the time of the Inca. It has evolved, in response to countless sociopolitical changes around it, since the llama was first domesticated in the Andes more than 6000 years ago. Since then it has adjusted to the rise and fall of the Wari state in the Ayacucho Basin (A.D. 600–800), the expansion of the Inca empire (A.D. 1450–1532), the Spanish Conquest of the sixteenth century, and the war of Peruvian independence from Spain (A.D. 1824).

At one and the same time, the llama herders of Ayacucho represent the survival of an ancient way of life and a group pushed farther and farther toward the margins of society by widespread economic and political change. Today they live in a region no one else wants—but they live in it on their own terms, still immersed in an Andean cultural tradition whose antiquity can be glimpsed in the sixteenth- and seventeenth-century Spanish documents. There is tremendous resilience in these herders, whose ancestors were, when you stop to think about it, the world's first meat-and-potatoes people.

Theoretical Frameworks

The herders of the Ayacucho puna present us with an opportunity to confront some of anthropology's most heated theoretical debates—those between culture and biology, and between culture and practical reason. One would think, because of the bleak reality of their subsistence, that it would be easy to show an economic rationale underlying everything they do. One would think, because of each herder's unending struggle to keep his herd alive and to pass it on to his offspring, that it would not be difficult to explain his behavior in terms of genetic fitness—both his and his llamas'. In this study, we shall see to what extent those expectations are fulfilled. Throughout, our theoretical rule of thumb has been, If it fits, acknowledge it; if it doesn't fit, don't force it.

During the 1960s there were numerous anthropological attempts to show that the behavior of non-Western societies made sense in terms of ecological adaptation. Not a few of these attempts involved the relationship between humans and animals (e.g., Leeds and Vayda 1965; Rappaport 1968). Some of the studies presented considerable supporting evidence, but others relied on assertion, introspection, or plausible reconstruction. As a consequence, there was a 1970s backlash from those who were unconvinced. Among others, Friedman (1974) made clear his impatience with all functionalist attempts to show the "rationality of institutions." Equally condemned were the "old functionalism," which attempted to show the rationality of institutions with respect to other elements of society (particularly the economy), and the "new functionalism," which attempted to show the rationality of institutions with respect to their environments.

For Sahlins (1976a:viii), another critic, "the distinctive quality of man [is] not that he must live in a material world, circumstance he shares with all organisms, but that he does so according to a meaningful scheme of his own devising, in which capacity mankind is unique." Sahlins did not challenge the obvious fact that humans must successfully eat and reproduce; what he challenged was the notion that an underlying economic rationality or "practical reason" was the motive for their behavior. For him the dichotomy was between this "materialist" notion and the contrasting "idealist" view in which means and motives are supplied by culture. In support of the latter view, Sahlins argued that the decisive quality of culture is not that it must conform to material constraints "but that it does so according to a definite symbolic scheme which is never the only one possible."

The llama herders of Ayacucho should be the perfect test case for any debate over "function," "adaptation," and "idealism." If ever a group had to work hard and make good economic decisions to preserve its way of life, it is they. And yet—as we shall see—the richness of their symbolic system and its effect on their behavior are a structuralist's dream.

Also in the 1960s, reacting adversely to Wynne-Edwards's (1962) theories of group selection, evolutionary biologists began to solidify their position on individual selection and the maximization of fitness (Williams 1966). It was not long before a resulting body of theory, called sociobiology, was being applied to explanations of human behavior. The attempt began with biologists (Wilson 1978; Alexander 1979) but soon included ethnographic and archaeological converts (Chagnon and Irons 1979; Dunnell 1980). Their approaches ranged from "soft core" to "hard core," with the latter drawing critiques not only from biologists (Lewontin, Rose, and Kamin 1984) and philosophers (Kitcher 1985) but also from anthropologists (Sahlins 1976b).

Sociobiological theory holds that the behavior of all animals, including humans, should aim at maximizing fitness: each human should behave in such a way as to maximize the spread of his or her genes (or the genes of his or her close relatives) through future generations. This can take the form either of large numbers of offspring or of heavy parental investment in a few offspring. A logical extension of the theory is that natural selection should lead to cooperation and altruism among large numbers of individuals only if they are closely related genetically, as among social insects.

However, altruistic cooperation among large groups of unrelated individuals has been observed in humans (Williams 1966), and various cultural behaviors have posed a problem for sociobiological theory. Hard-core sociobiologists have sometimes countered with complex explanations for these exceptions in an attempt to show that they do not violate the theory. Some of these efforts so closely resemble the elaborate devices of cartoonist Rube Goldberg that they have only engendered skepticism.

In search of more parsimonious explanations, a number of biologically minded anthropologists (e.g., Durham 1979, 1982; Rindos 1986) have proposed coevolutionary models for human biology and culture. The most extensive, and one of the most encouraging, is the dual inheritance model of Boyd and Richerson (1985). According to dual inheritance theory, humans attempt to pass on not merely their genes but also their culture, with natural selection operating on both. Altruistic individuals—the celibate priest, the marine who throws himself on the hand grenade—may have chosen to assure the survival of their culture rather than their own genes or those of their second cousin once removed. Moreover, group selection of cultural behavior can take place when the fitness of an individual depends on the cooperative behavior of other individuals in the group. If the incremental benefit of cooperating altruistically with genetically unrelated members of one's group exceeds its incremental cost, groups with the highest number of cooperators have a fitness advantage over neighboring groups (Boyd and Richerson 1985:230).

Once again, the herders of Ayacucho would seem to be made to order for an examination of the debate between culture and biology. Herders seek to have several sons and daughters, to pass on part of their herd to each son when he marries, and to make gifts of animals to their sons-in-law. They should therefore be concerned not only with their fitness, but also with the fitness of their llamas. And yet, as we shall see, they sometimes behave in ways that could enhance the success of unrelated neighbors. To add irony to the situation, their llamas are the domestic descendants of the guanaco, an animal whose behavior could well have been designed by a sociobiologist. This will enable us, in future chapters, to contrast the behavior of an animal with culture and an animal without it.

History of the Present Study

This book is the result of a collaboration. We should say a few words about the division of labor and make clear what the book is and is not. First of all, it is not the study of "our village"—not, in other words, the kind of multifaceted community ethnography that has been the mainstay of Latin American anthropology. Rather, it is a highly focused, problem-oriented study of the dynamics of llama herds and the relevant behavior of their herders. Its goal is to examine some of anthropology's current theoretical issues in the light of a fresh body of empirical data. It therefore pulls specific information from four or five communities rather than giving all the details of one community.

Between 1969 and 1972, archaeologist Richard S. MacNeish directed an interdisciplinary study in the Ayacucho Basin—the Ayacucho-Huanta Archaeological-Botanical Project. His study's goal was to reconstruct the transition from hunting and gathering to agriculture and animal domestication, and to document the subsequent evolution of complex societies in the region (MacNeish et al. 1981). Along with zoologist Elizabeth S. Wing, Kent Flannery took on the analysis of ancient animal bones and the reconstruction of early camelid domestication (Wing 1977, n.d.; Flannery n.d.; Flannery and Wing n.d.). Flannery discovered that there were very few data available on the size, composition by age and sex, or dynamics of modern llama herds which could serve as a guide to the past. After consulting with biologists at Peru's Instituto Veterinario de Investigaciones Tropicales y de Altura—whose concerns, of necessity, lay more with the commercially important alpaca and vicuña—Flannery decided to collect such data himself.

For the purpose of making comparative collections of Ayacucho fauna, MacNeish had assigned Flannery an expert hunter and jeep driver, don Elías Vásquez. Vásquez, a native Quechua speaker, knew the mountains of Ayacucho like the palm of his hand. In his hunting trips to the puna, he had come to know some families of llama herders well enough to break down their legendary distrust of strangers. Slowly and patiently, Vásquez helped Flannery penetrate the tiny estancias of Hatun Rumi, Paltamachay,

Toqtoqasa, and Pallqa. Between 1970 and 1972 they collected the data on herd composition that Flannery had wanted, and, of course, the inevitable happened. A whole new world opened up—a world of supernatural mountain spirits and were-llamas, of sacred snows and offerings of propitiation, of ritual corrals and Andean reciprocity—and that world cried out to be studied as well.

Meanwhile Joyce Marcus, having studied Andean prehistory while a Berkeley undergraduate, had buried herself in the ethnographic and ethnohistoric literature in preparation for a five-year project in Peru (Marcus 1987a, 1987b; Marcus, Matos, and Rostworowski 1983–1985). During this project, she also began to learn Ayacucho Quechua from highland informants who had immigrated to the coast. In addition to making more sense of Flannery's field data, Marcus recognized several widespread cultural patterns and beliefs that could be traced back to the sixteenth century and beyond. These contemporary patterns were thus part of a long cultural evolutionary history, not simply the modern herder's response to his increasingly marginal position.

Robert Reynolds, a computer scientist with a strong interest in anthropology, specializes in modeling long-term cultural and biological processes (Reynolds 1976, 1986). Drawing on the pioneering work of Zeigler (1976) and Holland (1975; Holland et al. 1986), he designed the algorithms that have allowed us to simulate herd growth under varied regimes of cultural behavior. These simulations have allowed us to test whether or not certain behaviors are "adaptive" rather than simply rely on plausible assertions. And while we cannot expect to change the mind of every highly committed ideologue, a test is certainly better than an assertion.

This, then, was the original division of labor. As the book stands now, however, the three authors' contributions are so intertwined that for simplicity's sake we have used the term "we" throughout.

The Limits of Our Study

The Quechua language has been divided into several regional variants (see Parker 1963, 1969; Torero 1964; Soto Ruiz 1976), two of the principal ones being the Ayacucho and Cuzco dialects. Ayacucho Quechua, spoken in the departments of Ayacucho, Huancavelica, and Apurimac, is one of the most homogeneous variants (Torero 1964). Its closest relatives are the mutually intelligible Cuzco dialects spoken to the southeast in the departments of Cuzco, Puno, Arequipa, and Apurimac (east of Abancay).

There are approximately one million speakers of Ayacucho Quechua (Soto Ruiz 1976:22), including the herders who are the subject of this study. We have largely confined our discussion to this region (Fig. 1.1) and have not made an extensive effort to point out how its concepts, kin terms, and additional cultural features differ from those of other parts of

Figure 1.1 Map of Peru, showing the location of the Ayacucho study area relative to other landmarks.

Peru. Anthropologists working in Cuzco will probably notice many differences, such as Ayacucho's *wamani* versus Cuzco's *apu* or Ayacucho's *masa* versus Cuzco's *cata* or *q'ata*. Sixteenth- and seventeenth-century dictionaries make it clear that much of the divergence between dialects has taken place in the last 300 years. Specifically, Cuzco Quechua seems to be the dialect that has changed the most; in the sixteenth century, it seems to have been much closer to the Ayacucho dialect.

Just as our ethnographic findings should not necessarily be expected to apply to other regions, the data we collected on herd dynamics are specific to Ayacucho and should not be uncritically applied to other parts of the Andes. All areas of puna on the rim of the Ayacucho Basin are narrow strips, bounded by lower-elevation farmland; they cannot be compared with the vast plains around Lake Titicaca or Lake Junín. Our loss rates from rustling, pumas, and mange are specific to Ayacucho conditions. Other regions must be studied in their own right and will undoubtedly prove to have their own variable rates. The ecology of herd management is such a subtle and region-specific affair that data from one area cannot be applied to another in "cookbook" fashion. For many of the same reasons, our figures on llamas should not be indiscriminately applied to alpacas. There have already been a number of important studies of alpaca herding in southern Peru (Flores Ochoa 1968, 1977, 1979, 1986; Orlove 1977). One animal is raised for its wool, the other for transportation, and that fact leads to important differences in herd dynamics.

Finally, our data on herd dynamics in the 1970s should not be projected back naively into the prehispanic era. In the latter part of Chapter 5 we hope to show that losses from rustling, pumas, and mange should have been much lower in Inca times, and that different management techniques were used to provide the ruler, the state religious apparatus, and the community with herds larger than any we saw in Ayacucho in the 1970s. Each epoch since the origins of domestication has had its own specific management techniques, and the one used at any given time and place was, to repeat Sahlins's phrase, "never the only one possible."

Unresolved Problems

Inevitably, there were other research directions we could not pursue because our time ran out. Among other things, we would like to know to what extent the Spanish introduction of sheep onto the puna has affected the quality of the range for llamas. Some Ayacucho herders raised both animals, because modern Peru affords sheep wool and mutton a higher prestige value. It was clear, however, that sheep simply did not occupy the important place in their ritual and cosmology that llamas did. By concentrating on llamas, we opened a window into Quechua culture and its prehispanic past.

We had hoped that during the 1980s we would be able to return to Ayacucho to collect additional data on a variety of topics. Unfortunately, violent conflict between the Peruvian police and the guerrillas of the Sendero Luminoso movement has made fieldwork in the mountains of Ayacucho impossible. Eight years of *lucha armada* have left thousands dead in the region and many small communities abandoned. At this point, even if any of our original informants are still alive, the disruption of their lives has been such that, even when the violence has ended, it is questionable whether fieldwork could pick up where it left off.

Two

Andean Nature

The Ayacucho region is a deeply dissected intermontane basin with many steep slopes and little level land. Local rivers like the Chihua, Cachi, and Pongor have carved deep canyons in the soft volcanic rock of the basin on their way to join the Río Mantaro northwest of Huanta (Fig. 2.1). As in so many parts of highland Peru, the differences in relief are accompanied by striking differences in temperature, rainfall, vegetation, and evaporation rate. Above all, they determine where people can farm, where they can herd, and which domestic species thrive.

So complex are the environmental gradients between snowcapped mountain peaks and the riverine floor of the basin that all published descriptions are simplifications. The human mind typically reduces a daunting mass of environmental information to a set of model or ideal categories, and this is as true of the Western ecologists who have studied the Andes as it is of the Indians. In this chapter, we look at the ways each group has classified the environments of the Ayacucho Basin.

Some researchers (e.g., Holland 1975; Holland et al. 1986) argue that a simplifying classification is one of the first steps in adaptation: a human group produces a workable coarse-grained model of a much more finely grained environment. For example, John Holland of the University of Michigan (personal communication) has visualized the problem as a nested set of Markov processes with progressively coarser structure. In the case of the Ayacucho Basin, the finest-grained structure would be a perfectly accurate characterization of the environment, including not only the gradients of temperature, rainfall, and evaporation but also the location of every type of rock, soil, plant, and animal. Somewhat coarser would be the models used by ecologists such as Weberbauer (1945), Tosi (1960), and the staff of MacNeish's Ayacucho Project (MacNeish et al.

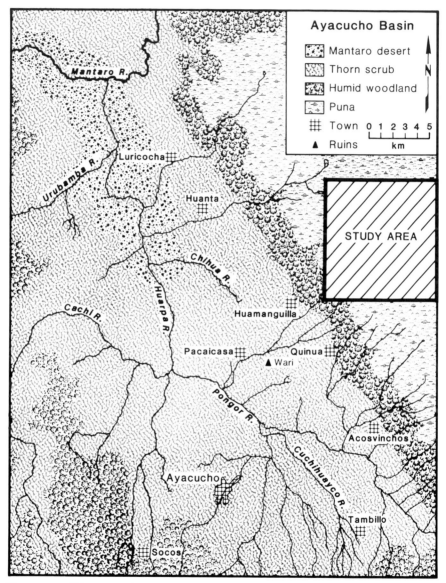

Figure 2.1 The Ayacucho Basin, with towns and environmental zones indicated. The study area, northeast of Quinua and Huamanguilla, is shown in detail in Figure 4.2.

1981:2–3; Flannery and Wing n.d.), who divided the basin into a series of environmental zones. Still coarser—yet just as relevant to the question of adaptation—would be the environmental classification of the Quechua-speaking Indians of the basin, which is based on a set of cosmological principles and the realities of land use (Quispe 1969; Palomino Flores 1970).

The "Western Science" Model

One of the most ambitious attempts to classify the Peruvian Andes into a series of environmental zones was undertaken by the Organization of American States (OAS) during the 1950s. This effort culminated in an important monograph by Joseph Tosi (1960), a work which utilized the classificatory methods of Leslie Holdridge and drew heavily on the pioneering botanical studies of Weberbauer (1945). More recently, the Oficina Nacional de Evaluación de Recursos Hidráulicos del Perú has published an ecological map of Peru which grew out of the OAS study (ONERN 1976).

Holdridge's method involves the use of a triangular graph whose three axes represent (1) mean annual precipitation in millimeters, (2) median annual temperature in degrees centigrade, and (3) total potential annual evapotranspiration in millimeters (Holdridge 1967). The intersection of lines from these three axes determines the "life zone" to which an area belongs. For example, ONERN's (1976) "pluvial tundra zone" is defined as having a mean annual temperature between 1.5° and 3.0° C, an annual precipitation between 500 and 1000 mm, and a total potential annual evapotranspiration roughly an eighth to a fourth of its precipitation.

Because the Peruvian life zones defined by Tosi (1960) covered a much broader area than the Ayacucho Basin, the various natural scientists of MacNeish's Ayacucho-Huanta project found it necessary to adjust them to fit the specifics of the basin. The final set of zones represents the consensus of geologist Nate Rutter, botanist Barbara Pickersgill, and zooarchaeologists Elizabeth Wing and K. Flannery. In order of increasing altitude, the environmental zones defined were the Mantaro desert (2250 m and below), the thorn scrub (ca. 2250–3100 m), the humid woodland (ca. 3100–4000 m), the low puna (4000–4500 m), and the high puna (above 4500 m). In a few cases, zones were divided into smaller facies depending on local conditions.

The *Mantaro desert*, lowest zone in the area, occurs in the deep rain shadow of the Huanta region. It is a region of alluvial lithosols with organ cactus (*Cereus*), acacia, and *Prosopis* (the leguminous tree called "algarrobo" in Peru and "mesquite" in North America). This xerophytic zone has little potential for agriculture apart from the narrow irrigated strip along the Río Mantaro which produces some maize, guava (*Psidium guajava*), and lúcuma fruits (*Pouteria lucuma*) when 300–500 mm of rainfall runs off into the canals between December and March.

Tributary canyons in the 2500–3000-m zone upstream from the Mantaro present a less desolate appearance. This is the *thorn scrub zone* (Fig. 2.2), which receives 500–700 mm of annual precipitation in the form of gentle rains between December and April and enjoys a relatively low erosion rate. The best developed soils are brown chernozems, and the potential for irrigation agriculture is high, even though evapotranspiration is two to four times the precipitation. Days are hot, nights are cool, and frosts can occur between August and November. This is the natural habitat of the Peruvian pepper tree (*Schinus molle*), which grows there in the company of woody legumes like *Cassia, Caesalpinia, Mimosa, Acacia,* and *Prosopis* whenever conditions are favorable. The city of Ayacucho itself lies at 2730 m in the middle of this zone.

Figure 2.2   Bordered by groves of molle trees, the Río Pongor winds through the thorn scrub near Pacaicasa. The highest peak on the mountain range in the left background is Cerro Yanahuaccra (see Fig. 4.6).

The staff of MacNeish's project recognized two facies within the thorn scrub: (1) a *dry facies*, covering slopes like the hillsides around Pikimachay Cave and featuring the maguey-like *paqpa* (*Furcraea*); and (2) a *riverside facies*, like that near the village of Pacaicasa. The riverside facies has a lusher appearance because the high water table encourages the growth of alder, willow, molle, and soapberry (*Dodonaea*). Irrigated orchards in the riverside facies produce limes, lemons, oranges, and grapes, and other fields are devoted to maize, wheat, barley, faba beans (*Vicia faba*), and squashes (*Cucurbita* spp.).

Because of its denser, weedier vegetation, this facies is rich in doves and pigeons, small rodents, hognosed skunks (*Conepatus rex*), white-eared opossums (*Didelphis albiventris*), Andean foxes (*Dusicyon culpaeus*), and wildcats (*Felis jacobita*); it must once have had many white-tailed deer (*Odocoileus virginianus*), today hunted almost to the vanishing point. Cave remains also indicate that guinea pigs (*Cavia porcellus*) were raised in large numbers in this zone, perhaps as far back as 4000 B.C..

Ascending the slopes to 3000 m, one reaches the very important *humid woodland zone* (Fig. 2.3). Here the annual rainfall is 700–1000 mm—somewhat higher than the thorn scrub, and with an evaporation rate only half of or equal to its precipitation, as the result of cooler temperatures. This zone must formerly have been an open woodland 6–10 m high, dominated by trees such as *cciñua* (*Polylepis*), *chachacoma* (*Escallonia*), *mutuy* (*Cassia*), and *Buddleia*. Smaller shrubs would have included barberry (*Berberis*), *pespita* (*Ribes*), *yanawarmi* (*Monnina*), *chilca* (*Baccharis*), *karwinchu* (*Brachyotum*), groundsel (*Senecio*), and *Solanum*. The weedy undergrowth would have been composed of grasses and herbs, the latter including composites, mint, cress, sage, *Crotalaria*, and *Urticaria*. Frosts are common in this zone during the Andean winter (May to October), and there are periods of prolonged fog and rain in summer (November to April).

This is by far the lushest of the local vegetation zones, permitting the growth of maize (to about 3500 m altitude) and such native Andean crops as *quinoa* (*Chenopodium quinoa*), *cañiwa* (*Chenopodium pallidicaule*), *oca* (*Oxalis tuberosum*), *olluco* (*Ullucus tuberosus*), *maswa* (*Tropaeolum tuberosum*), and common potatoes (*Solanum tuberosum*). The best-developed soils are brunisols, and there is a great deal of agriculture in spite of the lack of level land. Many important towns of the basin, such as Quinua and Huamanguilla, lie near the transition from thorn scrub to humid woodland.

Figure 2.3 *Polylepis* trees along a stream in the humid woodland south of Socos. The tree line, showing the transition from woodland to puna, can be seen clearly at the upper left.

The humid woodland must originally have been one of the richest faunal zones in the Ayacucho Basin. It is still lush, green, and filled with resources even after overgrazing by Spanish-introduced livestock. The zone still teems with viscacha (*Lagidium peruanum*), wild guinea pig (*Cavia tschudii*), white-eared opossum, dove, pigeon, Andean fox, and hognosed skunk. Prehispanic bones from Jaywamachay Cave also make it clear that guanaco (*Lama glama guanicoe*) and white-tailed deer were once very common in the area.

Still higher up, at about 4000 m, the trees of the humid woodland fade away and the *lower puna* begins (Fig. 2.4). The term "puna"—borrowed by ecologists from Quechua—refers to a tundra or Alpine meadow zone that occurs above the timberline. This is a land with at least 9–12 months of frost per year, where many plants hug the ground in rosette or "cushion" form for protection from the cold. Annual temperatures range from a mean low of 3.2° C to a mean high of 7.2° C, and evapotranspiration is only one half of or equal to the annual precipitation. Depending on whether it is Andean summer (November to April) or Andean winter (May to October), 800–1000 mm can fall in the form of rain or snow; at any time of the year there can be dense "fogs" which are, in reality, low-lying clouds that blanket the mountaintops. This is the zone in which most of the llama herders we studied lived, and we therefore look at it in a bit more detail than the other zones.

The best developed soils of the lower puna are arctic browns, some of which can be used for growing the small, bitter variety of potatoes used for *chuñu* (see Chapter 4). Weberbauer (1945) recognized four basic plant communities native to the zone. The first of these communities, sometimes referred to as "puna turf," occurs on flat areas which are relatively well drained. It consists of an undulating carpet of rosette and cushionlike herbs such as *Pycnophyllum, Arenaria, Geranium,* and *Lucilia* tightly interlocked and accompanied by a few slightly taller plants such as *Baccharis, Ephedra,* and *Astralagus.* There are also mosses and lichens in this assemblage, but they are outnumbered by herbs.

On sloping surfaces, and especially on rocky slopes, can be found a second community which Weberbauer called "tallgrass puna" (Fig. 2.5). The assemblage is dominated by bunchgrasses, one of the most prominent of which is *Stipa ichu.* This 50-cm tall feathergrass, known in Quechua as *ichu,* provides the Indians with raw material for ropes, lassos, baskets, and roof thatch. In between the relatively unpalatable bunches of *Stipa* grow a whole series of smaller and more delicate bunchgrasses which figure more

Figure 2.4 The lower puna near Toqtoqasa.

Figure 2.5 Along this stream near Toqto, one can find both overgrazed grassy puna (left foreground) and turf puna (right background).

prominently in the diet of guanacos, vicuñas, and llamas. Included are *Calamagrostis* spp., a series of fescues known locally as *chiriwar* (*Festuca* spp.), brome grass (*Bromus*), and meadow grass (*Poa*). Although impressive in its ungrazed state, this puna grassland is a fragile assemblage because of the cold temperatures and meager soil it has to endure. ONERN (1976:106) recommends that livestock be grazed on it at a density no greater than one animal per 6 hectares—a recommendation unknown to, and continuously violated by, the Quechua-speaking herders.

On flat areas which are poorly drained there develops a third community, the "puna peat moor." This humid vegetational assemblage is dominated by *Distichia muscoides*, a member of the family Juncaceae, which forms huge colonies of cushionlike plants so tightly fitted together that most other herb and grass species are kept out (Fig. 2.6). *Distichia* grows from the top, while the bottom of the plant is steadily converted into the peat known in Quechua as *champa*. Such peat moors are continuously spongy underfoot. Blocks of *champa* cut from them are widely used by the herders as fuel and construction material.

A fourth community occurs on rocky areas, which present so many microhabitats that the mix of plants is extremely varied (Fig. 2.7). Included are lichens such as *Rhizocarpon*; bryophytes such as *Gyrophora*; mosses and clubmosses; ferns such as *Polypodium*, *Polystichum*, and *Asplenium*; woody composites such as *Chuquiragua* and *Senecio*; herbs such as *Bomarea* and *Leuceria*; and stunted versions of some of the same bunchgrasses seen on the puna meadows.

Some animals of the puna are restricted to high elevations, while others are wide-ranging species which also occur lower down. The vicuña (*Vicugna vicugna*) and the huemal deer (*Hippocamelus antisensis*) are puna

Figure 2.6 *Chuñu* makers spread out their potatoes on a puna moor dominated by *Distichia*.

Figure 2.7   Rocky puna near Toqtoqasa.

natives, and the white-tailed deer also reaches this zone. The Andean fox and the hognosed skunk do well at this altitude, but the white-eared opossum cannot tolerate the 9–12 months of frost. Although doves and pigeons are usually not sighted on the puna, the bird life is otherwise rich; it includes several species of tinamou (*Nothoprocta* spp.), Ridgway's ibis (*Plegadis ridgwayi*), the Andean goose (*Chloephaga melanoptera*), the Andean gull (*Larus serranus*), and several species of teal (*Anas* spp.). The waterfowl are particularly common around small lakes and marshes, a special set of habitats which result from the low evaporation rate of the puna and its generous endowment of rain, hail, and snow. The bulrush, or *totora* (*Scirpus* sp.), which colonizes the marshes, serves as the raw material for several handicrafts; it also has an edible bulb. In some areas, dense stands of *totora* shelter colonies of wild guinea pigs.

Still farther up is the high puna, or "puna brava," a zone of Alpine turf, permanent glaciers, and windswept mountains above 4500 m. This is a region too cold even for root crops, where patches of snow linger late into the Andean summer in shaded valleys. Its mean annual temperature hovers between 2.5° and 3.5° C, and its 800–1000 mm of precipitation often come in frozen form. With a potential evapotranspiration only an eighth to a fourth of its precipitation, the puna brava is an extreme environment which nevertheless provides summer pasture for llamas and alpacas. The bunchgrasses and herbs of the lower puna gradually thin out as one climbs higher, but the lichens and mosses continue all the way to the glaciers. Interestingly enough, a number of wild flowers used in the native rituals of Ayacucho come from the Alpine tundra near the snow line; the *tarwi*, or lupine (*Lupinus*), among others, grows at this altitude.

The Quechua Model

For the native Andean people of the Ayacucho Basin, neither the life zones of OAS, ONERN, or MacNeish's project are of great significance. A more useful coarse-grained classification of the environment had already been made by their ancestors, along lines more meaningful to them.

From the floor of the Río Pongor to the upper limits of the *cciñua* and *chachacoma* trees—including all of the area we have called thorn scrub and humid woodland—runs the zone the Indians called *kichwa*, where all kinds of agriculture are possible. They do not divide this zone into vegetational communities, as we might, but into the part which is human community and the part which is not. The area of the village and its outskirts, modified by houses and hedgerows and canals, is called *llaqta*. Beyond are the *chakras*, fields cleared and planted with maize, faba beans, and potatoes. The native people do have terms for the sloping land along the banks of the river, where hot-country fruits and introduced plants such as prickly pear and agave can be grown: they call it *uku-mayu* ("deep river" or "inside the river") or *mayu patan* ("river's edge").

Seasonal contrasts in the *kichwa*, as might be expected, are related to the growing of crops. The rainy season, from December to April, is *poccoy* ("when the fruits ripen"). The dry season, from May to November, is *chiraw*, and frosts can be expected during June and July. August and February, as we see in Chapter 8, are considered dangerous months because of unstable relations between man and the supernatural.

A significant contrast is made between the *kichwa* zone, with its towns and agricultural fields, and the *sallqa*. *Sallqa* refers to the puna or tundra above the tree line, but the word means more than just "puna"; as Isbell (1978) reveals, *sallqa* also implies that the region is wild or uncivilized. It is therefore a term which characterizes the puna from the perspective of the *kichwa*-dweller, for whom the *llaqta* or "pueblo" represents civilization. There is no question that the relative lack of agriculture in the *sallqa* also helps to set it apart. Even the fact that *chuñu* potatoes can be grown on the lower puna seems unimpressive in light of the diversified farming in the *kichwa*.

Interestingly, when Ayacucho peoples find it necessary to distinguish between the lower and higher regions of the *sallqa*, they use the Spanish terms "puna alta" and "puna baja." One reason for distinguishing between the two is that, in many communities, cattle are grazed only on the lower puna, while sheep can be taken to the higher puna (Palomino Flores 1970). In ancient times, when llamas and alpacas were the only grazing animals, herders used both upper and lower puna while moving between summer and winter pasture. For this reason, it may be that there was little point in distinguishing between "puna alta" and "puna baja" until the Spaniards introduced cattle and sheep.

Finally, above the *sallqa* comes the *urqu*—the zone of snowcapped mountaintops and glaciers at the roof of the Andean world (Fig. 2.8). This is the abode of the aboriginal mountain spirits, the *wamanis*, the most powerful of whom are lodged within the most impressive peaks (see Chapter 3). Because the *wamanis* are thought to be the true owners not only of all domestic livestock but also of all wild animals, native Andean peoples do not assign animal species to life zones the way Western ecologists do. They know that certain animals can be found in certain places— for example, that a hunter looking for *wachwa* (Andean goose) and *yanawiku* (Ridgway's ibis) can find them near one of the *qochas*, or puna lakes—but in their cosmology, those birds belong more to a *wamani* than to an environmental zone.

As suggested earlier, certain flowers used in ritual must be collected from the *urqu*, often at the foot of the glaciers. Palomino Flores (1970) mentions three flowers from this zone—*kunuka*, *sallqantiway*, and *quri-waylla*—brought down from the high puna for use in rituals at Sarhua on the Río Pampas. The association of the *urqu* with powerful *wamanis* gives these flowers, as well as other products of the high mountains, a sacred power that the products of lower zones simply do not have.

Yet another important feature of the *urqu* is *riti*, or snow. Snow mantles the top of the Andean world and permanently covers the peaks occupied by the most powerful *wamanis*; it has powers of purification so great that they have been extended to white powders of other kinds, to white llamas,

Figure 2.8 Snowcapped mountains of the *urqu* overlook the rolling *sallqa* near Totora-
bamba. The gray oval near the center of the photograph is a typical high-altitude *Scirpus*
marsh.

to white alpacas, and to a host of other substances. It is no accident that
the Indians purify their ritual paraphernalia (described in Chapter 8) by
sprinkling them with a mixture of white clay and cornmeal called *llampu*.
In lieu of real snow, *llampu* is the purifier of choice.

That this should happen underscores one of the fundamental differences
between Andean classifications and those of Western ecologists. For Western science, life zones are defined by the nonrandom association of specific
plant and animal genera with the variables of soil, precipitation, temperature, and evapotranspiration which sustain them. For native Andean
peoples, as Palomino Flores (1970) reminds us, each life zone has a series
of cultural-symbolic phenomena associated with it, and the relevant animals belong to the supernatural beings who live in springs, lakes, and
mountain peaks. An ecologist might note that a town like Quinua lies at
the transition from thorn scrub to humid woodland, but the town itself
would not enter into his definition of either zone. For the Indian, however,

llaqta is its own zone; the town and its human modification of the landscape contrast with unmodified wilderness in a way that is more important than any finer divisions within the *kichwa* could be. Similarly, one cannot define the *urqu* without considering the *wamanis* who live there, for their presence charges the zone with danger and makes even the wild flowers of the *urqu* sacred. As for the *sallqa*—the treeless tundra whose people occupy us for most of this book—it is defined not as a complex of bunchgrasses, lichens, and peat moors, but as a place for wild herders who do not live in the *llaqta* like civilized men.

Three

Andean Culture

In the beginning, said Santa Cruz Pachacuti Yamqui ([1613] 1963), there was only Viracocha—the hermaphrodite Creator, progenitor of Sun and Moon. Equally male and female, Viracocha was able to give rise to a male line headed by the Sun and a female line headed by the Moon. Sun gave rise to Venus as the Morning Star, termed "Grandfather" and considered male; Moon gave rise to Venus as the Evening Star, termed "Grandmother" and considered female. Morning Star was in turn the father of Camac Pacha, "Lord Earth"; Evening Star was the mother of Mama Cocha, "Lady Sea." Finally, Lord Earth gave rise to Man, and Lady Sea gave rise to Woman. Because Man and Woman are descended from Viracocha through lineages that remained separate for four supernatural generations, Andean men and women should ideally take care to marry only spouses to whom they are unrelated over a distance of at least four generations (Fig. 3.1; Zuidema and Quispe 1967).

Also created in antediluvian times, and perhaps related to Camac Pacha, were the mountain spirits known as *wamanis*. The *wamanis*, true owners of all animals wild and domestic, live in mountain peaks and puna lakes and are the most powerful supernaturals with whom humans actually come into contact. There is a hierarchy of *wamanis* in Ayacucho, with the most powerful occupying the most impressive *nevado*, or snowcapped peak, in the region; inside the mountain, the *wamani* lives in a palace filled with incalculable treasure, occasionally emerging astride a giant viscacha with a gold and silver harness. Below the supreme *wamani* for the region are lesser peaks with slightly less powerful spirits, and below them are a whole series of local *wamanis* who are in charge of the llamas and sheep raised by specific households of herders. During two particularly dangerous months of the year—February and August—the earth opens and the *wamanis*

25

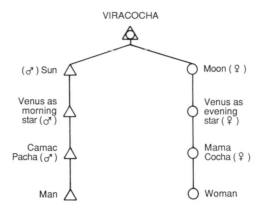

Figure 3.1 The descent of mortal man and woman from Viracocha (redrawn from Zuidema and Quispe 1967).

become hungry and walk the earth in search of offerings; at times they eat the hearts of men who walk alone in the mountains or show the *wamanis* too little respect. Indians wishing to hunt or raise animals successfully must take care to propitiate the *wamani* with whom their household is associated, addressing him as *Tayta Urqu*, "Father Mountain."

The *wamanis* live in the *sallqa* or *urqu*, linked to the mountain peaks and puna lakes and strongly associated with animals. In contrast, the Pacha Mama lives in the *kichwa* zone, where she is associated with both agriculture and fertility. At villages like Sarhua in the Río Pampas district of central Ayacucho, daily offerings are made to the Pacha Mama; when maize is being planted, farmers make a hole in the center of the field and bury coca, cigarettes, and chicha as an offering to her (Palomino Flores 1970:123).

Four hundred years of acculturation following the Spanish Conquest have not been sufficient to eliminate these prehispanic spirits. Catholic saints coexist with ancient supernaturals rather than replacing them, and the "dios" of the Spaniards lives in the *urqu* as do the *wamanis* (Zuidema and Quispe 1967). In ancient times there were major spirits who were always at their *wakas*, or shrines, and minor spirits who could be transported. Even today, major Catholic saints are associated with the *kichwa* and are immobile, indifferent, and little feared. Minor saints are associated with the *sallqa* and are mobile, emotional, fearsome beings who interact regularly with humans and animals (Palomino Flores 1970: 115–116). Structuralist anthropologists working in Ayacucho have pointed to this dichotomy of male deity/*sallqa*/herding and female deity/*kichwa*/agriculture as one of several important "structural oppositions" in Ayacucho Quechua culture.

Several other dangerous beings roam the highlands, among them the *amaru* and the *pistako*. The *amaru*, a mobile male spirit, lives at the entrance to the mountains and grows to maturity in underground chambers. He emerges as a landslide of mud and water which rushes downslope to punish communities that have misbehaved (Palomino Flores 1970:123). Such landslides, or *wayqos*, are a common occurrence in the Andes; significantly, they are explained not as natural phenomena but as the *amaru's* punishment for human misbehavior.

The *nako*, or *pistako*, is a terrifying figure in the Huanta-Ayacucho area. *Pistakos* are said to be tall, white (sometimes blond) foreign males, often dressed in leather jackets or yellow to khaki clothes. Their goal is to kidnap Indians, whom they boil to make candles "because human grease is better than any other kind." The term *nako* presumably comes from the Ayacucho Quechua verb *nakay* ("to decapitate" or "to draw and quarter"), a reference to the fact that *pistakos* are thought to cut up and hide the bodies of their victims in caves until they are ready to begin their boiling. *Pistako*, in turn, comes from the Quechua noun *pistaq* ("butcher"). It is not clear whether the *pistako* is a prehispanic survival or a product of the Spanish Colonial era, a time when hundreds of Indians were taken away by white strangers and never returned. Whatever the case, archaeologists on survey in Ayacucho soon learn not to wear yellow or khaki clothes, and ethnologists often must wait out a tense period until their informants conclude that they are not *pistakos*.

Human Society

Most Quechua-speaking villages of the Ayacucho Basin depend on the mixed strategy of farming and herding implied by the *sallqa—kichwa* opposition described above. Even towns such as Huamanguilla, with their emphasis on commerce, have a strong substructure of farming and herding which supports the economy.

Although our focus is on herders of llama, we should stress that those herders are in no sense a separate caste, lineage, or community. In the Andes, as pointed out by Murra years ago, herders never became a separate ethnic group as they did in the Near East; "full-time herders, even if they spent most of their lives in the *puna*, high above the peasant settlement, continued socially to belong to the village" (Murra 1965:189). Murra suspects that one group of sixteenth-century herders, the *yana* of Lake Titicaca, might eventually have developed into a separate group had the Spanish Conquest not intervened; but the Conquest ended that process. And in Ayacucho, despite claims of "structural opposition" between *kichwa* and *sallqa*, the herders of the puna are merely the highest-altitude members of a community that extends vertically through several environmental zones.

The basic social group into which Andean farmers and herders have traditionally been organized is the *ayllu*, a unit which retains its prehispanic name. Some confusion results from the fact that *ayllu* today can refer to either (1) a genealogically related group of extended families, which considers itself to share a common ancestor and a common *pacarina*, or place of origin; (2) a number of unrelated extended families living together in a restricted area, which frequently corresponds to a community, village, or barrio; (3) any group of friends, relatives, and neighbors one can "rely on" for *ayni*, or reciprocal aid; or (4) any group with a common leader or "head" (e.g., Acosta 1940; Ávila [1598] 1966, 1983; Cock 1981; Cunow 1929; Isbell 1977, 1978; Poole 1984; Rowe 1946; Skar 1982; Zuidema 1977).

If the *ayllu* is the fundamental unit of Andean social organization, why is it so difficult to define precisely? Among other things, (1) the term used today refers to different units in different regions; (2) the meaning of *ayllu* also varied from region to region in the Colonial era; and, finally, (3) the *ayllu* in Inca times was not the same as the *ayllu* encountered by twentieth-century ethnologists. Let us look first at the prehispanic *ayllu* and the ways it was transformed during the Colonial era, before looking at its different regional meanings today.

Two of the earliest sources providing information on the sixteenth-century *ayllu* are the 1560 dictionary of Fray Domingo de Santo Tomás (1951a:72r, 107v) and a 1598 work by Fray Francisco de Ávila (1966:257). Santo Tomás defines the *ayllu* as a "lineage, generation, or family." Ávila describes it as "a number of people who share a common origin, much as we might refer to 'the Mendozas' or 'the Toledos.' [The place of origin] is often the rocky outcrop or peak of a mountain, and [the *ayllu*] has its own priest, owns agricultural land, and holds its own fiesta every year." From these and other sources, Rowe (1946:253) has concluded that the six-teenth-century *ayllu* "seems to have been a general word for 'kin group' in Quechua, and its specific meaning was probably made clear by the con-text." He also found evidence that each *ayllu* claimed rights to a definite territory, with each married couple cultivating as much of it as they needed (1946:255).

Although *ayllus* in agricultural regions seem to have had rights to farm land, Rostworowski (1981:42–43) has suggested that this was not a uni-versal condition. On the Pacific coast, she argues, there were *ayllus* of fishermen who had rights to specific beaches rather than to farm land, as well as *ayllus* of craftsmen who may not have had any land at all. Thus, while many scholars have focused on the importance of territorial rights (e.g., Cobo 1890–1895; Cock 1981), others have stressed shared ancestry and descent from a common *pacarina* or sacred mythical place (e.g., Allen [Wagner] 1978; Rostworowski 1981:43).

How an *ayllu's* lands were divided among its members prior to the Inca period is not always clear. When indigenous populations came under Inca control, their agricultural land was divided into three parts—one to sup-port the state government, another to support the state religion, and a third for the commoners. Similarly, pasture lands for herds of llama and alpaca were divided into three parts, with the lands devoted to state government and religion sometimes larger than those belonging to com-moners. In some regions, the ordinary adult male family head was allowed up to ten animals and could keep their wool for his own use; even a man whose own camelids provided him with sufficient wool also received an allotment of wool from that state, just as did any other commoner (see Cobo 1890–1895: Bk. 12, Chaps. 28 and 29).

The arrival of the Spaniards brought changes to prehispanic institu-tions, and the *ayllu*, in turn, adjusted to changing conditions. Two Span-ish policies in particular had a profound impact. One, the *encomienda*, often involved the granting of Indians from dispersed regions and ethnic groups to individual Spaniards; the other policy, *reducción*, forced formerly dispersed populations to congregate in newly established communities. Both these policies altered prehispanic ethnic identities and changed the previously important boundaries between societies and territories. By the twentieth century, many of these new communities had come to be legally recognized as land-working collectives called *comunidades campesinas*.

Marriage and Incest

In prehispanic times, marriage outside the *ayllu* was forbidden to commoners (Garcilaso de la Vega [1604] 1960, 1966). Such *ayllu*-endogamous
weddings stood in contrast to the marriage of rulers, who often took wives
from other noble *ayllus* or *panacas*, with the resulting children belonging
to the father's family (e.g., Falcón [1580?] 1918; Fernández [1571] 1876;
Relaciones Geográficas de Indias [1881–1897] 1965: Vol. 1, pp. 100–101,
188–189; Rowe 1946:254; Acosta [1590] 1940; Cock 1981). From these
sources and others, we can expand our definition of the prehispanic *ayllu*
to include endogamy and possibly patrilineal descent.

Marriage within the *ayllu*, however, did not mean marriage with close
relatives. Just as mortal man and mortal woman had descended from
Viracocha through lines which were separate for four generations (Fig.
3.1), so also was it necessary to marry someone who was unrelated over a
distance of three or four generations. For example, Zuidema (1977:250)
describes the *ayllu* as a descent group consisting of an apical male ancestor
and four generations of descendants, with the males descending from their
fathers in a patriline and the females from their mothers in a matriline,
and with incest prohibitions up to the fourth generation—which means
that commoners could marry only third cousins or still more distantly
related kin. This marriage prohibition would mean that the nearest mar-
riageable relative would be FFFZddd.

Whether the prehispanic word *ayllu* had the very same meaning in
Cuzco Quechua and Ayacucho Quechua needs to be investigated. Certainly today, 400 years after the Spanish Conquest, there seem to be
regional differences. For the Ayacucho region of greatest interest to this
study, *ayllu* continues to refer to a type of kin group, while most ethnologists working in the Cuzco region emphasize the term's reference to a type
of territorial unit (e.g., Poole 1984). As we have seen, it is the social
aspect which determines who can and cannot marry. In the Río Pampas
area of central Ayacucho, those who are *ayllu* ("close kin") cannot marry,
while *karu ayllu* ("distant kin") are those who can (Isbell 1978). Isbell
defines the *ayllu* in Chuschi as a bilateral kindred up to the second cousin;
this means that *karu ayllu* are those who are more distantly related than
second cousin. In both the Río Pampas district and the Quinua-Huamanguilla region studied by us, there is parallel inheritance of surnames and
property, with sons inheriting from their fathers, and daughters from their
mothers. Those who share a surname cannot marry.

Fear of incest is so strong that it has created a monster called the *ccarccacha*. Should a man cohabit, for example, with a sister or a first cousin, each will be turned into a were-llama. Maintaining his or her human form by day, the *ccarccacha* is converted at night into a llama who circles the settlement, usually after 2 A.M., crying in a human voice. Because incest is thought to be more common among the "uncivilized" people who live permanently on the puna, dark nights there are particularly frightening, and the sound of strange hooves in the distance is enough to keep most people indoors. It is said that some brave men have been able to lasso a *ccarccacha* and hold it captive until dawn. Knowing that its incestuous acts will be revealed when it reverts to human form, the were-llama offers its captors "any reward, any treasure" to release it and keep its secret safe.

Given such supernatural sanctions, why would anyone commit incest? We were told that, after a tremendous drinking bout at a fiesta on the puna, two near relatives might be so drunk that they do not know what they are doing. "After all," said one informant from the *kichwa*, "some of those *estancias* on the puna are so small there aren't a lot of partners to choose from, and it gets mighty cold at night."

Masa and Llumchuy

In the lives of the native peoples of Ayacucho—and especially in the rituals described in this study—alliance relations with one's in-laws are of great significance. Seventeenth-century documents make it clear that this has been true from ancient times, and that kin terms and ritual obligations of in-laws have shown great continuity over the centuries.

Among Quechua speakers in general, the kin group can be characterized as ego-centered and bilaterally organized (see Bolton and Mayer 1977; Isbell 1977; Mayer 1977; Webster 1977). Membership is reckoned with emphasis on collateral relationships. Quechua terms for parents and their collaterals could be described as bifurcate-merging, with cross-cousins distinguished from siblings and parallel cousins.

Such bifurcate-merging and "Iroquoian" features are sometimes associated with unilineal systems of kinship. Among the bilaterally organized Quechua, however, the principle is one that merges collateral kin of the same sex and separates those of the opposite sex. Kin group membership is transmitted equally by either sex. Cross and parallel relationships between collaterals are crucial to the organization of the kin. Terminology between siblings of parallel sex is reciprocal, but cross-sex siblings are referred to by distinctive nonreciprocal terms (Webster 1977:28–32).

Because long lists of Quechua kin terms are available in Bolton and Mayer (1977), it would be superfluous to repeat them in detail here. Table 1 in Isbell (1977) and Tables 1 and 2 in Isbell (1978) give extensive lists of kin terms for a Quechua community in central Ayacucho; her terms differ from the ones used in this volume only because she has used the possessive form of address (e.g., "my brother" rather than "brother"). In the llama-herding communities we studied, just as in Isbell's village of Chuschi, Spanish terms such as *tío*, *sobrino*, *abuelo*, and *suegro* have begun to replace the Quechua terms for uncle, nephew, grandfather, and father-in-law (Table 3.1).

Two terms which have not changed since at least as far back as the seventeenth century—almost certainly because of their ritual importance—are *masa* and *llumchuy*. A man's "true" *masa*, or *yura masa*, is his son-in-law, his daughter's husband; the term can be extended, however, as in *mallki masa*, to his sister's husband, brother's daughter's husband, or sister's daughter's husband. A man's "true" *llumchuy* is his daughter-in-law, his son's wife; however, it too can be extended to his brother's wife, brother's son's wife, or sister's son's wife (Fig. 3.2).

Figure 3.2   The positions of *masa* (son-in-law) and *llumchuy* (daughter-in-law) in Ayacucho Quechua kinship (redrawn from Palomino Flores 1970).

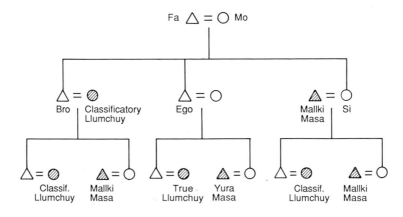

Table 3.1

Kinship terms used by modern Quechua speakers of the Yanahuaccra-Toqtoqasa region compared with those used by Quechua speakers of the sixteenth and seventeenth centuries

| English term | Modern Yanahuaccra-Toqtoqasa[a] | Sixteenth- and seventeenth-century terms[e] | | |
		Clemente Perroud and Chouvenc[b]	González Holguín[c]	Santo Tomás[d]
father	tayta	taita	(n.c.)	yayanc
mother	mama	mamá	mama	mama
husband (wife speaking)	qosa	josa (hari, yana)	(n.c.)	coça
wife (husband speaking)	warmi	warmi	huarmi	guarme
son (father speaking)	churi	churi	churi	churi
daughter (father speaking)	ususi	ususi	ususi	ussinc?
son/daughter (mother speaking)	wawa	wawa	huahua	guagua
first-born son	piwi churi	piwi churi	ppiui churi	(n.c.)
older son	kuraq churi	kuraq	curak churi	(n.c.)
younger son	sullka churi	sullka churi	sullka churi	(n.c.)
brother (brother speaking)	wawqe	wauje	huauqque	guauquin
brother (sister speaking)	turi	turi	tura	tora, tori
sister (brother speaking)	pana	pana	pana	pana
sister (sister speaking)	ñaña	ñaña	ñaña	(n.c.)

(continued)

[a] Terms collected in 1970–1972.

[b] Terms collected from Ayacucho informants and colonial documents by Clemente Perroud and Chouvenc (1970).

[c] Terms collected in the Cuzco area by González Holguín ([1608] 1952).

[d] Terms collected by Fray Domingo de Santo Tomás ([1560] 1951a).

[e] (n.c.) = term not collected.

Table 3.1 *(continued)*

English term	Modern Yanahuaccra-Toqtoqasa[a]	Clemente Perroud and Chouvenc[b]	González Holguín[c]	Santo Tomás[d]
		Sixteenth- and seventeenth-century terms[e]		
grandfather	machu	machu	(n.c.)	aposqui, macho
grandmother	paya	maman	paya	paya
grandchild	willka	willka	huhuayniypac hurin	haguaynin cari (male) haguaynin guarme (female)
father-in-law (male speaking)	kaka	kaka	caca	caca
father-in-law (female speaking)	(n.c.)	kiwach	(n.c.)	quihuachi
father's sister (nephew speaking)	ipa	ipa, ypa	(n.c.)	(n.c.)
mother-in-law (son-in-law speaking)	aqe	aje	(n.c.)	acque
mother-in-law (daughter-in-law speaking)	kiwach	kiwachi	quihuach	quiguahx
son-in-law, brother-in-law	masa	masa	catay	massa
"true son-in-law"	yura masa	(n.c.)	(n.c.)	(n.c.)
classificatory son-in-law: my sister's husband, my brother's daughter's husband, my sister's daughter's husband	mallki masa	(n.c.)	(n.c.)	(n.c.)
daughter-in-law	llumchuy	llumchui	cachun	llunchuy, cachonin

In a 1618 manuscript by Fray Pablo José de Arriaga (1968:54), who was reporting on "superstitions" and "idolatrous practices" of various provinces including Junín and Ayacucho, the preferred guests for certain Indian family rituals were said to be the *massa* and the *caca*. Ayacucho

Quechua dictionaries drawing on early ethnohistoric sources such as Guardia M. (1967:95) and Clemente P. and Chouvenc (1970:107) define *massa* as "son-in-law," "brother-in-law," or "husband's brother"; for contemporary Ayacucho, Soto Ruiz (1976:74) gives *masa* as "son-in-law." *Caca* or *kaka* is variously defined as "father-in-law," "wife's father," "mother's brother," or "wife-giver." *Llumchuy* is most frequently defined as "daughter-in-law." The strong implication is that fathers-in-law, sons-in-law, and daughters-in-law have ritual obligations to one another that have characterized Quechua culture for many centuries.

The ritual obligations of *masa* and *llumchuy* constitute a widespread phenomenon in the Andes. At Quinua and Huamanguilla (this study), at Chuschi and Choque Huarcaya in central Ayacucho (Isbell 1978; Quispe 1969), and at Tangor in the Department of Pasco (Mayer 1977), these affinal kin play roles so prominent that alliance relations seem ritually elevated above descent. Sociobiologists would probably argue, however, that this appearance is superficial. Since a man's daughter is carrying many of his genes, a father-in-law's economic support of his *masa* (including a gift of llamas at the time of the marriage) could be construed as an investment in his daughter's prosperity and fitness. As for a man's *llumchuy*, she will of course bear his son's children one day. Thus sociobiological theorists could justifiably claim to predict these close ritual relationships.

However, when there are economic advantages to be gained, these affinal relations also provide a framework into which affluent strangers can be fitted. For example, at Paruro in the Cuzco region, when a family wishes to incorporate a foreign female anthropologist, her social ties, and her material riches into the ritual system, she is labeled *qachun*, "daughter-in-law," by her informants (Poole 1984).

As Mayer (1977) points out, the obligations of father-in-law and son-in-law are viewed not in the jural idiom of explicit rights and duties but in the idiom of reciprocal exchange. This brings us to the concept of *ayni*, or "Andean reciprocity," one of the most basic and all-pervasive features of the Andean world view.

Ayni and Minka

Underlying all the systems of mutual assistance we discuss in later chapters of this book—and at the heart of several rituals of possible adaptive significance—is the concept of Andean reciprocity.

Among *ayllumasi*, or members of the same *ayllu*, reciprocal relations are usually of two types: *ayni* and *minka* (Fonseca Martel 1974; Alberti and Mayer 1974). *Ayni* is the indigenous term for delayed, symmetrical, reciprocal assistance—ritual or economic aid which will be returned one day. It is the Quechua equivalent of the Zapotec Indian concept *guelaguetza* (Martínez Ríos 1964; Beals 1970), a service performed for a member of one's kin group with the unspoken understanding that equivalent assistance will be returned one day—house construction for house construction, herding for herding, planting for planting.

Minka, on the other hand, is asymmetrical reciprocity in which work can be exchanged for food, drink, coca, goods, rights to use land, or even money. The wage relationship is the least preferred among indigenous people because it is seen as establishing a hierarchical relationship between a superior and a subordinate. If *ayni* is modeled on man's relations with his kinsmen, *minka* is modeled on man's asymmetrical relations with the *wamani*.

Farmers, Herders, Animals, and Spirits: A Summary

An Ayacucho community is composed of several *ayllus*, frequently as many as four. Where *ayllus* are large, they can be divided into "near kin" with whom one cannot marry and "distant kin" with whom one can. Where *ayllus* are small, the exchange of brides across *ayllu* lines is necessary. To avoid incest—and the frightening possibility of being turned into a were-llama—one must marry only those to whom one is unrelated over three or four generations. This preserves the cosmological model in which mortal man and woman have descended in separate lines from Viracocha through Camac Pacha and Mama Cocha.

Farmers and herders can belong to the same *ayllu* and the same communities. But while the farmer usually lives in the *llaqta*, or village, in the *kichwa* zone, the llama herder often lives with his animals in a tiny *estancia* in the *sallqa*. Virtually everyone in his *estancia* is too close a relative to marry. Thus the herder has two choices: he can marry a woman from the *kichwa*, who may find life on the puna too rugged, or he can marry someone from another *estancia*. The latter choice (preferred by most of the herders we knew) requires that friendly relations be maintained throughout a network of tiny *estancias* scattered over hundreds of square kilometers of puna (see Chapter 4).

The maintenance of such a network is accomplished by a set of obligations based on the concept of *ayni*. One has reciprocal obligations to one's *ayllu* members, and these obligations are extended by marriage to one's in-laws. Ritual relations between father-in-law, son-in-law, and daughter-in-law have traditionally been so important, at least since the early 1600s, that they require long trips across the *sallqa* to assist at ceremonies. Indeed, so important is ritual assistance that the term "in-law" can be extended even to non-kin who offer it. There is still another term—*kuyaq*—which is extended to non-relatives who "love" or "care enough" to act like honorary kinsmen (Isbell 1977). Such inclusion of strangers as honorary *ayllu* members is necessary because there is no other context in which one could extend *ayni* to strangers.

Living beside the herder's cottage in the *sallqa* are his llamas and sheep, the animals on which his livelihood depends. Of the two species, it is the llamas with which his relationship has the longest, deepest, and most indigenous roots. They belong not to the herder but to the *wamani* who lives in the mountain nearest his corral, with whom the herder's relations resemble *minka*. The *wamani* can make the herd thrive and increase, but he expects gifts and prayers in return. Once a year, during one of the two "angriest" months, man's relations with the *wamani* become unstable and must be renewed (see Chapter 8).

As part of the ceremony of renewal, there comes a day when some llamas are dressed up like humans and some herders briefly imitate llamas. Two animals may be "married" on a wedding bed; others may have alcoholic beverages forced down their throats; still others may be purified with a powder that symbolizes snow. Fathers-in-law, sons-in-law, and daughters-in-law fulfill their ritual obligations, and unrelated visitors who contribute to the success of the ceremony are treated as fictive kin. It is all consistent with the notion that everyone—even strangers and llamas—can participate if, for the sake of the ritual, they can all be considered members of the *ayllu*.

Four

The People of the Puna

Quinua and Huamanguilla are market towns in the eastern piedmont of the Ayacucho Basin. They depend for their livelihood on a mixture of agriculture, animal husbandry, craft activities, and commerce. Like so many central highland towns, they lie in the midst of the fertile *kichwa* zone, where cereals and root crops flourish among tree-bordered irrigation canals.

Both Quinua and Huamanguilla are backed up against a massive mountain range that separates Ayacucho from the *montaña* of the eastern Andes. The top of the range is a wilderness of rocky cliffs, alpine tundra, cold puna lakes, and Pleistocene glacial moraines. This, too, is an economically productive part of the Quinua-Huamanguilla area; it is where all the llamas and most of the sheep are grazed. Here animals are forced to use land that might otherwise be useless and simultaneously prevented from invading the crops of the *kichwa*.

The herders who keep these flocks usually have relatives in Quinua, or Huamanguilla, or in the *montaña* town of Tambo on the opposite side of the mountains. As we stressed in an earlier chapter, herders are neither a separate caste nor a different ethnic group from the people of the *kichwa*. However, because they live permanently on the puna and come to town only on certain occasions, they are thought of as uncivilized by the people of the town (Fig. 4.1).

Isbell, living in the village of Chuschi, heard the same derogatory comments from her informants: "The term *sallqa* has a double meaning in Quechua; it signifies the high puna and also means savage or uncivilized. People who live on the puna permanently and do not engage in agriculture in the *kichwa* zone are called *sallqaruna*, savage people." Among other things, the puna is regarded as a zone where "uncivilized acts such as

Figure 4.1   Somewhat ill at ease on the cobblestone streets of Huamanguilla, a family of herders from Paltamachay poses shyly for a photograph.

forbidden sexual activity occur. Villagers believe that incestuous acts oc-cur in the *sallqa*, and people engaging in such acts are condemned to roam the streets of the village at night in animal form" (1978:91). One can hardly blame the villagers for believing this, since the herders on the puna believe it themselves. Isbell's allusion to people in animal form sounds like a villager's version of the *ccarccacha*, or were-llama, which the herders believe results from incest.

In this chapter we introduce the *sallqaruna* who lived permanently on the punas above Quinua and Huamanguilla in the early 1970s. All of them raised llamas, which were used in pack trains, and some herded sheep as well. All grew *chuñu* potatoes on the puna, and a few had *chakras* at lower elevations for common potatoes. Virtually all were monolingual speakers of Ayacucho Quechua, and all believed more strongly in the aboriginal spirits of the Andes than they did in the Catholic saints. We picked them for study because they gave us the closest link to the prehispanic herder that we could find in the region. Occupying the lowest rung on Ayacucho's social ladder, they proved to be tough, fatalistic, self-reliant, stoic, deeply religious, and very suspicious of strangers.

Contributing to the toughness of Peru's high-altitude herders is a life of physical exertion in the face of continuous cold and oxygen deprivation. At 4500 m elevation (14,700 feet), oxygen pressure is decreased by as much as 40% compared to the pressure at sea level. The resultant hypoxia gives visitors to the puna alkalosis (with temporary infertility), chronic fatigue, weight loss, and more transitory disorders such as headaches and shortness of breath (Frisancho 1975:313). Highland natives have adapted to this by having greater chest size, an enlarged right ventricle of the heart, and larger lung capacity, especially larger residual lung volume; they also have red blood cell counts of 5–8 million per mm^3, substantially higher than the 4.5 million typical of lowlanders. These adaptations are acquired during the developmental years, and while it is not known how much is genetic and how much is a physiological response, "some individuals appear to be predisposed to high altitude sickness" while others "feel only mild effects that can be overcome with acclimatization" (1975:313).

Obviously, there should have been selection for the latter individuals over time. Baker (1968:30), who studied a similar high-altitude population in southern Peru, interpreted his results "as showing that some aspects of native adaptation [to cold and hypoxia] take lifelong exposure to the environmental conditions and may be based on a genetic structure which varies from that of lowlanders." Baker's study population showed high birth rates, high death rates, slow postnatal growth, and unusually high female death rates postnatally as well as prenatally.

The typical diet of Baker's study population consisted of 86% carbohydrates, 8% protein, and 6% fat. Similar proportions characterized the diet

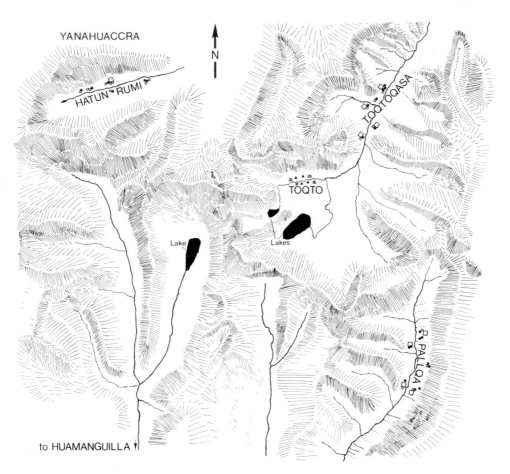

Figure 4.2   Hatun Rumi, Toqtoqasa, Pallqa, and Toqto all lie in this mountainous, 100-km² area northeast of Huamanguilla. Rectangular symbols represent cottages and corrals visible on old aerial photographs; small black triangles symbolize temporary shelters.

of the Ayacucho herders. We estimated their plant intake as 40% potatoes (in the form of soup, boiled potatoes, or freeze-dried *chuñu*); some men boasted of being able to eat a kilogram of potatoes a day, and while we have no reason to doubt them,[1] the most we ever observed was 0.5 kg. The rest of the plant intake was about 20% maize (usually as soup, boiled kernels, or chicha), 20% faba beans (*Vicia faba*, a Spanish introduction),

1. Sherry Ortner reports that some Sherpa men can eat a kilogram of potatoes in one day.

and the remainder divided among *maswa, oca, olluco, quinoa, cañiwa,* squashes, and wheat.

As so often happens, most of the meat raised by the herders wound up on the tables of townspeople. We estimated the herder's own meat consumption at 0–200 g per day. The 200 g were eaten on ceremonial occasions (4–5 times a year) or at childbirth, but several days per week could be meatless, except for whatever tidbits flavored the soup. On other days that same *chupi,* or soup, might include a 10–40-g piece of meat or rehumidified *charki* for each person.

In addition, each adult chewed perhaps 5–15 leaves of coca (*Erythroxylum coca*) on days when he or she could afford it. Mixed with lime and kept in the cheek as a slowly chewed quid, these leaves provide for the slow release of very small quantities of cocaine over a period of two hours or so (Barnett 1983). Andean Indians at all altitudes feel that chewing coca "helps people to stay awake and confers resistance against hunger, thirst, and muscular fatigue, as well as producing a degree of euphoria and mental excitement" (Bray and Dollery 1983:273). Although Bray and Dollery have shown that coca chewing is too widespread to be a response to the stress of high altitude, studies by Picón Reátegui (1968) suggest that it may temporarily raise skin temperatures. Ayacucho herders claimed that coca dulls their hunger while up on the puna brava (almost certainly because of its anaesthetic effect on the mouth and tongue), yet they also chewed it between courses of a ritual meal (see Chapter 8).

The herders we studied lived mostly at five settlements between 4200 and 4500 m elevation. All five, separated by deep canyons and high mountain peaks, were linked by marriage. In order to protect the privacy of our informants, we have omitted their surnames and changed a few other details which do not affect the study. We refer to the five settlements as Hatun Rumi, Paltamachay, Toqtoqasa, Pallqa, and Toqto (Fig. 4.2). All were studied between 1970 and 1972.[2]

Settlement Patterns

Herding communities on the puna are referred to by the Spanish Colonial word *estancia,* meaning "small ranch." *Estancias* are dispersed settlements

2. Because our narrative applies only to that period, we use the past tense. Use of the present tense would be inappropriate since, as we mentioned in Chapter 1, the guerrilla activity of the 1980s has forced the abandonment of many settlements in the region and changed the lifeways of others.

composed of widely scattered units called *kanchas*. Although *kancha* is the Quechua word for "corral," it has also come to refer to the whole "compound," or complex of buildings and corrals, used by an extended family and its herds. As we shall see, *kanchas* could vary greatly in size depending on the number of buildings, the number of corrals, and the presence or absence of walled gardens for *chuñu* potatoes (Figs. 4.3–4.5).

The herder's family lives in a rectangular structure called a *chuklla* (pl. *chukllakuna*), which has a thatched roof and walls made from either stones or blocks of *champa* (peat). In Quechua, the term *chuklla*, or "cottage," can be contrasted with the more elegant term *wasi*, or "house." A *chuklla* is more substantial than the pole-and-thatch hut used at temporary camps, but it falls short of the *wasi* used by a person of rank.

Hatun Rumi, Paltamachay, Toqtoqasa, and Pallqa were all *estancias* of llama herders. Toqto was an example of another puna settlement type, the temporary camp at which *chuñu*, or freeze-dried potatoes, were made. *Chuñu*-making camps were seasonal occupations established each year in July and August following the potato harvest. *Chuñu* making was an activity in which the women of the puna played an important role, and we have added Toqto to our list of settlements to underscore the fact that the *sallqaruna* practiced agriculture as well as herding.

Figure 4.3   The smallest *kancha* at Toqtoqasa, consisting of one elongated *chuklla* and a single corral. The parallel white lines are snow-filled furrows in old potato fields.

Figure 4.4 A medium-size *kancha* at Toqtoqasa, consisting of two cottages, a guardian's hut, and five or six corrals, one of which (upper left) was ceremonial.

Figure 4.5 A relatively large *kancha* at Hatun Rumi, consisting of a group of four cottages, a fifth cottage with attached potato garden (center), a guardian's hut (far right), and at least ten corrals in different stages of repair.

Figure 4.6   Yanahuaccra, Saya Runa, and the V-shaped Hatun Rumi valley, seen from the humid woodland above Huamanguilla.

Yanahuaccra

One of the most prominent landmarks of the Ayacucho Basin is a mountain named Yanahuaccra,[3] which overlooks Huamanguilla from an altitude of 4413 m. This peak can be seen from as far away as the highway near Pacaicasa (Fig. 2.2). At its summit is the monumental rock formation *Yana Waqra* ("Black Horn"), from which its name derives; not far to the west is its companion formation *Saya Runa* ("Standing Man") (Fig. 4.6). On the shoulders of the mountain below these stony peaks are a group of canyons and narrow glacial valleys through which the waters from melting snows and springs descend toward the Río Chihua drainage. Throughout these canyons, which run the environmental gamut from the upper *kichwa* to the high puna, the herders of Yanahuaccra once moved on an annual circuit from summer pasture to winter pasture to potato fields.

    3. This is the hispanicized spelling given on government maps rather than the preferred Quechua orthography.

Figure 4.7   The huge, glacially transported boulder for which Hatun Rumi was named, incorporated into one of the *kanchas* as the back wall of a corral.

Perhaps the most important *estancia* during the early 1970s was Hatun Rumi ("Big Rock"), which lay below and to the southeast of Yanahuaccra at an elevation of 4200–4300 m. Its stream valley had clearly been scoured by Pleistocene glaciers, which carried down the enormous boulder for which the *estancia* was named and left it perched in what was then the center of the community (Fig. 4.7). To each side of the stream were three Pleistocene end moraines which ran parallel to the drainage for part of its course, then were cut through by the stream where they converged down-valley (Fig. 4.8). The long, narrow valley—trending from southwest to northeast—was floored with Pleistocene gravels, and even in the late Andean summer one could find patches of snow on top of the ridge to the northwest.

The Hatun Rumi area was a diversified wet puna with many vegetational subfacies due to contrasts between rocky areas, seeps from springs which are permanently humid, and dry hillsides. In March 1971, Flannery and botanist Barbara Pickersgill followed a llama herd up the valley to see exactly what they were eating, and the dietary diversity was impressive.

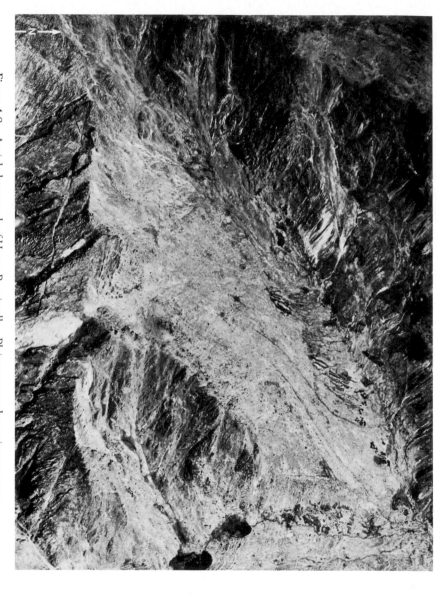

Figure 4.8 Aerial photograph of Hatun Rumi valley. Pleistocene end moraines appear as sinuous lines in the upper right quadrant. (North is at the top of the photograph.)

There were a whole series of grasses, then grazed fairly short, including *Festuca*; a member of the Malvaceae with small blue flowers; a club moss called "cola de chancho," probably *Lycopodium* sp.; an abundant white lichen called "papelito"; a member of the Gentianaceae; a wild geranium; several Compositae, including ground-hugging rosette forms; a legume, very low, possibly *Astragalus*; and an occasional *Arenaria*, one of the plants preferred by vicuñas in other parts of Peru (Koford 1957). This varied menu was eaten by the llamas as they strode nervously along, nibbling on the move, and it may be that the synergistic effect of this species mix improved their nutrition. In addition, this in-motion style of eating was less devastating to the puna vegetation than the way sheep eat, which frequently consists of standing in one place until the ground is bare. Many of the grasses at Hatun Rumi should have been at least 20 cm tall but were heavily overgrazed because the llamas had to share their range with sheep. For an example of the difference sheep can make, see Figure 4.9.

During 1970–1972, the *estancia* of Hatun Rumi comprised five *kanchas* strung out in linear fashion for a kilometer along the banks of the stream. Each *kancha* was the property of one extended family and consisted of one

Figure 4.9 Tall grass puna near Pari, Junín. To the left of the fence is ungrazed range belonging to a mining company; to the right is range heavily overgrazed by sheep.

to three *chukllakuna* built of volcanic tuff boulders pulled from nearby moraines, mortared with *champa*, and thatched with *ichu* grass brought in from a neighboring drainage. These cottages were accompanied by one to three corrals and at least one *chuñu* garden, both walled with the same moraine boulders. Some corrals also had guardian's huts of either stones or pole-and-thatch.

Residence at Hatun Rumi was patrilocal or neolocal; sons who split off from their father's household simply moved 200 m upstream or downstream. There were at least four paternal surnames at the *estancia*, all of them common in Huamanguilla, which was the town to which the herders were most closely affiliated. Huamanguilla lay only three and a half hours' walk below Hatun Rumi at an elevation of 3260 m. Before the land reforms of General Velasco, much of the Yanahuaccra area had been hacienda lands belonging to don Claudio P., a prosperous merchant of Huamanguilla; during land reform the hacienda was abolished and some occupants of Hatun Rumi were allowed to buy from don Claudio the very llamas they had formerly herded for him. Social ties between the Indians and their former patron remained strong, however, and when the herders of Yanahuaccra descended to Huamanguilla to buy tea, sugar, salt, and kerosene, they invariably returned to don Claudio's store.

Nor did land reform appear to have affected settlement patterns at Hatun Rumi, most of whose *kanchas* had been built long before the Velasco junta seized power. The canyon had been selected for its strong springs, its relatively sheltered position between higher escarpments, and its location along the route to higher grazing lands. Its *kanchas* could have been built farther apart, but as every herder of the early 1970s agreed, "we live closer together for mutual protection."

Seasonal Movements

Individual llama herds in the Hatun Rumi area averaged 25 animals, with a range from 18 to 35. In their daily grazing trips, the llamas were allowed to use a circle with a radius of about 2 km. Even if their range had not been shared with sheep, it is questionable whether this area would have been adequate for an entire year's grazing. The cold temperatures of the puna so inhibit plant growth that regeneration is slow, and areas close to the *estancia* soon become overgrazed. This is, however, only one of the reasons that the herders of Yanahuaccra changed settlements during the year; another reason was potato cultivation.

At least two types of potato were grown on the slopes of Yanahuaccra. A larger variety, grown in the upper *kichwa* zone, had no bitterness and could be cooked and eaten without extensive processing (we refer to these as "common potatoes"). A smaller variety, grown in the puna of Hatun Rumi, had greater frost resistance but tasted bitter and was therefore processed into *chuñu* (we refer to the latter as "*chuñu* potatoes," and in the section on the encampment at Toqto we describe the local making of *chuñu inglés*, or "white *chuñu*").

In the early 1970s, individual families at Hatun Rumi did not synchronize their seasonal movements. There was no time when the *estancia* was completely abandoned; rather, depending on the season, some families (or family members) were present and others absent.

One group of herders left Hatun Rumi in November to go to a higher *estancia* called Paltamachay ("Cave with a Lopsided Mouth"), situated in the puna brava above and to the north. There they spent the Andean summer, returning to Hatun Rumi in August for the *herranza* or annual llama-decorating ceremony (see Chapter 8). They remained at Hatun Rumi until November, avoiding some of the snow, sleet, and hail which the Andean winter brings to Paltamachay. This first group of herders usually grew *chuñu* potatoes in walled gardens near their *kanchas* at Hatun Rumi; these potatoes were harvested in July by family members who did not make the Paltamachay trip, and later the whole family made *chuñu* together in August.

A second group of herders treated Hatun Rumi as their summer *estancia*, remaining there from September until April. From May to July, this second group of herders kept their animals down at an encampment below Hatun Rumi, where they harvested common potatoes; in August, they returned to Hatun Rumi to harvest their *chuñu* potatoes. One important reason for their decision to spend the Andean winter in the upper *kichwa*—in addition to the fact that common potatoes do better there— was that this group of herders owned some cattle. Cattle need the richer forage of the *kichwa* zone and, because of their marriage ties with certain families in Huamanguilla, this second group of herders had access to lower pastures.

Let us now take a closer look at specific families from those two groups.

Kancha 2: Sebastián, Emilio, and Porfirio V.

The second *kancha* from the southwest at Hatun Rumi had two rectangular cottages which formed the north and east borders of an irregular stone-walled dooryard or patio. Along the west and south borders of the patio were two large corrals, and beyond this a small pig pen and several *chuñu* potato gardens. Another corral and garden, both older and in need of repair, lay farther away. This was clearly one of the older *kanchas* at the *estancia*, one which had undergone considerable modification and growth by accretion over the years (Figs. 4.10 and 4.11).

This *kancha* belonged to Sebastián V., a senior male in his mid 50s, who had four children by his first wife (later deceased) and three more by his second. Living with him were his eldest son, Emilio (early 30s); Emilio's wife and their four children; Emilio's younger brother Porfirio (early 20s) and his wife, still childless; and occasionally an unmarried brother-in-law. In August, the total number of persons occupying the household hovered at ten, making it one of the largest at Hatun Rumi.

In 1971, Sebastián owned 34 llamas, including 3 or 4 born in February of that year. Emilio and Porfirio each had smaller herds, bringing the total for the extended family to roughly 70 animals. Both sons had received their first llamas from their father at the time of their marriage. Neither had as yet given or received llamas through *suñay* (see Chapter 8), but they had witnessed others do it and knew that it had been a frequent occurrence in earlier times.

Figure 4.10   Layout of Sebastián's V.'s *kancha* at Hatun Rumi.

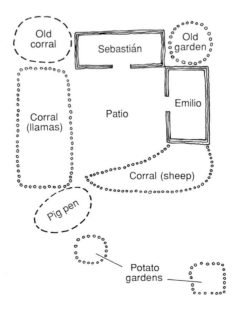

Figure 4.11 Porfirio, Emilio, their wives, and Emilio's children pose in front of their *chuklla* at Hatun Rumi. Note the llama hide thrown on the roof to dry.

Even though Emilio had his own herd, a wife, and four children, he had not yet split off from his father's *kancha* to establish his own separate household. With his father's advancing age and occasional illness, Emilio was needed around the compound. Perhaps more to the point, he and Porfirio had established a division of labor with Sebastián; while their father remained in Hatun Rumi from November to August to guard the *kancha* and help tend the *chuñu* potato gardens, Emilio and Porfirio took their herds up to Paltamachay, where they maintained a summer residence of their own.

Kancha 5: Modesto P.

The fifth (and most northeasterly) *kancha* at Hatun Rumi, separated from its nearest neighbor by 300 m, belonged to Modesto P. It comprised one *chuklla* of stone, turf, and thatch; one circular stone corral with a pole-and-thatch guardian's hut; 35 llamas; a herd of almost 100 sheep; 7 pigs; 3

guard dogs; and a family made up of Modesto, his wife, and an infant child.

Modesto's *kancha* (in contrast to Sebastián's) was the newest at Hatun Rumi; he had only recently split off from his father's household and established his own neolocal residence. Modesto had originally received llamas from his father and father-in-law when he married. Later, having accumulated a nest egg through wage labor, he took advantage of the Velasco government's land reforms by purchasing 25 more llamas and his herd of sheep from don Claudio P. It was this jump in herd size that had provided him with the economic base to establish his own household; indeed, his herd of sheep was unusually large for the community and made his balance of resources somewhat atypical.

Like all herders at Yanahuaccra, Modesto claimed not to know exactly how many llamas he had. However, since he revealed in casual conversation that every llama had a nickname, this ignorance was clearly feigned. All herders in the area, fearing both rustling and government taxation, were understandably suspicious of strangers who wanted to know how many animals they had. This made it necessary for us to count their animals as unobtrusively as possible.

Modesto was one of the herders who had rights to *chakras* for common potatoes at elevations below Hatun Rumi. He therefore did not make the trip to Paltamachay, choosing instead to spend November to March at Hatun Rumi; during most of the Andean winter, he was encamped near his potato fields in the upper *kichwa*.

Toqtoqasa

In the region of Apacheta, southeast of Yanahuaccra, the rim of the Ayacucho Basin is a sturdy wall 4500 m high. This is the watershed between the streams of the basin's interior and the drainages running north toward Tambo and the *montaña*. Roads climb up out of the *kichwa* zone near the pottery-making town of Quinua and ascend the wall of puna in a series of long, laborious hairpin curves. One route carries the traveler up a narrow valley leading from MacNeish's Ruyru Rumi Machay ("Cave below a Round Stone") to the *Scirpus* apron of Lake Yanaqocha, then continues over the crest which separates the two drainages. Below is an L-shaped glacial valley called Toqtoqasa ("Divided Pass"), which drains toward Tambo and the *montaña* through spectacular cliffs and rockslides (Fig. 4.12).

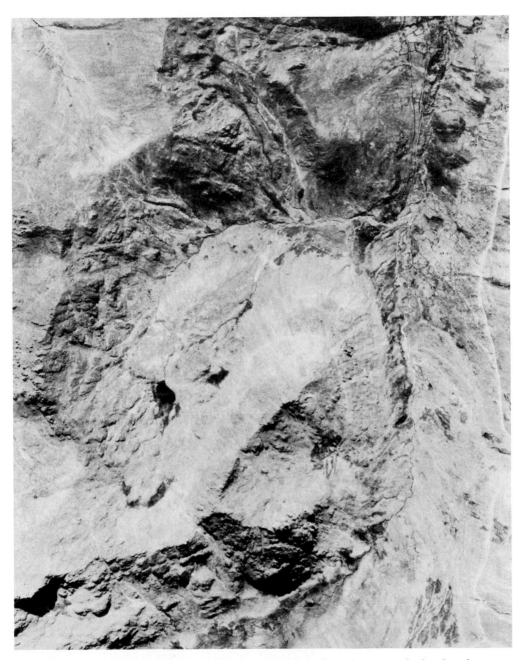

Figure 4.12   Aerial photograph of Toqtoqasa. Old corrals can be seen on both sides of the stream running toward the upper right corner. (Northeast is at the top of the photograph.)

The stream at Toqtoqasa, like the one at Hatun Rumi, runs parallel to (and eventually cuts through) three successive Pleistocene end moraines (Fig. 4.13). In 1970–1972 there were roughly twelve *kanchas* strung out along the stream for a distance of over two kilometers, producing an average spacing of 200 to 300 m between households. Also like Hatun Rumi, the *chukllakuna* and corrals at Toqtoqasa were built of boulders and rubble from the moraines and even set against the latter in some cases. The valley had several permanent springs feeding the stream and the familiar pattern of dry, gravelly puna alternating with areas of wet and spongy peat. Short grasses, lichens, and club mosses were the same as at Hatun Rumi, and footsteps on the scree above the *estancia* set off a similar flurry of startled viscachas. The day fieldwork began at Toqtoqasa, it sleeted; the day fieldwork ended, it snowed.

Household Settlement

Each of the twelve or so *kanchas* at Toqtoqasa consisted of from one to four rectangular cottages of moraine boulders, mud mortar, *champa*, and a roof of *ichu* grass over a wooden frame. *Chukllakuna* averaged 4 × 6 m

Figure 4.13   Three parallel end moraines at Toqtoqasa cross the photograph from upper left to lower right.

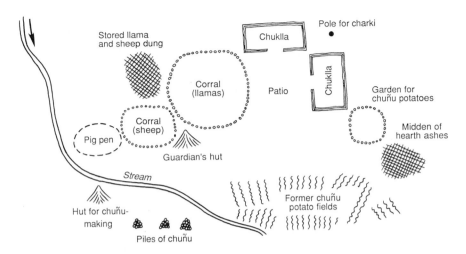

Figure 4.14   Idealized household unit at Toqtoqasa, showing some of the typical features mentioned in the text.

and ranged from square (4 × 4 m) to oblong (4 × 8 m). Such cottages have only one door on the long side, no windows, and no chimney; the smoke from cooking fires rises through the thatch of the roof, which lets smoke escape but does not allow snow to enter. As at Hatun Rumi, when multiple *chukllakuna* were present they were arranged around the sides of an irregular dooryard or patio.

Ten features characterized a typical household unit (Fig. 4.14). The first was the set of cottages already described; the second was a series of boulder-walled corrals for llamas, sheep, and sometimes a few pigs. At larger *kanchas* one special corral, a little farther from the houses, was reserved for the llama-decorating ceremonies to be described in Chapter 8. Still a third feature was a series of feeding troughs made from hollow logs, especially common when pigs were present.

Fourth of the typical features was a small, boulder-walled garden for growing *chuñu* potatoes. There might also be a set of fallow former potato fields downslope from the houses and corrals. These took the form of small patches with *surcos*, or furrows, running vertically downhill, patches often widely separated because of the thin and stony puna soil. Occasionally a sixth feature, the "*chuñu* hut," was found along the stream nearby. This was a small, conical hut or shelter of *ichu* grass like the ones at Toqto (see pp. 72–82), used to store freeze-dried potatoes.

Seventh of the features was a guardian's hut (sometimes built of boulders, but more often of poles and *ichu*) located in or near one of the corrals. In this hut one of the younger men slept, accompanied by his dogs, on nights when the family feared visits from rustlers or mountain lions. Dense foggy nights, when the corrals could not be seen clearly from the house, were considered particularly dangerous.

Still another feature was an upright pole with branches to hold drying strips of *charki*, or freeze-dried meat, out of the reach of dogs. *Charki* might also be thrown onto the roof of the cottage to dry; so were occasional skins of hognosed skunk, which were saved to be tailored into the pouches in which coca leaves were carried. Vegetables from lower elevations, such as maize and squash, were stored under the eaves of the *chuklla* roof.

Two final features of the *kancha* were a pair of middens kept carefully separate. One was a midden of ash from hearth fires, which was periodically removed from the houses and dumped in the same place week after week. The other was a midden of llama and sheep dung, periodically removed from the corrals and added to the growing pile, which would later be used as fertilizer for *chuñu* potatoes. Such use of fertilizer was systematic in the walled *chuñu* garden but much less systematic elsewhere. It is interesting that the llama herd's tendency to defecate in one location—a behavior used by their guanaco ancestors to reinforce territorial boundaries—now benefits potato agriculture.

These ten features defined the typical household unit; many should be archaeologically detectable and could be used to reconstruct the history of the *kancha* as a settlement type. They were complemented by the material culture with which the dark, smoky interiors of the *chukllakuna* were furnished.

Stepping into that darkness, one was first startled by a flash of brown-and-white guinea pigs as they ran squealing for cover (Fig. 4.15). One's second impression was that the cottage was used as much for storage as for sleeping, with sacks of maize and potatoes banked against the walls. Dependent on the markets of the *kichwa* for their coca, salt, sugar, tea, matches, kerosene, and indispensable alcoholic beverages, the herders of Toqtoqasa used their llama trains to bring wool, *charki*, and *chuñu* down to Quinua and Tambo in exchange for the products of the towns. The wooden chairs in their cottages, the carved wooden spoons, the enamel bowls and cups had all been obtained that way, and the pottery water jars had clearly been made by the *alfareros* of Quinua. In addition, however, the *chukllakuna* were furnished with many products the herders themselves

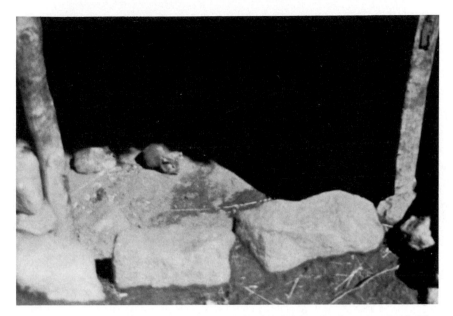

Figure 4.15   Guinea pigs scurry across a patch of sunlight in the doorway of a *chuklla*.

had made: ponchos and gunny sacks woven of llama hair, meter upon meter of rope woven of *ichu* grass, shallow circular baskets made from willow wands, *qenas* (indigenous flutes) carved from sections of cane.

Only one *kancha*—at the farthest outskirts of the *estancia*, just before the descent toward Tambo—had possessions beyond those described above. This was the household of Félix U., a weaver who owned a pedal loom of the type introduced by the Spaniards (Fig. 4.16). Félix and his two brothers lived in the *kancha* with their wives and children; the women spun yarn from llama and sheep wool, while the men worked the loom to produce clothing and textiles from the yarn. Félix had used the income from the sale of these textiles to make his *kancha* uniquely comfortable and well furnished, and we never saw another like it. Indeed, such striking evidence of acculturation was rare among the *estancias*.

Pastor and Martina W.: The Linking of *Estancias* through Marriage

The most southerly *kancha* at Toqtoqasa in 1970–1972, not far from the ascent leading back to Quinua, belonged to "don" Pastor W. and his wife, "mama" Martina V. de W. (Fig. 4.17). Their honorific titles reflected both their sexagenarian status and the fact that almost everyone in the *estancia* was somehow related to them. There were fewer surnames at Toqtoqasa

Figure 4.16   Spanish-style loom in the cottage of Félix V., at Toqtoqasa.

than at Hatun Rumi, and Pastor's was the most common; it was said to be common also in Tambo, the town whose ties to the *estancia* were strongest. Martina, however, was a woman from Yanahuaccra—a relative of Sebastián, Emilio, and Porfirio V.—who had moved to Toqtoqasa after her marriage to Pastor. Indeed, Pastor and Martina's family serves as a convenient example of the way that marriages could link four tiny *estancias* scattered over a wilderness of mountains (Fig. 4.18).

Let us begin with the marriage of Pastor and Martina, some time in the late 1920s. With that marriage, Pastor received llamas from his father at Toqtoqasa and his father-in-law in Hatun Rumi so that he could begin his own herd. While that herd grew, Pastor and Martina lived at his father's *kancha* in Toqtoqasa. But Pastor had now become a *masa*, or son-in-law, which obligated him to travel to his father-in-law's *kancha* at Hatun Rumi each August to participate in the llama-decorating ceremony. This was also an opportunity for Martina to visit her family.

As his herd grew, Pastor eventually established his own household and corrals at Toqtoqasa, and he and Martina went on to have five children: Manuel W. (their *piwi churi* or firstborn male heir); two daughters who died in their 20s; Teófila, married and living nearby in the early 1970s;

Figure 4.17 Martina V. de W. stands near the *charki* pole to the east of her *chuklla*, Toqtoqasa.

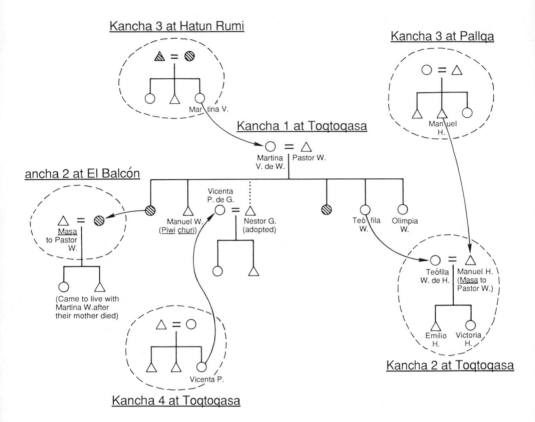

Figure 4.18 Kinship diagram showing the linking of Hatun Rumi, Pallqa, Toqtoqasa, and El Balcón by marriage. Hachured symbols indicate persons who died prior to 1970.

and Olimpia, who was still an unmarried teenager. They also adopted Nestor G., the *wakcha*, or orphan son, of more distant relatives, whom they treated as their own offspring.

Pastor and Martina's oldest daughter had married a young man from El Balcón, another *estancia* in the mountains some two days' walk from Toqtoqasa. Although she subsequently died as the result of a miscarriage, her husband continued to be Pastor's *masa*, and he sometimes returned in August to participate in the decorating of Pastor's llamas. The two surviving children of this marriage came to live with Pastor and Martina after their mother died, since there was no female relative at El Balcón willing to look after them.

Teófila, a younger daughter, married Manuel H. from Pallqa, another *estancia* not far to the southeast (see Fig. 4.2). Under normal conditions, Teófila would have gone to live with her husband at Pallqa, but there were no suitable locations there for Manuel to build a *kancha* of his own. Manuel therefore moved to Toqtoqasa and set up his own *kancha* only 200 m distant from that of don Pastor. He, too, became a *masa* on whom Pastor could rely; and little Emilio and Victoria, the children resulting from his marriage to Teófila, spent most of their time playing with their cousins around mama Martina's kitchen. Because it was not standard practice for a man to move to his wife's *estancia*, Manuel H. had to tolerate a certain amount of good-natured joking.

Finally, adopted son Nestor G. married Vicenta, a girl from a neighboring *kancha* at Toqtoqasa. Still not yet economically independent in 1971, he and Vicenta lived in Pastor's household with their two children. Thus there were at least ten people occupying Pastor's *kancha* in the early 1970s: Martina and Pastor; Manuel W.; Nestor G., Vicenta, and their two children; Olimpia; and the two children from El Balcón whose mother had died (Fig. 4.19).

This *kancha* consisted of four 4- × 6-m cottages arranged around a 5- × 20-m patio, surrounded by llama and sheep corrals, guardian's huts, and *chuñu* potato gardens. The need to marry someone "four generations removed" or "not sharing two surnames" (see Chapter 3) had extended the search for mates through four different *estancias*—Toqtoqasa, Hatun Rumi, Pallqa, and El Balcón—and linked an area of several hundred square kilometers of high-altitude tundra into a network of blood-kin and affinal obligations.

A Day in the Life

Dawn: on a typical morning late in the Andean winter, the first rays of the sun sparkle on heavy frost. Long shadows extend down over Toqtoqasa from the cliffs and crags to the east. In the utter silence, the air is like icewater in your lungs, your fingers too blue to move. Clusters of llamas, still serenely asleep with their knees tucked beneath them, appear to be frozen to the floor of the corral.

Little by little, the gray smoke from peat fires rises through *ichu* roofs as a morning meal is prepared. Men stand in the shadow of boulder walls, noisily blowing noses held between thumb and forefinger; women emerge, pitch basinfuls of used water onto the frozen dooryard, and disappear again. By 7:30 A.M. on a sunny day the herders are in the corrals, encouraging the llamas to stagger to their feet in that characteristically awkward way. In a few minutes they will be off to pasture at higher elevations, followed later by the sheep.

Had it been a rainy or foggy morning, the herds might not have been taken out until 10 A.M. Dense fog is particularly dangerous, since animals separated from the herder can be lost or stolen. Families with horses or donkeys, which are considered even more expensive, usually make sure those animals graze near the *kancha*; thefts of up to thirteen horses have occurred when the animals were allowed to stray too far into the hills and were overtaken by fog.

When such thefts occur, the herders, often armed with no more than a strong club, must try to track the rustlers and their stolen animals across

Figure 4.19 Occupants of Pastor's household share a morning joke before the herds are taken out to the still-snowy hills in the background. The carefully protected tree in this *kancha* is a rarity on the puna.

Figure 4.20   Sr. Vásquez examines the skin of a mountain lion killed by herders from Hatun Rumi.

the mountains in an effort to recover them. It is risky business, since the rustlers frequently lie in ambush for the unwary herder. Such dangers, however, do not seem to deter the people of the *estancia*, who regularly attack live skunks with dirt clods and kill mountain lions with rocks (Fig. 4.20). In 1971, Flannery and Vásquez came across two herders from Hatun Rumi skinning a puma who had eaten two of their sheep. In response to

Figure 4.21 Toqtoqasa, 8 A.M. The bad news: snow covers the llama range in the background, and the temperature is 2°C. The good news: breakfast will be preceded by "happy hour."

the inevitable question about how the predator had been killed, one herder answered matter-of-factly, "*Payta kaspikunawanmi wacctaraniku*" ("We hit him with sticks").

Breakfast at mama Martina's kitchen in Toqtoqasa begins with a shot of *cañazo*, the eye-opener of choice for frozen herders (Fig. 4.21). Although it is distilled from sugar cane, *cañazo* sells for about 50 cents a fifth and resembles nothing so much as paint remover. Following local protocol, Pastor takes a shot himself before offering it to a guest, "just to prove it isn't poison." Then one is handed a wooden spoon and an enamel bowl of *chupi*—thick soup composed of hominy, transverse slices of boiled corn on the cob, faba beans, a piece of *charki* or pork rind, boiled and cut-up potatoes, cabbage, and parsley. "*Chaynam ñoccanchicpa kawsayninchicca*"

("This is our life"), says mama Martina to a guest; "*Micuycuya kay mi-cuyta, amaya wischupacuychucca*" ("Do us the honor of eating it without disparaging us").

The second course is a dish of boiled *maswa* (*Tropaeolum tuberosum*), sweeter and more turniplike than potatoes, a plant whose wild relative still grows on the talus of Ruyru Rumi Cave. On other mornings, an alternative second course might consist of a wicker basket filled with tiny redskin potatoes which had been boiled, then simmered in salt and cooking oil to enhance their flavor.

Like Yanahuaccra, Toqtoqasa is overgrazed because the llamas must share their range with sheep. The llamas use a circle with a 2-km radius, but the location of the circle varies slightly every day. Whereas shepherds stick close to their flock of sheep, llama herders do not; they climb to a peak with a good view of the country, then sit or "hunker down" while the llamas stride along, eating. Anticipating the places their herd will eventually reach, the men arrive there first by taking shortcuts over cliffs and ridges, then wait for the llamas to catch up. The farthest distance from the *estancia* that llamas are allowed to stray—usually no more than 5 km—is determined by how far the herders believe their animals can travel and still be caught and returned to the *kancha* before dusk. Impending darkness or incoming fog, with its threat of predators, can cut the trip short. Infringing on the meadows of another *estancia* is avoided because of the bad relations it can cause.

While the men follow the herds, the women of Toqtoqasa carry out their tasks. Spinning wool into yarn, they sit in groups in the relative warmth of the dooryard and talk as they fill the spindles (Fig. 4.22). In August, when the *chuñu* potatoes have been harvested, some women may do the freeze-drying at home, although not on the scale seen in the *chuñu* camp at Toqto (see below). Along the banks of the stream, the potatoes lie in piles 30 cm high and 50 cm in diameter, frozen as hard as rock (Fig. 4.23). The women spread them out as the morning sun thaws them, treading on them with bare feet to squeeze out the water, giggling to each other "*Chiriwachkan llumpayta*" ("It's making me very cold"). The process goes on day after day until the desiccation is complete. At noon the women take a coca break beside the conical *chuñu* hut, sitting crosslegged with their multilayered woolen skirts arranged to provide a depression for the bag of leaves. This is the pause that refreshes: to *chacchar*, to fill one's cheeks like a chipmunk, to speak in animated tones about past chapters in the ongoing soap opera of life at Toqtoqasa. The men, looking down on the scene from the grazing lands above, assure a visitor that the conversation below is sheer gossip, "*warmipa rimaypayllanmi.*"

As afternoon shadows lengthen, the herders and their flocks descend from the Apacheta highlands and cross the stream into Toqtoqasa. Their stoicism reinforced by their own cheekfuls of coca, they have ignored cold and hunger for eight hours and perhaps missed their *cañazo* more than anything else. As for the llamas themselves, even if they have spent the whole day grazing together, each herd of 15 to 40 animals separates itself from the rest and seeks its own corral.

An evening meal, imperceptibly different from the *chupi* served at breakfast, is already cooking over a fire of *champa* in each kitchen at Toqtoqasa. Now is the time for anyone who has a *qena* to bring it out— or, in the case of the least impoverished families, a small transistor radio. By the light of a kerosene lamp, someone searches the radio dial for Ayacucho, Huancavelica, or Huancayo. With luck, they may soon be

Figure 4.22   A young woman of Pastor's household spins raw wool into yarn on a spindle.

Figure 4.23 Their *chuñu* potatoes laid out in piles along the banks of a puna stream, three members of a Toqtoqasa household squeeze out the liquid with their feet.

listening to the melancholy sevenths and minor chords of a *waynu* sung in Quechua.

Then, very suddenly, it is sleeting—gentle and sporadic sleet whipped around by the wind, but sleet nevertheless. From that point on there is little to do but go to sleep, even if it is only 8 P.M. After all, when night falls on the *estancia*, nothing stirs out on the puna except rustlers, mountain lions, were-llamas—and perhaps an occasional *pistako*.

Pallqa

En route from Quinua to Tambo, on the puna beyond Ruyru Rumi Cave and shortly before the ascent to Lake Yanaqocha, lies a north–south trending valley named Pallqa ("bifurcation" or "divide"). The altitude is about 4250 m, and in 1970–1972 the *estancia* consisted of eight to ten *kanchas* strung out for about 1.6 km along a small stream (Figs. 4.24 and 4.25). The herders of Pallqa used Quinua as their closest market town and

Figure 4.25 A large *kancha* at Pallqa, consisting of five cottages, a patio, a circular ceremonial corral, and seven or eight rectangular corrals. The llama herd is assembled in one corral on the left; in the center of the photograph is an oval *chuñu* potato garden, with a huge pile of llama dung stored as fertilizer.

had close relations with the people of Toqtoqasa; many of them processed their *chuñu* potatoes at Toqto. Pallqa was obviously an *estancia* of considerable time depth, with numerous abandoned *kanchas* suggesting that the population had once been larger. Because of the coming and going between Pallqa and various "summer *estancias*" at still higher elevations, it was difficult to get accurate estimates of the population at any one time.

Félix M. and Agustina H. de M.

One of the most extensive *kanchas* at Pallqa belonged to Félix M. and his wife, Agustina. This was one of the most economically secure families in the region; both husband and wife had inherited large llama herds from their fathers and managed them well. The combined total for the two herds was 50–60 animals, which provided a very extensive llama train. Félix kept a group of eight horses and donkeys so that he and his sons and

Figure 4.24 Aerial photograph of the Pallqa valley. The dark patches on both sides of the stream are old potato fields. The steepness of the terrain is reflected in the hairpin curves of the Quinua-Tambo road, which appears as a white line to the left of the stream. (Northeast is at the top of the photograph.)

brothers could ride while they accompanied the llama caravan on its trips. He kept a dozen head of cattle but, unlike some of his neighbors, owned no sheep.

Félix and Agustina's *kancha* (Fig. 4.26) exemplified the relatively prosperous extended household. Three boulder *chukllakuna*, whose corners adjoined, formed one border of the innermost corral—the small one where pregnant llamas were kept during the final days before parturition. Forming an L around this corral was a larger one where the rest of the llamas were kept; it allowed room for both Félix's and Agustina's herds to remain separate and contained two huge piles of llama dung used to fertilize the *chuñu* potato garden near the cottages.

A long, narrow corral for the horses and donkeys ran parallel to the long axis of the llama corral. Beyond this was a corral for the cattle which extended to the near wall of Félix's brother's cottage. The presence of his brother's *chuklla* made it unnecessary for Félix to build a guardian's hut near his cattle corral.

Félix, Agustina, one married son, and two unmarried daughters occupied the three *chukllakuna* near the small corral. Their network of kinsmen, *masas*, and *llumchuys* was extensive, and they had added fictive kin to this group by adopting the Latin American peasant custom of *compadrazgo*. In Chapter 8 we describe an important ceremony at this particular *kancha*.

Toqto

South, or upstream, from Toqtoqasa—very near the divide between the waters of Tambo and Ayacucho—lies a small intermontane depression with a series of puna lakes. Surrounded by peaks reaching to 4500 m, its major landmark is Lake Yanaqocha, which supports flocks of *yanawiku* (Ridgway's ibis) and *wachwa* (Andean goose). Streams draining these high bodies of water converge at a place called Toqto, where the cold current meanders across a strip of spongy but almost level land before descending toward Toqtoqasa.

In 1970–1972, Toqto was the site of a seasonal camp for the making of *chuñu inglés*, or "white *chuñu*." Some of the features that led to its use were unlike those characteristic of other settlement types. Many sites on the puna were chosen for settlement because they were warmer and a bit more sheltered than the average place; in contrast, *chuñu* camps were frequently

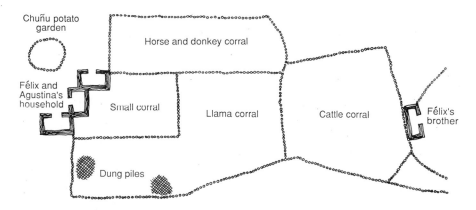

Figure 4.26   The layout of Félix and Agustina's *kancha* at Pallqa.

found on the bottom of natural depressions where cold air tended to settle and therefore increased the chances of a hard frost. Another important feature was that the camp needed a stream which could easily be dammed up with stones and earth, producing a temporary basin where thousands of potatoes could be submerged.

Since it takes only about 17 days to make *chuñu* (14–15 under ideal conditions), the dam does not have to be permanent, nor do the shelters built by the occupants. What they constructed at Toqto were conical huts averaging 2.5 m in diameter at the base, capable of holding one person comfortably or three not so comfortably. The frame was composed of 8 to 12 wooden poles whose bases were set in the earth at intervals around the outside of the circular floor and whose upper ends were tied together to form the conical peak; a horizontal lattice of cane or willow wands linked the lower sections of the poles, and the whole structure was thatched from ground to peak with *ichu* grass (Fig. 4.27). Since all these materials were easily transportable, such a hut could eventually be dismantled and its parts carried back to the *estancia* from which the *chuñu* makers had come. We were struck by how much these huts resembled archaeological structures from Peruvian preceramic sites such as Chilca (Donnan 1964) and Asia (Engel 1963). In the Cuzco region, similar temporary shelters are referred to as *astana* (Orlove 1977:89–90 and Fig. 12).

Toqto was used mainly by families from Pallqa and Toqtoqasa, who traveled there in July and August to process their potatoes. Many brought

Figure 4.27 The *chuñu*-making encampment at Toqto, showing the typical spacing between two families' temporary shelters of poles and *ichu* grass. Large circles of peat have been removed for fuel in the vicinity of each hut. On the mountain slopes in the distance, one can see abandoned corrals from an earlier era.

the construction poles with them on horseback or donkeyback and built small corrals for those animals on the outskirts of the encampment. Some even brought their llamas and sheep along, especially if there were no relatives back in the *estancia* to take care of them during the two to three weeks of *chuñu* making.

Prehistoric camps for making white *chuñu* have not been reported archaeologically, but they should potentially be identifiable. One would have to look for an area with a dammable stream, where cold air settles and frosts are heavy, and which has remnants of boulder corrals but no traces of domestic architecture other than postmolds. Such sites are likely to appear so meager that most archaeologists will not be attracted to them, but if located they could provide some interesting economic information on a region. The presence of water sets such camps apart from most areas where *tokosh*, or "black *chuñu*," is made. Since *tokosh* is not flushed in water (and retains some bitterness as a result), it can be made almost anywhere.

Chuñu Production

There are several varieties of potato grown in the *sallqa* and upper *kichwa* zones of the Ayacucho Basin. Some varieties, like the *wanya papa*, are whiter, less bitter, and less frost tolerant; others, like the *maura* or *mauna papa*, are darker, more bitter, and more frost tolerant. The Indians prefer the whiter and less bitter varieties, but these can usually only be grown at *kichwa* altitudes. In general, the more frost tolerant the phenotype, the stronger the bitterness.

Making potatoes into white *chuñu* flushes out the bitterness, but it would be simplistic to assume that it is only puna potato growers who practice such freeze-drying. The fact is that the preservation of food by drying—whether it involved root crops, *charki*, fish, or crayfish—was a widespread pattern in the ancient Andes and remains important today at every altitude. During the early 1970s, some farmers in Ayacucho's *kichwa* zone protected their potato crop from "gusanos" (probably grubs and nematodes) by taking it up to the puna and converting it into *chuñu* at camps like Toqto. This is such an inexpensive way to combat potato worms that it came to the attention of General Velasco's land reform officials, who in August 1971 provided the occupants of Toqto with wheelbarrows to speed the processing of a greater volume of potatoes.

Because the main focus of our study was the dynamics of llama herding, we did not collect data on the growing of common potatoes in the upper *kichwa* by herders from the Yanahuaccra area. Our data are limited to the gardens of dark, bitter potatoes at the *estancias* of Hatun Rumi, Pallqa, and Toqtoqasa, and they are frustratingly imprecise because the herders did not think in terms of kilograms or hectares. Their units of measurement were the (probably aboriginal) basket (25 cm in diameter and 10 cm deep), the Spanish *costal* (gunny sack), and the *carga de llama*, which we estimated at 24–25 kg.

Planting of potato gardens took place late in November or December, toward the end of the Andean spring. The seed potato used in planting was ideally about 40 g in weight and worm free. Areas for planting were selected on the basis of having at least 50 cm of soil, good drainage, and a soil color which was interpreted as indicating fertility. Given the thin soils of all three *estancias*, these requirements seriously limited the area of potential potato fields; this is perhaps why one walled garden, within the *kancha*, was usually fertilized with llama dung and might even have earth of the appropriate color added to it. Outside the *kancha*, scattered fields such as those shown in Figure 4.28 had to lie fallow for seven years (or even longer) before their fertility was restored.

The fields were prepared with the *lampa*, an Andean hoe, and each consisted of a set of furrows running vertically downhill, separated by parallel ridges of raised earth in which the planting was to take place. The distance between these ridges was one pace (about 70 cm), and within each ridge the tubers were planted about 40 cm apart; this spacing provides about 9.6 plants per m². Potatoes were usually ready to harvest by July, in the Andean winter.

Perhaps the single most variable set of figures we collected were the yields of these potato gardens. In the poorest gardens at Hatun Rumi, a good individual plant might yield only 0.25–0.50 kg. At lower elevations, or in the best of the Pallqa gardens, a good individual plant could yield a kilogram of tubers. In the *kichwa* zone, a plant in good soil with heavy doses of fertilizer could yield 3 kg. It would be tempting to try to calculate the yield per hectare, were it not for the fact that no family had fields even remotely that large. Most available patches of appropriate soil were no more than 100 m², and the most any family used was a few such patches.

The question, "How much potato land do you have to plant to satisfy your family's annual needs?" drew no useful replies. At all *estancias*, herders agreed that potatoes from their own gardens always ran out before the next crop came in. Adults at Toqtoqasa could eat as much as half a kilogram of potatoes per day, but this figure was lower when other foods were available. This meant that households such as Pastor and Martina W.'s could theoretically consume 4 kg per day, or 1460 kg per year. To harvest this quantity of potatoes, they would have to have cultivated roughly 2920 plants, or about 2.8 hectares, which was many times the area they had actually planted.

The herders made up their potato deficit through exchange with their relatives and neighbors in the villages of the *kichwa* zone. There potatoes grow so well that a kilogram sold for only 4 to 6 soles in 1971; a llama, by

Figure 4.28 This large *kancha* at Toqtoqasa is surrounded by patches of potato fields from previous years, temporarily highlighted by the light snow in their furrows.

contrast, was worth 500 soles. Wool, hides, mutton, and *charki* were all sought by the potato farmers, as was white *chuñu*. By freeze-drying their potatoes, the herders of Pallqa and Toqtoqasa could triple or even quadruple the value of a *carga de llama* (Table 4.1). In villages at lower altitudes, the "flour" of ground white *chuñu inglés* was highly prized as a base for soup, as a filler in the manufacture of ice cream, and as an ingredient in numerous *criollo* dishes. And in the tropical forest below Tambo, where insect pests made the growing of potatoes impossible, getting a kilogram of white *chuñu* was said to be "like getting a kilo of the finest Swiss chocolates."

Table 4.1
Approximate values of various locally produced
commodities in the rural Ayacucho Basin, 1971

Commodity	Price (soles)[a]
One adult llama	500
One large adult sheep	500
One kilogram of potatoes	4
One kilogram of *chuñu*	15
One kilogram of white maize	6
One kilogram of dark maize	4
One kilogram of faba beans	4–6
One kilogram of wheat	5
One kilogram of peas	4
One kilogram of coca leaves	30
One liter of cheap *aguardiente*	15
One liter of good *cañazo*[b]	20

[a]1971 Peruvian soles, then worth 3–4 cents U.S.
[b]"Good" is, of course, a relative term

Chuñu Processing

Once the huts at Toqto were set up and the pack animals had been
unloaded and corraled, the business of *chuñu* making could begin (Fig.
4.29). First the potatoes were laid out on the ground, scattered only one
layer deep. One really good night of frost was said to "burn" the potatoes
"almost as if they had been cooked," but just to be sure, they might be
left for two nights. This was particularly true if the sky happened to be
overcast, for then the blanket of clouds would prevent the escape of heat
from the earth; what everyone hoped for were clear, starry nights with
hard frost.

After this initial freezing, the potatoes could be clustered in small pyramidal piles of about thirty potatoes each. Although this is done to
facilitate treading on them, such clustering is also a longstanding Andean
custom, one whose conceptual roots are almost certainly prehispanic. In
contrast to most North Americans, who tend to spread items out uni-
formly, Quechua speakers tend to divide their potatoes, *ollucos*, or chile
peppers into small groups or separate piles. There are a number of verbs
used to describe these activities, such as *rakiy* ("to separate or select"),
sapachay ("to separate or isolate"), *sapaqchay* ("to separate, select, or
differentiate"), *suntuy* ("to pile up"), and *tawqay* ("to pile"). Often An-

Figure 4.29 A single family's encampment at Toqto: one conical shelter of *ichu* grass, a pile of possessions stored beneath a waterproof poncho, a woman's work area for cooking and peat cutting, and a man's work area for sorting basketloads of *chuñu* potatoes.

dean people carefully separate the small potatoes from the big (*rakisqa ñutu papata hatunninkunamanta*).

Over the course of the next day, the barefoot women trod repeatedly on the piles of thawing potatoes to squeeze out the water (Fig. 4.30). Then the potatoes were carried to the dammed-up stream and submerged, either in baskets or sacks or simply loose (when available, the land reform wheelbarrows might be used for this task, as shown in Fig. 4.31). Here the potatoes lay underwater for six or seven days, while the cold water flushed

Figure 4.30   An extended family squeezes the liquid from small piles of potatoes which have been allowed to freeze overnight on the puna moor at Toqto.

out the bitter juices. The potatoes were tasted periodically to see how this process was advancing; at this time the skin, by now half flaked away, might be completely removed.

Finally, the potatoes were removed from the water (Fig. 4.32), laid out again on the ground one layer deep, and left for several days during which they froze and thawed, froze and thawed. At this point the potatoes had turned snow-white and very hard, shrinking as they became completely desiccated. Those whose skin had not previously been removed could now be rubbed briefly between the palms of one's hands until the last fragile traces of skin had vanished. Finally, scattered over the carpet of puna like so many hard white pebbles, the potatoes had become *chuñu* (Figs. 4.33 and 4.34). They were then raked up into the usual pyramidal piles (*sun-*

tukuna or *tawqakuna*), placed in the pair of 12.5-kg bags which together made up a 25-kg load, and packed on a waiting llama, one bag per side. Each animal, in other words, left Toqto carrying a burden worth more than two-thirds the value of the llama itself (see Table 4.1).

Two days after *chuñu* making ended at Toqto, only the circular areas of missing turf showed where the huts had stood. Llama droppings, hearth ash, shriveled potato peels, and a few other biodegradable reminders of

Figure 4.31 Using a wheelbarrow provided by the Velasco government's land reform program, one family pours its load of partially processed potatoes into the cold waters of a dammed-up stream.

Figure 4.32   Using his traditional wicker basket, a *chuñu* maker at Toqto retrieves potatoes which have been underwater long enough to have their bitterness flushed out.

human activity were sprinkled across the campsite. A few whitened potatoes still shimmered underwater, but the stream had already begun to
erode the temporary dam. In one sense Toqto was an ephemeral place, a
"functionally specific activity locus" in archaeological jargon. At the same
time, it is worth noting that even if it were used as a *chuñu* camp for only
one human generation, it could have more than 100 posthole patterns
under its regrown layer of turf.

Birth and Death on the Puna Brava

PALTAMACHAY, MARCH 8, 1971, 10 A.M.: All but one of the llamas are
grazing on the high puna near this summer *estancia*, half an hour above
Hatun Rumi. One animal, a brown 15-year-old gelding, has been kept

near the settlement. This elderly llama is now so lame and arthritic that he has declined in importance as a burden carrier; his teeth, worn down almost to the gum line, foretell a period of increasingly inefficient eating and steady weight loss. For some time it has been clear that this particular llama will eventually have to be made into *charki*, and now seems as good a time as any. Fast approaching are the fiestas of Semana Santa, when great quantities of meat can be sold to the townsmen of the *kichwa*.

Emilio V., Porfirio V., and their cousin Martín induce the llama to kneel down; then they tie all four of the animal's feet together and roll it over on its side. At Yanahuaccra, llamas are not killed by cutting their throats, as sheep are killed; that is a custom introduced by the Spaniards. Instead, Emilio cuts through the back of the neck, searching with a sharp knife for the juncture between the atlas vertebra and the occipital condyles of the skull. He then cuts the spinal cord much as a bullfighter finishes off a wounded bull, except that it is done with a horizontal slash instead of

Figure 4.33   Spread out on the surface of the puna after its removal from the water, this finished *chuñu* has now turned white.

Figure 4.34 Production of units of *chuñu* is frequently staggered, as shown in this photograph. In the left background, a batch of finished *chuñu* is spread evenly over the puna. In the right foreground, new piles of roughly thirty potatoes each are ready for squeezing by foot; two men form the piles while three women begin the squeezing.

the bullfighter's vertical stab. Although the pain is mercifully brief, the startled llama gives off a series of high-pitched screams which end only when the cord is cut.

Quickly the three men untie the llama's feet so that they can thrash about freely while the animal lies dying on its side. This is important, for the kicking feet are thought to indicate that the llama's spirit is "running back to its corral." Only when it has kicked for the last time is its spirit thought to be home, and the butchering can begin.

Now the men begin to extend the cut, already begun at the back of the animal's neck, around toward the jugular vein. At a signal from Emilio, the wives of all three herders move in from the periphery of the scene and begin to participate actively in the butchering. Emilio's wife kneels with an earthenware jar to catch the blood from the jugular vein and carotid artery, perhaps three or four liters in all. A shotglass is filled with the first spurt of blood, which will be thrown on the ground as an offering to the *Tayta Urqu*. The rest will be used to prepare a dish now called by its

Spanish name, *picante*—first the blood will be cooked alone, then potatoes and other vegetables will be added to produce something like blood pudding. The care with which the blood is collected makes it clear why cutting the animal's throat would have been inappropriate; the llama had to be immobilized first so that no blood would be spilled. There can be little doubt that much of this ritual has survived from prehispanic times. In the Inca period there was even a ceremony called the *capacocha* in which a gourd container of camelid blood had to be carried hundreds of kilometers over mountain trails by porters who risked execution if so much as a drop were spilled (Duviols 1976; Rostworowski 1988).

The llama now has a deep cut running completely around the neck, making the removal of its head a logical next step. Having done this, the men prepare to open the abdomen. This is not done by splitting the belly open (as a Spaniard would disembowel a sheep), but by making two long, parallel cuts along the cartilage joining the ribs to the sternum and lifting the sternum out as a strip.

The removal of the sternum makes it easy to open the rib cage, exposing the heart and lungs. A further cut is made all the way down the abdomen to the pubic bone. The huge camelid stomach, borne quite far forward, is removed; the women receive and wash the heart, lungs, liver, and other organs. Now the men, who have done most of the work to this point, put down their knives and sit back to enjoy a coca-chewing break. The women, sitting on the opposite side of the carcass, continue cleaning and tying up the various parts of the intestines. Virtually all the internal organs, as well as all the available sinew, is saved and put to some use. The bladder is washed and saved as a waterproof container; in ancient times, such bladders were used to hold mineral pigments which would have hardened into useless lumps if exposed prematurely to moisture. Last of all the organs to be removed are the kidneys, which had previously been hidden by everything else.

Their coca break over, the men now begin to skin the llama. The work is unhurried, patient, each herder careful not to cut through the hide or otherwise damage it. As soon as the hide is free, the women spread it on the ground, hair side down, and place the animal's internal organs on it. Now tied loosely in a bundle, the llama skin will be used to carry the organs back to the *chuklla*.

Emilio and Porfirio have begun in the meantime to quarter the llama. Little time is spent searching for articulations, such as the point where the head of the femur enters the acetabulum of the pelvis. Instead, a few blows with an axe fracture the pubic bone, ultimately separating the pelvis into two halves, each of which is carried away with a hind limb. Similar axe blows shatter the blade of the scapula and leave each forelimb free. The llama now consists of four separate limbs, a head, a spinal column with rib cage attached, and a folded skin full of internal organs. All this will be carried back to the kitchen of Emilio's *kancha*, where the women will begin cutting the meat into long narrow strips. These will be hung from poles out of reach of the dogs, drying in the bitter cold air of the *sallqa* until they have become *charki*.

PALTAMACHAY, MARCH 8, 1971, 12:30 P.M.: The leisurely butchering has taken three men two and a half hours, including a 15-minute coca break; most of the women's work lies ahead of them. Emilio and Porfirio wash their hands and say goodbye to Martín, whose collaboration has earned him a share of the meat. He will remain in the *estancia* while his two cousins catch up with the rest of their llama herd in the rocky pastures above.

Emilio and Porfirio know exactly where their animals are likely to be— grazing beside their in-laws' herds and watched over, in an act of *ayni*, by those same in-laws. In a narrow, unroofed anticline above Paltamachay, where patches of snow survive in the permanent shadows below the serrated edge of the andesite cliffs, some 50 or 60 llamas stand straddle-legged with their mouths buried in fescue. Unimpressed by the arrival of Emilio and Porfirio, they stride forward briefly and lower their heads again.

Only one part of the scene seems out of place: one llama is down on her knees with two of Emilio's in-laws beside her. A white-and-tan 5-year-old female, she is part of Emilio's herd. Pregnant, but not thought to be at full term, she had given no indication in the corral this morning that anything was about to happen; now she is giving birth on the cold grass of the high puna.

Emilio's greeting of his in-laws is laconic. They know he appreciates their watching of his herd and will reciprocate one day; little needs to be said. The men kneel to assist in the birth of a new female, still too wet and bloody for her coat color to be clearly discerned. Emilio cuts the umbilical cord with the same knife he had used earlier to decapitate the old gelding. Removing his poncho, he collects the afterbirth for transportation to its place of ritual burial. After a period of waiting that seems impossibly short, the tiny female struggles to her feet and begins to nurse.

PALTAMACHAY, MARCH 8, 1971, 2:30 P.M.: Holding his poncho bundled under his arm, Emilio climbs slowly to the top of the anticline. Along the base of the sawtoothed cliff, a faint white footpath leads to a triangular crevice between two massive boulders. The smoke-blackened chamber—too small to enter—barely qualifies as a *machay*, or cave, but it still contains former offerings in the form of decomposing candles and cigarettes. Unfolding his poncho, Emilio gently removes the llama's afterbirth and places it inside the crevice. He knows that when he visits the opening again, perhaps in a year, the afterbirth will be gone; the *Tayta Urqu* will have taken it back.

Emilio retraces his steps downslope to the base of the ravine where three herds of llamas are grazing together. Porfirio and his in-laws are standing beside the newborn llama, watching it shiver in the wind as it nurses. As its wooly coat dries, it is becoming clear that it will be *qarwa*, or light brown.

A group of North American ranchers, standing around a skinny newborn filly as she struggled to maintain her bowlegged stance, might have cracked a joke or laughed, recalling some appropriate anecdote. Not the herders of Paltamachay; their expression is merely stoic, impassive, noncommittal. At some future time, momentarily freed from their daily routine by a few chota pegs of *aguardiente*, these men will giggle and squeal like teenagers. But not today. Today is simply a day when one llama went down to its knees to die and another went down to its knees to give birth. For the herders, it is just another day at the office.

Five

The Guanaco and the Llama

When humans first entered the Andes, they discovered and hunted two native wild members of the camelid family, the guanaco (*Lama glama guanicoe*) and the vicuña (*Vicugna vicugna*). The guanaco (Fig. 5.1) was the more widespread of the two, ranging from northern Peru to Tierra del Fuego and living in arid or semiarid habitats from sea level to 4000 m. The vicuña, restricted to the high altiplano between 3700 and 4900 m, had a much more limited range. Both species are now in danger of extinction, which makes it fortunate that both have also been the subject of intensive behavioral studies (Koford 1957; Raedeke 1979; Franklin 1983; Wilson and Franklin 1985.)

After many thousands of years of hunting, the Indians of Peru succeeded in producing two domestic camelids, the llama (*Lama glama glama*) and the alpaca (*Lama pacos*). The llama, used as a beast of burden as well as a food animal, tolerates the same wide range of habitats as the guanaco and could therefore be used to transport products between the altiplano and the coast. The alpaca, considered more important for its fine wool than for its meat, thrives only at high altitudes and suffers malaise when brought down below 1000 m.

Zoologists are generally agreed that the llama's wild ancestor was the guanaco (Herre 1952, 1961; Wing 1977). The origins of the alpaca are more controversial (Moore n.d.). There are reasons for believing that it, too, may be descended from the guanaco, with subsequent selection for long wool rather than for burden-carrying stamina (Wing 1977:847). Most zoologists believe that the vicuña has never been successfully domesticated; it resisted all attempts at domestication by the Inca and continues to be difficult even to hybridize with the alpaca (Fernández Baca and

Figure 5.1   A group of young guanacos (photograph courtesy of William L. Franklin).

Novoa 1968). However, because of the alpaca's fine wool, love of high altitudes, and obligate water requirements, a few scholars would like to see at least some vicuña genes in its ancestry.

The Early History of Domestication

Because studies of domestication in the Andes are in their infancy, we do not know when or where camelids were first brought under human control. At the archaeological site of Jaywamachay Cave, in the *kichwa* or *Polylepis* woodland of the Ayacucho Basin, hunters killed scores of guanaco and deer during the period 9000–5800 B.C.; however, there was no evidence of domestication at that time (MacNeish *et al.* 1981; Flannery n.d.). The first hint of domestication in Ayachucho came from a second site, Piki-machay Cave, in levels dated 4500–3100 B.C. (Wing 1977:848). Jane Wheeler reports a similar date of around 4300 B.C. for early camelid domestication at Telàrmachay Cave near Junín, Peru (*El Comercio* 1980:1). Such early domestic camelids probably still looked a lot like the guanaco, since they had presumably not yet undergone selection for the wide range of coat colors and fiber qualities we see in today's llamas and alpacas (see p. 97 and Table 5.1).

Included among the problems facing early herders would have been the need to modify certain wild camelid behaviors. In this chapter, we look first at the herd dynamics of the wild guanacos studied by Franklin, Rae-deke, and others. We look second at the dynamics of the domestic llamas kept by herders on the Ayacucho puna in the 1970s. In the process, we consider two questions: (1) What aspects of wild camelid behavior had to be changed to produce domestic herds like the ones we saw? (2) What human behavioral patterns have arisen to provide successful management for those herds? And finally, just to keep today's herders in perspective, we look briefly at the sixteenth-century descriptions of Inca herding at the time of the Spanish Conquest.

The Dynamics of Guanaco Herds

Over much of Peru, including Ayacucho, guanacos have been driven nearly to extinction by overhunting and competition from domestic ani-mals. Small populations survive at Calipuy in the upper reaches of the

Santa River and on the Pampa Galeras Vicuña Reserve in southeastern Ayacucho (Franklin 1975). Larger populations in southern Chile have recently been studied, one on Tierra del Fuego (Raedeke 1979) and another on the extreme southern mainland (Franklin 1983).

One key to the guanaco's wide geographic range is the flexibility of its social organization. Responding to local environmental conditions, guanacos may be sedentary while resources are rich and migratory when conditions worsen. Local populations are usually organized as *family groups, male groups,* and *solo males.*

Family groups consist of a single adult male (sometimes called an "alpha male") with a number of adult females and their recent young (Fig. 5.2). Family groups on Tierra del Fuego average one alpha male, 5–6 adult females, 1–2 yearlings, and 3–4 young of the current year. On the main-

Figure 5.2   A guanaco family group—composed of a territorial male, a number of females, and their offspring less than 15 months old—grazes near a stream in southern Chile (photograph courtesy of William L. Franklin).

land, sedentary family groups fluctuate between 2.9 in winter and 12.8 in summer, averaging 7; migratory family groups average 16 animals. About 55% of the mainland guanacos occur in family groups.

Alpha males range between 6 and 11 years of age, averaging 8. They are extremely territorial individuals who, because of their ability to select and defend areas of good forage, can attract females to their group. The size of their territory is correlated with forage production, and, where territories are small and rich, the alpha male spends a lot of time establishing dung piles along its borders and chasing his neighbors away. Where territories are large and poor, less time is spent in defense of territory, presumably because the border is so long.

Interestingly, the size of the family group is not correlated with either forage availability or territory size (Franklin 1983). The alpha male tolerates a certain amount of coming and going by females, but when a certain group size has been reached he drives newcomers off. In addition, when yearling males and females have reached 11–15 months of age, the alpha male expels them from the family herd.

The young males expelled by the alpha come together in male groups, which may vary in size from several guanacos to 60 individuals (Raedeke 1979). The larger groups tend to occur when many young males have recently been driven from family groups; the norm is closer to 15–20 animals. On the mainland of Chile, such male groups amount to 41% of the guanaco population (82% of the males). They serve as the pool from which new alpha males can be recruited as the vigor of older alphas declines. Members of male groups continually spar with each other, practicing the chest ramming, body slamming, spitting, and biting they will use when they eventually challenge an alpha (Wilson and Franklin 1985).

During the years they spend in the male group, young males are excluded from the best forage areas by the alpha males in the family groups; they also cannot mate. During the nonbreeding season, young females may temporarily fall in with male groups, but once the breeding season begins they flee the unwanted attentions of these junior males and may seek the protection of a family group.

Eventually, a male who is physically and sexually mature enough separates himself from the male group and spends time as a solo male. Such males are the explorers who try to find a new area of good forage and establish themselves on it, thereby taking the first step toward attracting a group of females. Alpha males spend a great deal of time battling these and other challengers; one 11-year-old male studied by Raedeke

(1979:136) had 78 visible scars from previous fights. Eventually, an old alpha is defeated and a new family group is formed.

At Tierra del Fuego, breeding takes place between January and March, with a peak in February. Given a gestation period of roughly 11 months, births are strung out between early December and mid-February, with a peak early in January. Females who have suckled young the previous year are less likely to breed than those who have not, especially in areas of poor forage.

Theoretically, guanacos of both sexes can reproduce in their second year; however, most do not. Females in the wild usually do not have the nutritional support to breed this early, and males under 5 are unlikely to have access to females. Once guanacos begin to breed, however, there is little drop-off in the fecundity of older age classes, at least through year 12 (Raedeke 1979). Thus females usually do not breed before their third year and usually do not give birth every year, but they can remain fertile to a relatively advanced age. We shall see that these statements are also true of the llamas we studied on the Ayacucho puna.

Guanacos sleep in thorn scrub or woodland areas when such cover is available, coming out onto the steppes or meadows during the day. Here the various groups graze with 50 to 200 m separating their members, a spacing similar to that seen among llamas. When the range is exhausted, or covered for extended periods by snow, some guanaco populations migrate to greener pastures. In the course of migration, the animals may temporarily form a mixed group of all ages and both sexes as they move from one range to another. Franklin (1983:612) reports seeing winter migratory groups of as many as 176 and suspects that in ancient times there may have been migratory herds of thousands. It is important, however, to remember that such groups are not permanent. Once having found good forage, the alpha males again establish family groups on territories, which are defended on a sedentary basis for as long as conditions permit.

Looking past the various kinds of guanaco groups, Raedeke estimates the local population as consisting of 112 males to every 100 females. For every 100 adult females, there are 37–51 infants of both sexes, 18–26 yearling females, and 11–15 females 2–3 years of age. Most guanacos are dead by 12 years, although a few old males might last to 16 or 18. The leading cause of death is starvation, which accounts for 81% of all deaths on Tierra del Fuego. Other sources of mortality include accidents, illegal hunting, and mange. The mange—caused by the same mites seen in domestic llamas (see pp. 102–104)—can be observed on 13.3% of the guanacos but kills only the 2.8% whose resistance is low. Finally, there is infant mortality. Difficult to estimate accurately, it probably contributes to the fact that in any one year only about half the adult females have offspring that survive.

This, then, is a brief look at the social dynamics of the wild camelid that was apparently domesticated by 4000 B.C. in the Andes. Clearly, its behavior presents some serious obstacles to producing domestic herds.

The key to guanaco populations is the family group, in which virtually all breeding takes place. Yet this group cannot grow to the size a herder would like, since the alpha male systematically expels all yearlings when they reach 11–15 months. Nor can it include a mixture of adult males and females, since the alphas and the other males would fight incessantly over the females. Maintaining a group of 8 to 10 burden-carrying males for a pack train would be impossible under those conditions. Of course, a guanaco male group would have roughly the same makeup as a llama train, but male groups cannot breed. Early herders would therefore have been faced with two alternatives: either maintain two types of herds—"family" and "male"—or figure out how to create a mixed-sex herd in which males do not injure each other and yearlings are not expelled.

And then there is migration—the instinct for guanacos to pick up and move en masse when they feel their forage is exhausted. Under domestication it has to be the herders, rather than the alpha males, who decide what size the herd territory will be, and when to move, and where to move. It has to be the herders who decide when 8–10 males, loaded with burdens, will be led off to another valley, leaving the females and their young behind in the corral. In the next section of this chapter, we consider how the Indians have altered camelid behavior enough to make llama herding possible.

Domestic Llama Herds in Ayacucho, 1970–1972

As might be expected, the age and sex profiles of domestic llama herds in Ayacucho are different from those of their guanaco ancestors. We have seen that competition among male guanacos creates two kinds of herds, one consisting of the dominant male and a number of females, the other consisting of subdominant males. The llama herders we studied did not want two kinds of herds, especially when one kind consisted only of males. They did not want their yearlings expelled at 11–15 months, nor did they want to put up with constant fighting among males for possession of females. Herders agreed that, because several herds might graze on the same range during the same day, when a female was in heat she might be attacked by males from neighboring herds. In the ensuing melee, both males and females could be badly bitten, injured, or even killed.

Herders counteracted this innate camelid behavior by castrating almost all the males in their herds when they were between 3 and 4 years of age. Whether a particular male was gelded or not was determined by the herders' evaluation of his general conformation over the first three years of life;

Figure 5.3   A herd of llamas at Pallqa, composed mainly of females and *capón llamas*.

Table 5.1
Terms for llama coat color, Yanahuaccra, 1970–1972

Term	English equivalent
yuraq	white
yana	black
oqe	gray (this same color, actually a brownish gray, was also used for white-tailed deer)
qarwa	light brown
paqo	dark brown
allqa	with two colors, both forming large patches
muru	with two colors, the second taking the form of smaller spots
chipro	with two colors, the second color taking the form of small specks or "freckles"

the male who most closely approximated the herders' view of the ideal phenotype would be left to become an *ayno*, or herd sire.

The gelded males became *capón llamas*, the main animals used as burden carriers in llama trains. *Capones* (obviously a Spanish loan word) often grew to be larger than *aynos* but remained intimidated by the more aggressive ungelded males. Rarely would a herd of 25 to 40 llamas in the Ayacucho *sallqa* contain more than one or two *aynos*—usually of different ages, so that the younger would be less likely to challenge the older until the latter was past his prime (Fig. 5.3). Through this strategy, the herders accomplished two goals: they created a single, manageable herd of males and females by eliminating the competition typical of wild guanacos, and they ensured that the males who sired future offspring would be chosen by the herders' criteria, not by natural selection. This allowed them to select for less aggressive males who would not expel their own yearlings.

Ayacucho herders did not know about dominant and recessive genes. The only kind of dominance they understood was male dominance; thus they believed that a baby llama would be born "whatever color its father happened to be." Llama coat color was not a matter of great importance to them, although they had a vocabulary of at least eight colors and combinations thereof (Table 5.1). This represents a considerable difference from Inca times, when llamas of various pure colors were requisite for particular sacrificial rites and coat color was therefore accorded more significance.

Starting Up a Herd

There were several ways a young man in one of the Ayacucho *estancias* could start up his own herd. Most commonly he received a few llamas from his father, and frequently from his bride's father as well, on the occasion of his marriage. The number of animals received depended on economic circumstances—as few as one or two llamas from one father if times were hard, as many as four from each father if both were doing well.[1] Even in the worst-case scenario, when no animals were available, there were alternatives for the groom. He could, for example, work until he had the resources to purchase a young female llama from a relative, affine, or neighbor. This young female would be left in the seller's herd for several years, until she had produced two or three offspring. At this point the young man could remove the female and her offspring from the herd and recompense the seller for having taken care of them during the intervening years. With luck, the young man would by then be able to buy or inherit a few more llamas to add to this nucleus.

Another common way of receiving one's first herd was by inheriting it. Inheritance of animals was supposed to be patrilineal, with the llamas being divided among the sons after a father's death. In such cases, the *piwi churi*, or firstborn son, often received more animals than his younger brothers. If the boys were very young, their widowed mother might keep the animals and give them to her sons in installments as they married. In cases where both parents died, the *piwi churi* might take charge of the herd, but even he would be expected to keep giving the animals away as his younger brothers married. Should a man die with no male heirs, his herd would be divided among his relatives on both sides of the family, with some consideration given to individual needs.

How many animals did a young man need to begin his own herd? This turned out to be a meaningless question. All herders believed that "two, a male and female," were enough; but their observed behavior said differently. Anyone with that few animals continued to live at his father's *kancha* and keep his llamas with his father's herd. A more meaningful question turned out to be how many animals a young man needed to split off from his father's *kancha* and found his own. For reasons made clear in

---

1. We found no evidence that marriages were ever arranged to augment a shrinking herd with an infusion of in-laws' animals, as happened among the Chukchi reindeer herders studied by Leeds (1965). Nor were llamas given by a groom to his father-in-law as a form of brideprice, as happens among cattle herders such as the Nuer (Kelly 1985).

Chapters 6 and 7, that number was larger—at least four females and two males, perhaps more. Two or three animals was simply not a viable unit. Lose one female from such a tiny herd to mange or predators, and he would soon be back in his father's *kancha*.

The Growth of a Herd

Once a young man had a herd, his life became a continual effort to protect the animals from thieves, mountain lions, accidents, and mange while their numbers increased to 25 to 40. Compounding his problem was the fact that all domestic animals have low fertility on the puna. Veterinarians at Peru's I.V.I.T.A. (Instituto Veterinario de Investigaciones Tropicales y de Altura) regard 50% fertility as typical for llamas at puna altitudes. What this means is that each fertile female will probably have no more than one offspring every other year, on the average, throughout her productive lifespan. Of course, this is not solely a female problem; male fertility is also low, even among llamas born and raised on the puna.

Herders in the Yanahuaccra-Toqtoqasa region agreed that, in any given year, each of their female llamas had about one chance in two of giving birth, and they did not expect any of them to give birth two years in a row. Since females began bearing young around 3 years of age, this meant that even a good female might have no more than four to six offspring during her lifetime. Everyone agreed that llamas could live to 20 years, but most did not; their usefulness began to decline by 15 years of age. When a llama's teeth have been worn down to the point where it can no longer forage effectively, the animal begins to get thinner and thinner until its strength is gone. The Ayacucho herders watched their animals carefully for signs of this downward spiral, and those llamas who had reached it—whether they were females who could no longer nurse young, or males who could no longer carry burdens—were eaten before they got any thinner. Almost all herders agreed that they would rather eat their own aged llamas than sell them. They had strong feelings about the integrity of the herd, and some felt that bad luck might befall the other animals if one of their number was sold to a stranger.

The gestation period for llamas is 10½ months. In the Yanahuaccra-Toqtoqasa area, births occur any time between January and March, usually with a peak in February. A tiny, newborn llama was referred to as an *uña*; by the age of 1 year it had grown to be a *malta*. Older age classes of llamas were referred to by a series of expressions that included both indigenous Quechua terms and Spanish loan words (Table 5.2).

Table 5.2
Terms for llamas of all ages and both sexes, Yanahuaccra, 1970–1972

Term	English equivalent
uña	infant llama, either sex (literally, "nursling of a quadruped")
malta	yearling of either sex (literally, "not yet fully grown")
china llamacha	young female llama (diminutive)
orqu llamacha	young male llama (diminutive)
china llama	adult female llama
orqu llama	adult male llama
paya llama	old female llama
machu llama	old male llama
criillo	female who has borne young (from Spanish *criollo*?)
qomy	sterile female llama
ayno	herd sire (uncastrated adult male llama)
urwi	sterile male llama
capón llama	gelded male llama (from Spanish *capón*, "neutered male animal")
carga llama	burden-carrying llama (from Spanish *cargar*, "to carry")

Three years was a crucial age for both males and females. After this point, females were likely to be fertile and males would be carefully evaluated to see whether they should be gelded or left as young *aynos*. Those gelded—the *capón llamas*—could begin carrying burdens as part of a pack train by age 4 and might accompany the older llamas on trips even before that. In spite of the relatively light burdens carried by *carga llamas*, many would develop extensive arthritis and bone spurs after ten or more years of service in the pack trains.

Obstacles to Herd Growth

A young man at Yanahuaccra or Toqtoqasa hoped that his herd would grow from 5 or 6 llamas to 25 to 40 by the time his *piwi churi* was ready to marry. However, in addition to the problems of low fertility already discussed, herders faced losses of animals from at least three main sources: mountain lions, rustlers, and mange.[2]

---

2. Baby llamas are also susceptible to intestinal diseases caused by organisms such as *Clostridium*. Because there were no outbreaks during our fieldwork, we have no basis for calculating the percentage of deaths from this cause.

The puma or mountain lion (*Panthera concolor*) could have been a major predator on Andean camelids in prehispanic times; it was still taking its toll in the early 1970s. Long since driven out of the lower elevations of the Ayacucho Basin, pumas survived in the *puna brava* above 4500 m. There it was not unusual to find a male–female pair making their den in a high-altitude cave, and changing caves several times over the course of a 5-year period to elude human hunters. Because of these movements, there were times when pumas might creep down on the herds of Hatun Rumi two or three times in one year, then disappear for a year before moving back into the area. What bothered the herders most is that, when a mountain lion broke into a corral, "*wañuchin iskay kimsata chayman huc apanayquipacc*" ("he might kill two or three llamas before carrying one off"). Nights with dense fog and no moon were particularly dangerous, and on such nights herders frequently slept in their guardian's huts in the corrals with their dogs nearby. Losses to mountain lions among the herds we studied seemed to average roughly 2 animals out of every 100 per year.

Llama rustling was another source of loss and was one of the main reasons given for clustering households into *estancias* for mutual protection. Thieves were said to enter the region two or three times per year and, when successful, to steal anywhere from one llama (a common occurrence) to eight (rarely). As with mountain lions, the rate of loss averaged 2 animals per 100 per year. Such theft was particularly frustrating to the herders of places such as Hatun Rumi and Toqtoqasa, since they knew their limited knowledge of Spanish would make it difficult to get help from the police or the judicial system.

Who were the rustlers? Clearly not relatives, or affines, or neighbors from the *estancias* of the puna, but people from the *kichwa* who needed capital for some festival such as Semana Santa (Easter week). The animals would be slaughtered and the meat distributed to fiesta goers, leaving no evidence of the crime. And who better to steal animals from than those dumb hicks on the puna, defenseless herders who couldn't even speak Spanish? Well, almost defenseless. "Sometimes, once in a great while," one herder from Toqtoqasa told us in 1971, "we catch one of them." "And what happens then?" he was asked. Without a smile, and with eyes as cold as the frozen pile of *champa* on which he sat, the herder extended his index finger and drew an invisible line across his jugular vein—not the way he sacrificed llamas, but the way the colonial Spaniards had taught his ancestors to butcher a pig.

Still a third source of animal loss was one of the two skin diseases, both called *qarachi* in Quechua and *sarna*, or mange, in Spanish. Both diseases are caused by mites in the 200–450-micron size range, so small that it was not until the nineteenth century that the link between the mite and the disease was definitely established. Because it is possible that at least one of these mites was introduced into the Andes by the Spaniards, let us look at them in some detail.

The itch mite, *Sarcoptes scabiei* (Fig. 5.4), is suspected of having evolved along with humans over many millennia and secondarily transferred to man's domestic animals. Today it occurs as a series of races which are specific to man, dogs, cattle, pigs, sheep, goats, Old World camels, Andean camelids, rabbits, and horses; these races can attack mammals other than their specific hosts, but usually they do not cause permanent infestations when they do so (Baker and Wharton 1952:363). The female *Sarcoptes* can bury herself in the epidermis in less than three minutes; she continues to dig at the rate of 2 to 3 mm per day until she has produced a burrow up to 3 cm long in the horny outer layer of skin (Belding 1942:765). Here she lays eggs which within 8 to 15 days have become adults ready to dig their own burrows. The early infestation produces no itching; after a month or so, however, the host becomes sensitized to the mite's waste products, and an intolerable itch, accompanied by hair loss, begins. Called scabies in humans, and mange in domestic animals, the infection is density dependent and spread by close contact, such as that between sheep in a corral or soldiers in crowded barracks. This condition is common in Old World history and tends to come in cycles. Because its association with humans is so old (and because there is an indigenous Quechua word for mange), *Sarcoptes* may have arrived in the Andes with the first Indians and later transferred to their llamas. However, there is a race specific to sheep, *S. scabiei* var. *ovis*, which was probably introduced by the Spaniards.

The scab mite, *Psoroptes equi* (Fig. 5.4), occupies a niche somewhat different from that of the itch mite. Instead of burrowing into the skin, *Psoroptes* pierces the skin and feeds on the serum that oozes from the wound. These mites live underneath the gradually thickening scabs formed by the exudation of serum at the site of the punctures (Baker and Wharton 1952:371; Banks 1915:131). A race specific to sheep (*P. equi* var. *ovis*) seeks wooly areas, producing a disease called "sheep scab" which results in scabbing, wool loss from biting and scratching, emaciation, and

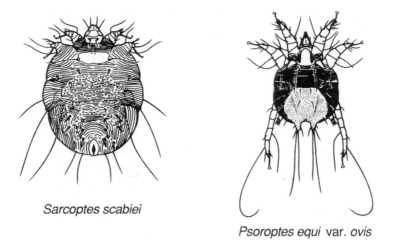

Sarcoptes scabiei

Psoroptes equi var. ovis

Figure 5.4 Two mites responsible for mange in Peruvian llamas: *Sarcoptes scabiei* and *Psoroptes equi* var. *ovis* (actual size, <450 microns).

sometimes death. By rubbing against posts, trees, and fences, sheep re-move patches of wool containing mites and eggs, and these are transferred to healthy sheep who brush against the same places (Banks 1915:131). The disease is also density dependent, spreading more rapidly the greater the size and crowding of the herd, with losses heaviest in autumn and early winter.

Psoroptic mange occurs in Peru today, but we feel that a strong case can be made for its having been introduced by the Spaniards. Sheep scab has a clear historic relationship with Old World sheep and is much less likely to have arrived in the Andes with the first Indians than is scabies. In a later section of this chapter we suggest that the first outbreak of *Psoroptes* in llamas and alpacas came in 1544–1545, following the introduction of European sheep into the Andes. This allows us to propose that losses of llamas to mange in prehispanic times may have been considerably lower than those of the early Colonial period, and perhaps even lower than today's losses.

In the 1970s in Ayacucho, herders tried to treat *sarna* with a whole range of folk remedies, mostly concoctions of tobacco or sulphur (Fig. 5.5). In the region of Yanahuaccra and Toqtoqasa, the largest herds were

Figure 5.5 While the rest of his herd waits patiently, Modesto P. of Hatun Rumi treats one of his llamas with a home remedy for sarcoptic mange.

the most likely to suffer. In herds of fewer than 20 llamas, only about 1 animal in 100 had mange; in herds of greater than 30, the frequency was closer to 5 animals per 100.

Herd Profiles

Despite all the obstacles to growth, Ayacucho herds did grow to reach 15–40 animals, with an average size around 25. Such herds were "mature" populations, usually with no more than 25% young animals. A typical herd of 25, for example, might at any one time have about three *maltas* and three *uñas*, with the rest of the herd consisting of adults.

In terms of archaeological faunal analysis, such a herd would be a population in which 75% of the members had virtually all the epiphyses of their limb bones fused—in other words, not unlike a wild guanaco herd. They would not show the high frequencies of yearlings (up to 50%) displayed by early domestic goat herds from the Near East (Hole, Flannery, and Neely 1969). In those herds, raised mainly for meat, young males were

eaten in such quantities that the steepest drop-off in "survivorship" occurred between 1 and 4 years of age. In contrast, when animals were raised
mainly for wool or milk, as in the case of some later Near Eastern herds
(Redding 1981; Zeder 1985)—or for burden carrying, as in the case of the
Yanahuaccra-Toqtoqasa herds—most animals were not eaten until their
productive years were behind them. This results in herds composed largely
of adult individuals.

Finally, we must deal with the question of maximum herd size. The
herders of Yanahuaccra, Pallqa, and Toqtoqasa regarded 25 animals as a
good herd, 15 as on the small side, and 35–40 as excellent. But why were
there no herds of 50, or 75, or 100? What determined the upper limit of
herd size? Was it the quality of the grazing land, the competition from
sheep, the damping effects of predators and mange, or some combination
of those factors? At the end of this chapter, we suggest an answer.

To the herders of Ayacucho, this limit was perceived as a supernatural
sanction for human ambition. "Allin kusikuycha kanman allin achcata kaptincca" ("Wouldn't we love to have more!"), one occupant of Hatun Rumi
said in 1971. "Allin allin kusikuycha, pachak pachak ñoccanchikpa kaptincca"
("Wouldn't we like to have hundreds!"). "Don't we watch them for the
Tayta Urqu! But once a herd has grown to a certain size, no matter what
we do, it won't grow any more; rather, there may even be some kind of
reduction, a divine punishment (castigo de dios)." Men were punished for
wanting too much, for being too greedy, for not restraining their ambition.
The same wamani—señor de los animales—who gave men llamas to herd
might recall some of them if his human caretakers grew so arrogant that
they forgot to whom the flocks really belonged.

Llama Trains

The people of the sallqa have always relied heavily on the products of the
kichwa, and the years 1970–1972 were no exception. Crucial to the pro-
curement of those products were the trains of carga llamas which moved
products of the puna down to the quebrada and brought products of the
kichwa villages back. The herders of Toqtoqasa, for example, took llama
loads of potatoes, chuñu, wool, and charki down to Quinua or Tambo and
brought back loads of maize, faba beans, wheat, salt, matches, kerosene,
coca, and cañazo. No ritual on the puna could be carried out without aqa,
or chicha, the aboriginal "hard cider" made from maize, which could not
be grown above the kichwa. Fortunately, the villagers at lower elevations
were eager for sallqa products; farmers in the deep quebradas of Huanta
were so glad to get the potatoes that they sometimes ate them "as if they

had been fruit." And villagers of the basin who wanted to provide their guests with *pachamanka*, or pit barbecue, sought sheep or llamas from *estancias* in the puna.

Not all the llamas in a herd were used for transport. Females were excluded, not simply on the basis of strength, but also because they were too important for breeding to risk death or injury on the trail. Llamas under 2 years of age were also left behind, and so usually were the *aynos*; however, if the train was one or two animals short, *aynos* might be included. This meant that the typical llama train was composed mainly of gelded males or *capón llamas*, accompanied by male *maltas* 2–4 years of age, who were allowed to come along with the train in order to get used to the trip.

As previously mentioned, *capón llamas* were usually gelded at 3 years of age and began carrying burdens when they reached 4 years. Llamas are perhaps the least efficient pack animals known, since the maximum burden they tolerate on a long trip is about 25 kg (55 pounds). In Ayacucho, this burden was typically divided into two sacks each weighing one *arroba* (12–13 kg), with one placed to either side of the spine for balance.[3]

Herders knew that if they overloaded a llama he would sit down and refuse to budge. Indeed, even when llamas had been correctly loaded, there might come a time after several hard days' travel when one animal would tire and sit down on the trail. When that happened, herders knew it was useless to beat or kick him; he would die before he would get up. The strategy was for one herder to go on with the rest of the train while another hid where the llama could not see him. From hiding, this second herder would toss several small pebbles so that they fell beside the animal. Startled, the reluctant llama would then spring to his feet and run after the rest of the train, burden and all.

The number of llamas taken along on a trip depended on the amount carried; it could be as few as 2 or 3 animals or as many as 15 to 20 geldings from a total herd of 30 to 40 llamas. Often several herders made the trip together, their combined animals giving the impression of a train of 40 to 50. However, when they reached their destination, the animals from each herd almost invariably separated themselves from the group and slept beside their herd mates.

Every llama train had its leader, called by the Spanish term *delantero*, "he who goes in front." *Delanteros* were said to be self-selected, not trained;

3. The *arroba* is a surviving Spanish Colonial measure amounting to roughly 25 pounds.

herders insisted that even as *maltas*, going along with the train for practice, certain animals liked to be right at the front of the pack. Interestingly, there was no correlation between being a *delantero* and being an uncastrated herd sire, or *ayno*—the *ayno* might be number one with the females, but the *delantero* was usually a *capón llama* with a natural instinct to lead the train. Herders had a special regard for the *delantero*, providing him with an embroidered bib, or *pechera*, which he wore on his chest while on the road. During the *herranza*, or llama-decorating ceremony, the *delantero* was the first animal decorated, and his bib was included in the ritual table prepared for the *wamani* in the ceremonial corral.

Perhaps no sight in the Andes is more pleasing to the eye than a train of llamas moving along a narrow trail between the *sallqa* and upper *kichwa*, the herders in their brown ponchos with several meters of coiled lassos over one shoulder, their camelids striding through the *Berberis* and *Polylepis* in a slow ripple of gray, brown, and white (Fig. 5.6). Sadly, it is a sight that is doomed to vanish, simply because one donkey can carry four times what a llama can carry, and a battered pickup truck is stronger still. It takes 40 llamas to carry a metric ton of potatoes from Yanahuaccra down to Huamanguilla. Obviously, there are more efficient ways to do it— though none quite as pretty.

Herds in the Sixteenth Century: Some Comparisons and Contrasts

So far we have looked at the herd dynamics of wild guanacos and modern Ayacucho llamas. The bridge between those two populations is the domestic herd of the prehispanic era, about which we know very little. Not until the sixteenth century, when the Spaniards had arrived but many Inca patterns were still in existence, do we have eyewitness accounts of aboriginal herding. And those accounts describe a "governmental" level of herd management not seen anywhere in Ayacucho today.

To provide some perspective on today's herders, we now look briefly at their sixteenth-century ancestors, who have been richly described by Murra (1965) and included in a classic synthesis by Rowe (1946). Some of the sources those authors used were the writings of Acosta ([1590] 1940), Cieza de León ([1550] 1862, [1550] 1943), Cobo ([1653] 1956), Diez ([1567–1568] 1964), Garcilaso ([1604] 1960), Polo ([1559] 1916a, [1571] 1916b), and Zárate ([1555] 1853).

Figure 5.6 A train of nine *capón llamas*—accompanied by three men, a woman, and two donkeys—en route from Toqtoqasa to Quinua with 250 kg of *chuñu*.

Qhapaqllama and *Waqchallama*

Just as farmlands in Inca times were divided among the state, the church, and the community, so were herds of llamas and alpacas (Rowe 1946:267). There were also privately owned herds, but since these were usually smaller, they did not generate as much interest among Spanish census takers.

The Inca spoke of *qhapaqllama*, "the herds of the mighty," in referring to the animals owned by state and church. Animals belonging to individuals or *ayllu* at the commoner level were called *waqchallama*, "herds of the weak." Wild guanacos and vicuñas were known as *intipllama*, "beasts of the Sun," and they could be captured only during royal hunts called *chaku* (Murra 1965:203).

Herds owned by individual commoners seem to have been no larger than the ones we saw in Ayacucho, and private ownership of up to ten animals was allowed without taxation or governmental requisition (Rowe 1946). *Qhapaqllama* herds, however, were enormous. Tens of thousands of state-owned llamas were used for military transport (see below), and tens of thousands of state-owned alpacas produced wool for distribution to the ruler's subjects. Various shrines and temples owned thousands of animals, hundreds of which were sacrificed each year during religious ceremonies, and hundreds more of which were used to support the temple staff.

During the military expansion of the Inca empire, llamas included in the spoils of war were sometimes given by the ruler to *curacas*, local hereditary lords, probably to reinforce their loyalty. These royal grants, which could be inherited by the grantee's kin, remained separate from the herds belonging to the *curaca's* community. Often a *curaca's* herds were so large that they had to be managed for him by crews of his subjects. It was apparently not unusual for a *curaca* to receive 200–300 llamas from the ruler in a given year (Diez [1567–1568] 1964).

According to Murra, there were several ways a commoner could obtain his own herd. First, he could receive llamas from his father. There was also evidence that animals were expected at the time of marriage. Alternatively, he could receive llamas from a local lord as recompense for having labored in his fields. All three of these options are similar to ones we observed in Ayacucho in the 1970s. In addition, in the sixteenth century a man could receive llamas from the *sapsi*, or community herd—a flock that was counted in public twice a year. Community herds were organized under *ayllu* and moiety sponsorship, with the tasks of herd management rotated among community members. Those flocks thus served as a kind of reserve population whose size was a matter of public record. No such institution existed among the Ayacucho herders we studied, although village and *cofradía* herds of Old World domestic animals were known in the Río Pampas area (see Chapter 8).

In the Aymara-speaking Lupaca region from which Murra drew much of his information, a man was likely to be herdless only if he had lost his animals through some disaster, if he was too young to have his own household, or if he was ethnically alien to the community. There were no "aliens" in the Ayacucho *estancias* we studied, but there were young men waiting to inherit their first animals and older men who had endured disaster.

Ancient Herd Sizes

The specific figures given for sixteenth-century llamas indicate that the *waqchallama* herds were mostly in the size range of the flocks we saw at Yanahuaccra in the 1970s. Among the Lupaca, Diez ([1567–1568] 1964) lists families with no animals, others with 2 or 3, others with 10 or 20, and some with 50 or 100 (Murra 1965:192). Larger herds of 500 to 1700 were owned by a few families—almost certainly the households of *curacas*, especially when one considers how many herders it would take to manage such numbers.

As various authors suggest, the Spaniards were eager to record the large herds belonging to communities, lords, and government institutions and far less concerned with documenting the smaller herds owned by commoners. There are some data on the latter, such as Ortiz de Zúñiga's ([1562] 1957:326) visit to Huánuco, where he found 100 persons living in two hamlets with only 33 llamas among them; the local ethnic leader himself had only 6.

Most descriptions of impressively large herds in the sixteenth-century literature seem to refer either to community flocks or to the *qhapaqllama* of church and state. They also deal, most often, with the vast grazing lands of southern Peru and adjacent Bolivia, especially the area of Lake Titicaca.

Consider, for example, the 1567–1568 document by Garci Diez de San Miguel, which deals with the west shore of Titicaca (Murra 1965). At Xuli, Diez found a "community herd" of 16,846 domestic camelids. This is an immense herd, but since Xuli consisted of 3242 households, it amounts to only five animals per household. At nearby Hilaui there was a community herd of 2122 camelids for 1470 households, amounting to less than two animals per household. Thus we are talking about vast herds, but not vast numbers of animals per family, except in the case of the *curacas*.

While each *ayllu* is said to have "kept separate its own animals," there are hints that some "*ayllu* herds" were really conglomerates of individual household herds. For example, Murra (1965:191) says that "any individual llama was publicly and ceremonially earmarked"—presumably by cutting a notch in its ear as is still done at Ayacucho during the August *chupa* or *waytakuy* (see Chapter 8). Yet those animals, often known to belong to particular households, spent most of the year grazing on the range together "all mixed up" (Murra 1965, citing Ortiz [1562] 1957, and Diez [1567–1568] 1964). This raises the possibility that some "*ayllu* herds" of 1000—seen by the Spaniards and assumed to be one herd—were in reality 50 herds of 20 animals each from 50 households, all grazing together.

We raise this point because, on the basis of our experience in 1970–1972, we consider it very unlikely that 16,846 camelids constituted a single herd. The number of *aynos* needed to service such a herd would lead to a level of fighting impossible to control. Such vast numbers of camelids would also require a strategy of management very different from that seen at Yanahuaccra or Toqtoqasa, and the sixteenth-century documents describe just such a strategy.

The animals of a given moiety or *ayllu*, Murra reveals, were segregated according to sex and age. Pregnant females grazed separately from burden-bearing males; so did nursing females and their *uñas*. Thus, by dividing their camelids into age- and sex-specific subherds, the sixteenth-century communities partially recreated the "family group" and "male group" of the wild guanaco, plus adding a few other groups as well.

Almost certainly, the large herds belonging to church and state must have been managed this way. The Inca could afford to do this because they had the luxury of abundant manpower. Full-time herders could be assigned to groups of burden-carrying males, groups of pregnant females, and groups of mothers and nursing young, each of which had their own specific requirements. In today's world, where the state has little interest in llamas, each family of herders at Yanahuaccra is on its own with its 15–35 animals. Only alpacas, with their valuable wool, are commercially important enough to make "industrial" management techniques worthwhile.

Ritual and Coat Color

Guanacos come in essentially one color scheme: fawn or chestnut above, white on the underbelly (see Fig. 5.1). This is a camouflage coloring which protects the guanaco from predators. After domestication, when humans began protecting the domestic camelids from predators, selection pressure was relaxed and previously deleterious color variants came to the fore.

We have seen that although today's Ayacucho llamas have a variety of colors and combinations, the herders attach relatively little significance to them. Such was not the case in Inca times, when the herds assigned to the state religion were selected and bred for specific colors. "If a lamb is born of a different color from its parents, it is put with those of its own color as soon as it has been reared. In this way the flocks were easily counted and recorded by means of the knots [of the *kipu*], the threads being of the same color" (Garcilaso [1604] 1966:260).

Temple herds were divided into flocks of uniform coat color, each of which was managed by full-time specialists. Every month, llamas were sacrificed to one supernatural being or another, and the calculi, or "bezoar stones," removed from their stomachs at the time of sacrifice were kept as amulets. These stones were called *ilya* (Rowe 1946:297), essentially the same term used today for small llama-shaped amulets used by Quechua speakers in Ayacucho (see Chapter 8).

The Sun preferred white llamas, so every year in October, 100 spotless white beasts were sacrificed to him. Viracocha preferred brown; each August and September, 100 brown animals were sacrificed to protect the newly planted maize against frost. Particolored llamas were sacrificed to Thunder (Rowe 1946:306; Cobo [1653] 1956; Murra 1965). Pure black was also prized for sacrifice because the animal was black "all over," even to the snout (Garcilaso [1604] 1966:360). When the Inca ruler traveled, he was sometimes accompanied by a pure white llama dressed in scarlet, with golden earrings and a necklace of red seashells. Often the mummies of the dead kings continue to own herds of llamas, which were used to support the custodians who curated the mummy bundles.

Apparently it was ritual color symbolism that led to this careful selective breeding by the prehispanic church, which in turn produced the variety of coat colors we see today. Alpaca breeders, who depend on the international demand for certain colors of wool, still pay close attention to coat color. Llama herders at Yanahuaccra can name all the colors, but their major concern is how much the beast can carry and how often it misbehaves.

Obstacles to Herd Growth

We have seen that pumas, rustlers, and mange were three of the sources of mortality most feared by the herders of Ayacucho in the 1970s. When we turn to the role of those mortality factors in the sixteenth century, a different picture emerges.

At periodic intervals the Inca rulers are said to have organized great communal hunts, called *chaku* in Quechua. As many as 30,000 Indians might be organized into lines of beaters, who encircled an area up to 30 leagues in diameter and closed in until they could literally take the game with their bare hands. The main purpose of the *chaku* was to capture guanaco, vicuña, and deer; some of those wild animals were killed, but most fertile females were released, and vicuñas in particular were set free after being shorn of their wool. In the course of the hunt, however, countless pumas, foxes, wildcats, and spectacled bears were also captured, and those predators "were all killed at once in order to rid the country of such vermin" (Garcilaso [1604] 1966:326). Since such hunts were held in each district every four years, this systematic extermination of predators would have depressed the fox and mountain lion population significantly.

In addition to this, sixteenth-century authors indicate that banditry was rare under Inca rule. Everyone who belonged to an *ayllu* was taken care of by his kinsmen, and even the poor and blind were given useful tasks by the state. The widespread assignment of useful tasks to marginal citizens, combined with severe punishments for criminals, meant that "neither Spaniards nor Indians ever feared to sleep in the open with no other company or security than their comrades, for there were no thieves or bandits" (Garcilaso [1604] 1966:515). Elsewhere, the same author reports that the herders in charge of the domestic camelids "diligently warded off wild beasts" and slept securely because "thieves were unknown" ([1604] 1966:268). Obviously this is an exaggeration, for Guaman Poma de Ayala ([1614] 1980:1038–1039) mentions thieves who stole llamas. Nevertheless, it would seem that rustlers were not the problem they are in Ayacucho today; had they been, the documents would undoubtedly contain many more anecdotes about them.

And then there was *qarachi*, or llama mange. As we suggested earlier, the antiquity of the *Sarcoptes* mite, its long association with man, and the existence of a Quechua word for mange all make it necessary for us to assume that it antedated the Conquest. In the case of *Psoroptes*, however, we suspect that it was not present before the introduction of European sheep. Consider Garcilaso's account of a mange outbreak in llamas and alpacas during 1544–1545—only a decade after the Conquest—described as "a very dire disease, hitherto unknown":

> It afflicted the flank and belly and then spread over the whole body, producing scabs two or three fingers high, especially on the belly, which was the

part most seriously affected and which came out in cracks two or three fingers deep, such being the depth of the scabs down in the flesh. Blood and matter issued from the sores, and in a few days the animal withered and was consumed. The disease was highly contagious, and to the horror of both Indians and Spaniards it accounted for two-thirds of all the animals. (Garcilaso [1604] 1966: 513)

This passage from Garcilaso is an almost perfect description of "sheep-scab," or psoroptic mange, and its timing and virulence strongly suggest an introduced mite for which the native camelids had developed no resistance. In desperation, the Indians attempted to halt the outbreak by slaughtering or burying alive the infected animals (Acosta [1590] 1940). Thus, although *Sarcoptes* mange may have been a problem even in ancient times, it is unlikely that prehispanic herds ever had to face a *Psoroptes* epidemic like the one in 1544–1545.

To be sure, there must have been plenty of prehispanic obstacles to herd growth—freezing weather, intestinal parasites, and the stress of altitudinal change all must have taken their toll. We are struck, however, by the possibility that the three mortality factors most feared by the herders of Yanahuaccra and Toqtoqasa today would have been less of a problem in the Inca period.

Ancient Llama Trains

In the sixteenth century, before mules and donkeys had become common in the Peruvian sierra, most transportation of cargo was by human porters or llama trains. Once again, the uses of llamas were different depending on whether they belonged to the state or the local *ayllu*. The ruler's pack animals carried supplies from the provinces to the capital, and thousands of state animals were pressed into military service; "army llama trains carried burdens and food and were themselves eaten in emergency" (Murra 1965:206). Some idea of the size of these military llama trains can be gained from Zárate's ([1555] 1853) estimate of 15,000 animals associated with one Indian general.

As for the pack trains belonging to various *ayllu*, once the rainy season ended they left the highlands for the coast or the *montaña* in large numbers. The Indians calculated that eight drivers were needed for every 100 animals (Rowe 1946:219). These pack trains must have been large, for Diez ([1567–1568] 1964) mentions one *mallku* or ethnic leader whose various *ayllu* supplied him with forty or fifty drivers (Murra 1965:201). This number of drivers would have been enough to manage 500–600 llamas.

Alpaca wool, llama and alpaca *charki*, common potatoes, and *chuñu* were among the major products leaving the highlands. Llama trains returned from the *montaña* with coca and from the coast with maize. Traveling only 15–20 km a day, the llamas and their drivers could take two to three months to make the round trip between sierra and coast—which explains the importance of drying most products to avoid spoilage.

Significantly, when llama trains reached sea level they often found the *yunga*, or coastal natives, as eager for the llamas themselves as for the products they bore. In ordinary years a choice llama, worth 18 Spanish ducats in Cuzco (Garcilaso [1604] 1966: 515), could be exchanged on the coast for five bushels of grain (Murra 1965:201; Diez [1567–1568] 1964). Coastal peoples bought llamas for food or for sacrifice, the result being that many coastal archaeological sites have camelid bones in their refuse middens, even when no camelids were raised locally. Llama trains on the coast were probably fed kernels, leaves, and stalks of maize while they waited to return to the sierra, since their normal forage does not grow in the coastal desert.

Clearly there were also smaller llama trains which made shorter trips, for Garcilaso ([1604] 1966:515) mentions Indians who had only "twenty-five animals to load and unload." This would be the size of an average train in the Ayacucho area in the 1970s. Once again, some of the huge llama trains described by the Spaniards might, on closer inspection, have turned out to represent the combined trains of ten to twenty individual herd owners.

A number of authors (e.g., Tschopik 1946:533; Flores Ochoa 1979:95) give 40–45 kg as the maximum that a llama can carry, and this figure has been widely cited by others. Based on our experience in Ayacucho, we regard this as a prodigious burden; in fact, Flores Ochoa says that on "long trips" of thirty days or so llamas carry only 25–30 kg. Although we do not rule out the possibility that a big, strong *capón llama* could carry 45 kg, we suspect that 25–30 kg was a more common load, especially on steep slopes. Drivers simply could not risk overloading their llamas. "To avoid tiring them, each flock has forty or fifty unladen animals, and whenever any beast is found to be flagging its burden is at once removed and transferred to another, before it lies down; for once it does this, there is no solution but to have it killed" (Garcilaso [1604] 1966:513).

We see several possible sources of confusion in the sixteenth-century authors' coverage of this subject. First, some documents deal with travel over relatively level land, such as the plains around Lake Titicaca; llamas "travel best between Cuzco and Potosí where the land is flat," as Garcilaso

([1604] 1966:513) expressed it. The burden a llama could carry over such *pampas* is greater than the load he could carry on the rugged terrain between Ayacucho and Pisco. Second, there is the problem of the Spanish folk measure *arroba*, already discussed earlier in this chapter. Garcilaso gives a llama's burden as "three or four *arrobas*." What size were these units? Possibly they were the 12.5-kg *arrobas* of our informants, but that is not certain.

In the sixteenth century, llamas were considered useful pack animals from 3 years of age up to 10 or 12 (Rowe 1946:219). That is virtually the same age span considered optimum at Yanahuaccra and Toqtoqasa. Were the burden carriers gelded *capón llamas*? We consider it possible, since Fray Domingo de Santo Tomás ([1560] 1951a) collected a number of sixteenth-century Quechua terms for such surgery: *chacani gui* or *corani gui* ("to castrate"), and *chacasca* or *corasca* ("a castrated animal").

Because llama trains traveled so widely in the Andes, the animal had been distributed from Ecuador to Chile by the time the Spaniards arrived. We may never know exactly where it was first domesticated. Earlier authors (e.g., Latcham 1922) theorized that its origins lay in the Titicaca Basin, but our oldest faunal evidence so far comes from Ayacucho and Junín. In fact, early domestication may have taken place over a large area of the guanaco's original range.

To base theories of early domestication on the llama's sixteenth-century distribution is to risk being misled by the regional economic specialization of the Inca period. Llamas are found at high altitudes today because that is where they interfere the least with agriculture and where Spanish culture has made the fewest inroads. They did very well at lower elevations in prehispanic times. There are even records of herds kept by highland immigrants at coastal oases (Diez [1567–1568] 1964), but as Murra (1965:188) points out, "special arrangements would have to be made to feed such coastal animals." Guanacos and llamas do well over the whole area between the puna and the *chaupi yunga* (coastal piedmont), but the hot coastal desert itself is outside their normal range.

Summary

Earlier in this chapter, we asked why there were no herds of 50, 75, or 100 llamas at Yanahuaccra and Toqtoqasa. We wondered if the upper limit of herd size was fixed by mange, predators, rustlers, competition from sheep, or some combination of those factors. To this we can now add a related question: Why were herds so much larger in Inca times?

First of all, the *waqchallama* herds of individual commoner households were evidently not significantly larger than the ones we saw. Even some of the so-called *ayllu* herds may have been conglomerates formed by allowing the flocks of 50 to 100 families to graze together "all mixed up." The herds that *were* larger were the *qhapaqllama* herds of the state, the church, and the *curacas*; and they were managed by a herding strategy completely different from the one used at Yanahuaccra in the 1970s. Using large teams of herders, the state separated its animals into groups that were all males, all females, all pregnant females, or all nursing females and their *uñas*. In addition, the herds attached to ancient temples were kept separate by color to provide animals for sacrifice. Such governmental management of llamas gradually broke down after the Spanish Conquest.

Second, the largest herds described by the Spaniards were usually found on huge areas of flat or gently rolling puna, such as the plains around Lake Titicaca—not on smaller areas of more precipitous terrain such as the punas of Yanahuaccra. Moreover, the llamas the Spaniards recorded were not sharing their range with sheep. An area of puna that today supports 100 llamas and 100 sheep could almost certainly support more llamas if the sheep were removed.

Third, the Inca herds were not faced with the same mortality factors prevalent in Ayacucho in the 1970s. We have seen that the huge royal hunts, or *chaku*, of the prehispanic state led to the killing of hundreds of pumas, foxes, and wildcats. We have also seen that under Inca rule bandits were rare enough that some chroniclers found that fact worthy of mention. Finally, we have suggested that the scab mite *Psoroptes equi* was unknown before the Spanish introduction of sheep. Thus, mortality rates from pumas, rustlers, and mange should have been lower in Inca times.

We conclude, therefore, that the upper limits on llama herd size in the *estancias* we studied were probably set by a combination of factors: small areas of rugged puna, forage depleted by sheep, predators not controlled by systematic hunting, Spanish-introduced diseases, modern rustlers, and the breakdown of the Inca herd management system. The *sallqaruna* of Yanahuaccra and Toqtoqasa are cultural descendants of the herders of *waqchallama*, "flocks of the weak." Deprived of the protection of the Inca state, and even of the calamity reserves of the *sapsi* herds, they can appeal today only to their *wamanis*. In the chapters that follow, we examine the way their cultural behavior affects the dynamics of their herds.

Six

Herd Dynamics I:
The "Oliver Twist" Model

During 1970–1972, the sizes of llama herds in the Quinua-Huamanguilla region were recorded along with data on losses to old age, rustlers, mange, and mountain lions. These static figures, however, failed to answer some of our original questions about llama herding. How long, we wondered, might it take a new herd to grow from a handful of inherited llamas to a group of 20 or 30? Was there a minimum size for a new herd, below which it might never get off the ground? Once having reached 20–30 animals, would a herd remain stable indefinitely? Why did herds not grow to 100 or even 200 llamas?

Since we could not spend 50 years at a puna *estancia* to answer these questions empirically, it seemed to us that the best alternative was to simulate the growth of a llama herd on the computer. Using the data we had collected in the early 1970s we could simulate a sample of herds, one large enough to see whether the variable rates given in Chapter 5 would generate herds with the characteristics of the ones we had studied. In this chapter, we describe the first stage of that simulation.

We experimented with herds that, at the start of simulation, consisted of anywhere from 2 to 6 inherited llamas (see below). Based on our interviews with I.V.I.T.A. veterinarians, we decided that each female would have a fertility rate of 50%, with the additional stipulation that she would not bear young two years in a row. Based on data collected from our Yanahuaccra-Toqtoqasa informants, we decided that no llama should live more than about 20 years. In any given year, its chance of being taken by rustlers would be .02 and its chance of being eaten by pumas would be .02. Its chance of dying from mange in any one year would be .01 if it was in a herd of fewer than 20 llamas, .02 if it was in a herd of 20 to 30 llamas, and .05 if it was in a herd of greater than 30 llamas. This gave us a useful series of random variables, one of them density dependent. Even if a llama managed to escape death from one of these causes, its likelihood of dying of old age would increase by .025 each year, so that it had reached 0.5 by age 20. Few llamas lasted that long, and those that did had only one chance in two of surviving for another year.

The Algorithm

We now present the actual algorithm used to simulate the growth of a herd. We realize that not all readers will want to read through this section in detail. On the other hand, we feel obligated to present the algorithm for those readers who have an interest in our methods. Those who have no interest can simply skip ahead to "Determining Minimum Herd Size" (p. 127).

The basic component of the simulation is the individual llama. While each herd grows from a small initial group of 3-year-olds, all subsequent llamas are born within the herd and begin at age 0. The program monitors the state of each individual llama in the herd with the passing of each year to ascertain whether it is still there or whether it has been unlucky enough to be removed by rustlers, pumas, mange, or death from old age according to the probabilities given above.

For each time step t (which represents a year in the simulation), the state of each llama can be described, and the size of the herd is determined by the llamas still alive plus any new ones that have been born. As an example of the descriptive variables associated with each llama, let us consider the variables for LLAMA (i), the ith llama within a herd of n animals.

AGE (i): This variable can take values from the set $\{1,\ldots,20\} \cup \{-1\}$. (It is assumed in the model that few llamas live more than 20 years.) The value -1 is used to denote llamas that have died during the current model year.

SEX (i): This variable describes the sex of each llama. It can take values from the set $\{M,F\}$.

The above variables apply to all llamas in the herd. For female llamas, two additional variables are used to enforce reproductive constraints:

BIRTH_FACTOR (i): This variable has a value of 1 if the female gave birth in the previous time step and 0 if she did not. This variable is used to enforce the constraint mentioned earlier that females are not likely to give birth two years in a row.

NUMBER_OF_OFFSPRING (*i*): This variable describes the number of successful births for a female. Each birth results in one successful offspring added to the model. Because of the constraints and mortality factors already mentioned, it is unlikely that any given female will give birth to more than five offspring during her lifetime. Such a figure is consistent with the situation observed for real herds given earlier.

The state of the herd can now be described as a function of the state values for its component llamas. The following variables reflect the state of the herd in a particular year *t*:

HERD_SIZE (*t*): The number of llamas in the herd at time step *t*.

JUVENILE_FEMALES (*t*): The number of females under 3 years of age in the herd at time *t*.

ADULT_FEMALES (*t*): The number of females between 3 and 12 years of age inclusive at time *t*.

OLD_FEMALES (*t*): The number of females over 12 years of age at time *t*.

JUVENILE_MALES (*t*): The number of males under 3 years of age in the herd at time *t*.

ADULT_MALES (*t*): The number of males between the ages of 3 and 12 inclusive at time *t*.

OLD_MALES (*t*): The number of males over 12 years of age at time *t*.

Given the above state variables, how are they updated each year? The update process is described by the model's *transition function* (Zeigler 1976). Here the transition function determines how the state of an individual llama is adjusted based on its current state and the state of the external environment. The general form of the function is

$$s\,(i, t + 1) = f\,(s\,(i, t), e\,(t))$$

This statement specifies that the overall state of LLAMA (*i*) at time $t + 1$, $[s\,(i, t + 1)]$, is a function f of its own inherent state at time t, $[(i, t)]$, and the state of its environment at time t, $[e(t)]$.

The environmental component $e(t)$ for a given llama consists of two basic parts. The first portion represents the influence that the current herd structure has on the transition function. The second portion represents the influence of the environment external to the current herd structure. Thus the transition function for an individual llama can be reexpressed as

$$s\,(i, t + 1) = f\,(s\,(i, t), \text{HERD}\,(t), \text{EXTERNAL}\,(t))$$

Factors external to the current herd structure which affect the mortality of a given llama are as follows:

PREDATION_PROB (t): The probability that the llama will fall prey to predators (such as pumas) during time step t.

SEPARATION_PROB (t): The probability that the llama will become physically removed from the herd during time step t (e.g., due to rustlers).

MANGE_DEATH_PROB (t): The probability that the llama will die from mange during time step t. Although mange is a density-dependent variable, it is here treated as an external factor because it is independent of the age and sex makeup of the herd.

The substitution of each set of variables into the equation for their representative terms gives the following:

$$s\,(i,\,t\,+\,1)\,=\,f\,(s\,(i,\,t),\,\text{HERD\_SIZE}\,(t),\,\text{JUVENILE\_FEMALES}\,(t),$$
$$\text{ADULT\_FEMALES}\,(t),\,\text{OLD\_FEMALES}\,(t),$$
$$\text{JUVENILE\_MALES}\,(t),\,\text{ADULT\_MALES}\,(t),$$
$$\text{OLD\_MALES}\,(t),\,\text{MANGE\_DEATH\_PROB}\,(t),$$
$$\text{PREDATION\_PROB}\,(t),\,\text{SEPARATION\_PROB}\,(t)$$

The transition function f can now be described. Since f takes a different form for males and females, we can reexpress it as a combination of functions f_m and f_f as follows:

$$f\,(s\,(i,\,t),\,\ldots)\,=\,\begin{cases} f_m\,(s\,(i,\,t),\,\ldots)\text{ if SEX }(i)\,=\,M \\ \\ f_f\,(s\,(i,\,t),\,\ldots)\text{ otherwise} \end{cases}$$

Now each of the two transition functions are described in algorithmic fashion in order to reflect the corresponding actions that our program takes to implement each. The transition function for male llamas f_m is described first. There are two state variables for males. One is sex, which is a static variable; the other is age, which is dynamic and is modified at time $t\,+\,1$ as follows:

$$s\,(i,\,t\,+\,1)\,=$$
$$f_m\,(s\,(i,\,t),\,\text{HERD}\,(t),\,\text{EXTERNAL}\,(t))\,=\begin{cases} \text{AGE}\,(i)\,=\,\text{AGE}\,(i)\,+\,1\text{ if} \\ \text{DEATH}\,(s\,(i,\,t),\,\text{HERD}\,(t), \\ \text{EXTERNAL}\,(t))\,=\,0 \\ \\ \text{AGE}\,(i)\,=\,-1\text{ if DEATH} \\ (s\,(i,\,t),\,\text{HERD}\,(t), \\ \text{EXTERNAL}\,(t))\,=\,1. \end{cases}$$

The DEATH function determines whether the llama dies during this time step. If the function determines that the llama does not die this year, the routine returns a 0 and the AGE of the llama is incremented by 1. If the DEATH function determines that the llama dies, a 1 is returned and the AGE of the llama is set to -1; that llama is removed from the herd at the end of the time step.

The DEATH function has the following structure:

$$
\text{DEATH } (s(i, t), \text{ HERD } (t), \text{ EXTERNAL } (t)) = \begin{cases} 1 \text{ if PREDATOR\_DEATH } ((s \, (i, \, t)), \\ \text{PREDATOR\_PROB}) = 1, \text{ or} \\[1em] \text{if SEPARATION } ((s \, (i, t), \text{ SEPARATION\_} \\ \text{PROB}) = 1, \text{ or} \\[1em] \text{if MANGE\_DEATH } ((s \, (i, \, t), \\ \text{MANGE\_PROB (HERD\_SIZE} \\ (t))) = 1, \text{ or} \\[1em] \text{if NATURAL\_CAUSES } ((s \, (i, \, t)) = 1 \\[1em] 0 \text{ otherwise} \end{cases}
$$

Each of the four functions that determine llama mortality requires the generation of a random number. The function that generates random numbers from 0 to 1 is denoted as "rand (seed)"; the way each of the four functions uses it is now described.

The PREDATOR_DEATH function, given below, returns a 1 if rand (seed) is greater than 0 and less than PREDATOR_PROB. This indicates that the llama has died as the result of predators:

$$
\text{PREDATOR\_DEATH } (s \, (i, \, t), \text{ PREDATOR\_PROB}) = \begin{cases} 1 \text{ if rand (seed) } < \text{PREDATOR\_PROB} \\[1em] 0 \text{ otherwise} \end{cases}
$$

The SEPARATION function represents the loss of a llama via its unintended separation from the herd, as for example by rustling. The form of this function is similar to that for PREDATOR_DEATH:

$$\text{SEPARATION } (s\ (i,\ t), \atop \text{SEPARATION\_PROB}) = \begin{cases} 1 \text{ if rand (seed)} < \text{SEPARATION\_PROB} \\ \\ 0 \text{ otherwise} \end{cases}$$

The MANGE_DEATH function determines whether or not the llama will die of mange during time step t. The probability that the llama will contract mange is a function of herd size; the larger the herd, the more likely it is that a given llama will come in contact with an infected animal.

$$\text{MANGE\_DEATH } (s\ (i,\ t), \atop \text{MANGE\_PROB (HERD\_SIZE } (t))) = \begin{cases} 1 \text{ rand (seed)} < \text{MANGE\_} \\ \text{PROB (HERD SIZE) } (t)) \\ \\ 0 \text{ otherwise} \end{cases}$$

The NATURAL_CAUSES function determines whether or not the llama will die as a result of natural causes. The probability of death, NATURAL_CAUSES_PROB, is a function of the llama's current age. This function allows the probability to increase as a llama becomes elderly:

$$\text{NATURAL\_CAUSES } (s\ (i,\ t)) = \begin{cases} 1 \text{ if rand (seed)} < \\ \text{NATURAL\_CAUSES\_PROB} \\ (\text{AGE } (i)) \\ \\ 0 \text{ otherwise} \end{cases}$$

The basic transition function for females f_f is similar to that for males and has the following format:

$$s\ (i,\ t+1) = f_f\ (s(i,t), \text{HERD}(t), \text{EXTERNAL}(t), \text{BIRTH (HERD } (t), s(i,t))$$

There are four state variables that describe a female llama. Sex is a static variable. The variable AGE is updated in the same manner as for males. The remaining two variables, BIRTH_FACTOR and NO._OF_OFFSPRING, are updated as follows:

BIRTH_FACTOR (i) = 1 if BIRTH (HERD (t), $s\ (i,t)$) = 1

BIRTH_FACTOR (i) = 0 if BIRTH (HERD (t), $s\ (i,t)$) = 0

NO._OF_OFFSPRING = NO._OF_OFFSPRING + 1 if BIRTH
                (HERD (t), $s(i,t)$)   = 1

The DEATH function for females is the same as that for males. Females, however, also have a BIRTH function, which determines if they will give birth during time step t. The BIRTH function is described as follows:

$$\text{BIRTH (HERD}(t), s(i,t)) = \begin{cases} 1 & \text{if } 2 \leqslant \text{AGE}(i) \leqslant 12 \\ & \text{and BIRTH\_FACTOR} \\ & (i) = 0 \text{ and ADULT} \\ & \text{MALES}(t) > 0 \text{ and} \\ & \text{rand (seed)} < .50 \\ \\ 0 & \text{otherwise} \end{cases}$$

Note that the probability of giving birth is .5, based on the situation observed in I.V.I.T.A.'s veterinary studies and by us in the field in 1970–1972. If the generated random number is less than .5, the llama gives birth to 1 offspring this year.

The BIRTH function affects the state of the individual llama in the following manner:

if BIRTH (HERD$(t), s, (i,t)) = 1$, then

BIRTH_FACTOR $(i) = 1$

NO._OF_OFFSPRING $(i) = $ NO._OF_OFFSPRING$(i) + 1$

otherwise BIRTH_FACTOR $(i) = 0$

The BIRTH function affects the state of the herd if the value returned by the function is 1. In this case, the GENERATE_NEW_LLAMA function is triggered. The GENERATE_NEW_LLAMA function creates a new llama in the following manner:

$$s(\text{NEW\_ID}, t) = \begin{cases} \text{NEW\_ID} = \text{GENERATE\_NEW\_ID} \\ \text{AGE (NEW\_ID)} = 0 \\ \\ \text{if rand (seed)} < .5, \quad \text{then} \\ \text{SEX (NEW\_ID)} = \text{"F"} \\ \text{BIRTH\_FACTOR (NEW\_ID)} = 0 \\ \text{NO.\_OF\_OFFSPRING (NEW\_ID)} = 0 \\ \\ \text{otherwise SEX (NEW\_ID)} = \text{"M"} \end{cases}$$

The GENERATE_NEW_ID function assigns a unique identity to each new llama, whose progress through time will now be followed.

The overall structure of the computer program that implements this model[1] can now be described, as follows:

```
Read (SIM_LENGTH)
t = 0
Read (HERD_SIZE (t))
For i = 1 to HERD_SIZE(t) ƄƄ READ (s(LLAMA (i))) End For
COMPUTE (HERD_SIZE (t))
While t ≤ SIM_LENGTH
Do
   if HERD_SIZE (t) > 0 then
   for each LLAMA (i)
```

$$\text{if SEX (LLAMA } (i)) = \text{"FEMALE", then}$$
$$\text{Do}$$
$$s(\text{LLAMA } (i), t+1) = f_f(s(\text{LLAMA } (i),t),\text{HERD } (t),\text{EXTERNAL}$$
$$(t),\text{BIRTH (HERD } (t), s(i,t)))$$
$$\text{if BIRTH (HERD}(t), s(i,t)), \text{then}$$
$$\text{GENERATE\_NEW\_LLAMA}$$

$$\text{End Do}$$

$$\text{else}$$
$$s(\text{LLAMA } (i), t+1) = f_m(s(\text{LLAMA}(i),t),\text{HERD}$$
$$(t),\text{EXTERNAL } (t)$$

```
                        End for
COMPUTE (EXTERNAL(t))
COMPUTE (HERD_STATISTICS)
PRINT RESULTS
t = t + 1

End Do
```

As can be seen, to run the simulation model one must specify (1) the characteristics of the initial herd with which the operations begin, (2) the probabilities associated with the various model activities, and (3) the number of time steps over which each run is to take place. The probabilities associated with the random processes in the model were set to conform as closely as possible with the data collected in the field in 1970–1972, as follows:

1. The implementation language was selected to be PL/1, and all runs of the program were performed by Reynolds on an AMDAHL 470 computer under the MTS operating system at Wayne State University.

```
PREDATION_PROB          = .02
SEPARATION_PROB         = .02
MANGE_PROB              = .01 if HERD SIZE ≤ 20
                          .02 if HERD_SIZE > 20 and ≤ 30
                          .05 if HERD_SIZE > 30
NATURAL_CAUSES_PROB = AGE (i) * .025
```

It should be noted that all experiments with probabilities in excess of these led to the generation of herds much smaller than those observed in the field in 1970–1972, which suggests that the variable rates we collected were reasonably accurate. One of the strengths of a simulation is that anyone who wants to can change the variable rates and see what the outcome would be.

Determining Minimum Herd Size

As previously stated, one of the questions we hoped to answer was whether or not there was a minimal size for a new herd, below which it might never get off the ground. "Getting off the ground" was here defined as growing to 15 or 16 animals, like many herds we saw in the field. We considered an initial herd size to be adequate if it gave the herd a 75% chance of growing to 15 or 16 llamas.

We experimented with initial herds ranging in size from 2 (one male, one female) to 6 (2 males, 4 females). All llamas in the initial herd were assumed to be 3 years of age, so all would have their fertile years ahead of them. The following combinations were tried:

HERD_SIZE	HERD_CONFIGURATIONS
HERD_SIZE = 2	{1 M, 1F}
HERD_SIZE = 3	{1M, 2F}, {2M, 1F}
HERD_SIZE = 4	{1M, 3F}, {2M, 2F}, {3M, 1F}
HERD_SIZE = 5	{1M,4F}, {2M,3F}, {3M,2F}, {4M,1F}
HERD_SIZE = 6	{1M,5F}, {2M,4F}

Each of the herd configurations given above was tested in a systematic fashion, beginning with HERD_SIZE = 2. Within each HERD_SIZE category, the first configuration tested was the one with the largest proportion of females. The next configuration tested had one less female and one more male. The last configuration tested for each HERD_SIZE was the one with the largest proportion of males. The first configuration that displayed an acceptable success (i.e., 75% or more of the runs grew to 15 or 16 llamas) was taken as the minimum size necessary for an initial herd.

It soon became obvious that HERD_SIZES of 3 or less would stand little chance of success, and they were therefore not tested extensively. The remaining nine configurations were each tested in sequence. The process stopped with a HERD_SIZE of 2 males and 4 females, since that was the first configuration that yielded a herd of 15 or 16 animals at least 75% of the time. This configuration of 2 males, 4 females is referred to by us as the "minimum reproductive core" for generating a herd given this set of mortality factors.

Herd Longevity and Stability

As stated above, herds which began with 2 male and 4 female llamas and were subjected to the variables of predation, rustling, and mange already described had a 75% chance of growing to 15 or 16 animals. However, even herds that grew to this size (or larger) did not achieve stability at that point. The history of every herd was one of continual fluctuation over time, apparently reflecting not only random losses to one of the external variables but also random imbalances in the sex ratio. We allowed herds to run for 100 model years to see if an equilibrium was ever achieved, and it soon became clear that, given a long enough time, all herds would eventually go to zero—even if they had reached 30–40 animals at some point in their history. This was one of the most interesting discoveries to emerge from the initial simulation.

We performed nine runs of the simulation which began with 5 animals (1 male, 4 females). Most runs did not last 100 model years. Even those that did last that long oscillated wildly (e.g., from 36 animals down to 8 and up to 36 again). The greatest size achieved by any one herd was 45 animals, and that particular herd ended before year 90.

We then performed fourteen runs of the simulation which began with the 2 male, 4 female minimum reproductive core. Although three-fourths of these herds grew to 15 or 16 llamas, only 3 herds were still going after 100 model years. In fact, 7 of the herds (i.e., half the runs) lasted 50 years or less, with 3 of them vanishing by year 35. Of the remaining 7 herds, 4 lasted for less than 80 years, leaving only the 3 surviving herds already mentioned. The greatest size reached by any one herd was 35–40 animals.

We have selected six runs as typical of this simulation and illustrated them in Figure 6.1. In Figure 6.2 we have graphed the history of the

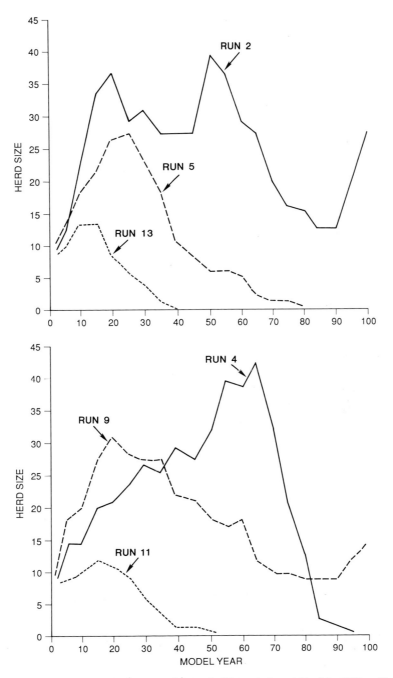

Figure 6.1   Outcomes of Runs 2, 5, and 13 and of Runs 4, 9, and 11 of the "Oliver Twist" model.

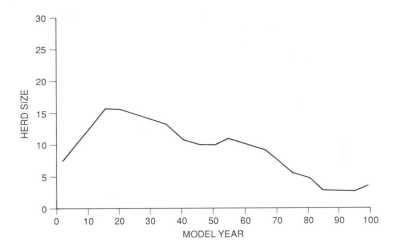

Figure 6.2 Average performance of all herds over all runs of the "Oliver Twist" model.

average herd for all fourteen runs. Note that the average herd reached a peak size of about 15 animals by years 18–20, gradually declined to below 10 animals by years 45–50, rose slightly until roughly year 56, then declined and fell below 6 (the minimum reproductive core) by year 75. Our results suggest that, once a simulated herd contains fewer than 4 fertile females or 2 fertile males, its likelihood of rebounding is low.

Examination of all simulation runs revealed that the main reason for a herd's demise was an imbalance in the sex ratios. Because each herd was such a small population, chance factors (such as a mange epidemic and a puma attack occurring in the same year) could randomly remove enough fertile animals of one sex or the other to create such an imbalance. Should a herd lose all but one of its fertile males or all but three of its young females in a given model year, it was in big trouble.

A Sample Herd History

As an example of how random mortality factors can affect a herd, we offer Box 6.1. This illustration gives the statistics from a 3-year period (model years 33–35) in the history of a simulated herd. By the end of year 32, the

Box 6.1 Computer output from Model Years 33–35 of a typical "Oliver Twist" run, which shows how random mortality factors can produce an imbalance in the sex ratios, leading to a fatal decline.

THIS IS YEAR #   33
OF BIRTHS THAT TOOK PLACE IS   1
FOLLOWING ARE THE # OF DEATHS BY PUMAS
CASUALTIES   2
NUMBER IN HERD =   21
MANGE PROB =   0.020
                0   LLAMAS WERE KILLED BY MANGE
FOLLOWING ARE DEATHS BY RUSTLERS
CASUALTIES   1
NUMBER OF DEATHS BY NATURAL CAUSES =   0

---------------------- FEMALES -------------------
ID NO.	AGE	BIRTHFACTOR	NUMBER OF BIRTHS
25	20	0	3
26	18	0	3
33	14	0	3
40	11	0	2
42	10	1	3
52	3	0	0

---------------------- MALES -------------------

ID NUMBER	AGE
28	17
30	16
32	15
34	14
36	13
37	12
39	12
43	9
44	9
45	8
48	6
49	6
50	6
53	3

THERE ARE   0 JUVENILE FEMALES
THERE ARE   3 ADULT FEMALES
THERE ARE   3 OLD FEMALES
THERE ARE   0 JUVENILE MALES
THERE ARE   9 ADULT MALES
THERE ARE   5 OLD MALES

Box 6.1 (*continued*)

THIS IS YEAR #   34
OF BIRTHS THAT TOOK PLACE IS   1
FOLLOWING ARE THE # OF DEATHS BY PUMAS
CASUALTIES   0
NUMBER IN HERD =   21
MANGE PROB =   0.020
                              0   LLAMAS WERE KILLED BY MANGE
FOLLOWING ARE DEATHS BY RUSTLERS
CASUALTIES   0
NUMBER OF DEATHS BY NATURAL CAUSES =   0

```
------------------- FEMALES -------------------
```

ID NO.	AGE	BIRTHFACTOR	NUMBER OF BIRTHS
25	21	0	3
26	19	0	3
33	15	0	3
40	12	1	3
42	11	0	3
52	4	0	0
55	1	0	0

```
-------------------- MALES --------------------
```

ID NUMBER	AGE
28	18
30	17
32	16
34	15
36	14
37	13
39	13
43	10
44	10
45	9
48	7
49	7
50	7
53	4

THERE ARE   1 JUVENILE FEMALES
THERE ARE   3 ADULT FEMALES
THERE ARE   3 OLD FEMALES
THERE ARE   0 JUVENILE MALES
THERE ARE   7 ADULT MALES
THERE ARE   7 OLD MALES

Box 6.1 (*continued*)

THIS IS YEAR #   35
OF BIRTHS THAT TOOK PLACE IS   0
FOLLOWING ARE THE # OF DEATHS BY PUMAS
CASUALTIES   1
NUMBER IN HERD =   20
MANGE PROB =   0.010
                        1   LLAMAS WERE KILLED BY MANGE
FOLLOWING ARE DEATHS BY RUSTLERS
CASUALTIES   0
NUMBER OF DEATHS BY NATURAL CAUSES =   1

```
------------------ FEMALES ------------------
```

ID NO.	AGE	BIRTHFACTOR	NUMBER OF BIRTHS
26	20	0	3
33	16	0	3
40	13	0	3
42	12	0	3
52	5	0	0

```
-------------------- MALES --------------------
```

ID NUMBER	AGE
30	18
32	17
34	16
36	15
37	14
39	14
43	11
44	11
45	10
48	8
49	8
50	8
53	5

THERE ARE   0 JUVENILE FEMALES
THERE ARE   2 ADULT FEMALES
THERE ARE   3 OLD FEMALES
THERE ARE   0 JUVENILE MALES
THERE ARE   7 ADULT MALES
THERE ARE   6 OLD MALES

herd had reached 22 animals. One new llama was born in year 33, but 3 animals were lost to pumas or rustlers, leaving a herd of 20, as follows:

0 juvenile females
3 adult females
3 old females
0 juvenile males
9 adult males
5 old males

This herd already had a problem, since 5 of the 6 females were at least 10 years old. Model year 34 went reasonably well, but in model year 35 there were no births and 3 llamas were lost due to the cumulative actions of pumas, mange, and natural causes. The result was to reduce to 2 the number of females between 3 and 12 years of age. This shortage of females in their most productive years gave the herd little chance of rebounding. In fact, from this point onward the herd gradually dwindled until the last llama died at year 80.

Conclusions

This early phase of our simulation answered a few questions and raised others. To begin with, it showed us that the figures on llama birth and mortality we had collected in 1970–1972 must be reasonably accurate, since by using them we could generate herds with maximum size ranges similar to those observed at Yanahuaccra and Toqtoqasa.

Second, it showed us why herders could not really start out with one male and one female and expect eventually to have a herd. Any group smaller than 4 young females and 2 fertile males had a chance of less than 75% of growing to a herd of 15 or 16 animals. Smaller initial herds were best left with one's father (or older brother's) llamas until they had reproduced sufficiently.

Third, it showed us that even herds that did grow to 15–30 animals were not stable flocks that could last indefinitely. All herds were inherently unstable populations whose sex ratios were subject to the vagaries of pumas, rustlers, and mange (and the larger the herd, the greater the chance of mange). Not only could they never grow to 100 animals, their population curve was one of continual oscillation between growth and decline. Given a long enough time, all would inevitably reach equilibrium at zero.

Still another insight that emerged from the simulation was the fact that these long histories of oscillations would have been out of focus, not only to the herders themselves, but also to any anthropologist who spent only a few years with them. We can see the pattern today because we ran each simulation for 100 model years, but no anthropologist is likely to spend more than five years on the puna. He or she would observe some herds of 10 llamas and some of 35, without necessarily realizing that those figures were just momentary fluctuations on an ever-changing curve.

Even the herders themselves were unlikely to witness more than 30 or 40 years in the history of the herd they managed—a herd they hoped to pass on, intact and thriving, to their children. Should that herd crash to extinction after only 30 years, a Yanahuaccra herder would attribute it to the displeasure of the *wamani* and blame himself for improperly executing the necessary rituals. In fact, in the eyes of Western science, his herd would simply have fallen prey to the inevitable risks of small populations.

The questions raised by this early simulation established the design for future versions. Could this high a proportion of herds truly fail in real-life situations? Would camelid domestication ever have grown and spread across the Andes if it were this risky? Beyond this, could the average herder really survive if (as the simulation suggested) it took his initial herd of 6 animals some 15–20 years to become a flock of 15–25? We suspected that the answer to all three questions was no. There was something missing in our first simulation—something that would speed up herd growth and decrease risk.

We remembered that the Chukchi reindeer herders studied by Leeds (1965) had from time to time faced a similar situation of declining herds. They had settled on two solutions: (1) arranged marriages, which allowed the consolidation of one's shrinking herd with a spouse's larger herd, and (2) periodic capture of wild reindeer to incorporate into one's domestic herd. We found no evidence that the herders of the Ayacucho puna ever arranged marriages for this purpose, and it has been a long time since there were any wild guanacos left to capture in the region. Such continual inputs of wild camelids into domestic herds might have been possible during the early periods of prehistoric domestication, but it was no longer an option for the people of Yanahuaccra and Toqtoqasa. What they needed were occasional inputs of one or two llamas from someone else's herd.

We decided that we should expand our simulation to see if, in fact, occasional small inputs of new breeding stock could make a difference in the case of the herds that had failed. That simulation, called the "Santa

Claus" model, is described in Chapter 7. For the purpose of identifying the original simulation given in this chapter, we refer to it as the "Oliver Twist" model. It is, after all, a model in which impoverished herders cannot get an additional llama—not even by asking the *wamani*, "Please, sir, may I have some more?"

Seven

Herd Dynamics II:
The "Santa Claus" Model

In Chapter 6 we learned something about the long-term dynamics of llama herds. By using the variables for birth and mortality collected at Yana-huaccra and Toqtoqasa, we were able to generate herds whose maximum sizes were in the range of the ones observed in 1970–1972. We learned, however, that such simulated herds would neither increase indefinitely nor remain stable at sizes of 15 to 30 animals. Instead, the curve of each herd's history showed a series of random oscillations—rising to 15, dropping to 6, rising to 30, dropping to 10—until one fatal downswing put it out of business. Because each herd was such a small population, it was only a matter of time until mortality factors such as predation, rustling, or mange produced an imbalance in the sex ratios. Every herd, even one that lasted until year 100, was inevitably doomed to extinction. In biostatistical terms, its "equilibrium population size" was zero.

The "Oliver Twist" model also gave us an idea what the minimum reproductive core necessary for survival might be. Specifically, a herd with 4 young females and 2 fertile males had a 75% chance of growing (or rebounding) to 15–16 animals. We considered 75% to be a sufficiently high percentage, because it seemed likely that in the real world at least some herds must have failed.

What we wanted to generate next were the conditions under which an average herd could be guaranteed an equilibrium population higher than zero. Indeed, given the minimum core mentioned above, it was clear that that equilibrium would have to be at least 6 animals (4 females, 2 males) and probably more.

Suppose, for the sake of argument, that the owners of each of our simulated herds also believed that a herd with fewer than 4 young females and 2 fertile males had little chance of survival. At Yanahuaccra, we had seen that such tiny herds would be quickly combined with that of a close relative. But suppose that a herder could obtain one additional llama of the appropriate age and sex whenever his herd dropped below 2 males or 4 females, ensuring that he would always have the minimum reproductive core. Would this be enough to produce a non-zero equilibrium?

We decided to answer this question by running just such a simulation. We established an imaginary donor—in effect, a kind of "Santa Claus"—with a supply of llamas so large that he could provide each shrinking herd with an appropriate animal whenever it fell below our 4-female, 2-male minimum. Each llama donated by Santa possessed full reproductive capability. In our model, this meant that each LLAMA was of AGE = 3 and, for females, BIRTH_FACTOR = 0 and NUMBER_OF_OFFSPRING = 0.

This second model can be implemented by a simple addition to the "Oliver Twist" algorithm, which was described in detail in Chapter 6. Donation of new llamas takes place after the generation of HERD_STA-TISTICS and prior to PRINT_RESULTS in the pseudoprogram given for "Oliver Twist." We describe these modifications in the next section; once again, those readers who wish to may skip ahead to the final section, "Results."

Additions to the Algorithm

The donation of new llamas by Santa Claus consists of two phases, REQUEST and DONOR. The REQUEST phase, which occurs when a herd drops below the minimum reproductive configuration, can be modeled by the following function:

REQUEST (t, # males, # females) when

$$\text{\# males} = \begin{cases} 0 \text{ if no. fertile males} \geq 2 \\ 2 \text{ minus no. fertile males otherwise} \end{cases}$$

$$\text{\# females} = \begin{cases} 0 \text{ if no. fertile females} \geq 4 \\ 4 \text{ minus no. fertile females otherwise} \end{cases}$$

The DONOR function at time t is simply

DONATE (t) = g (REQUEST (t, # males, # females))

where *g* generates the requested number of maximally reproductive llamas of each sex requested.

Results

We produced fifteen runs with the "Santa Claus" model. These included reruns of the fourteen herds originally run with the "Oliver Twist" model, since we were curious to see whether the presence of an inexhaustible donor could save those herds which had gone to extinction in our previous simulation. In addition, we ran a fifteenth herd to increase the sample.

This time, all fifteen herds survived 100 model years. We have picked six runs to illustrate (Fig. 7.1) and compare to their "Oliver Twist" counterparts (Fig. 6.1). Notice that, following an initial spurt of growth, after about 50 years most herds begin to oscillate around a mean population size of 22 animals. That is not to say that Santa's donations bring the curves to a steady plateau. Of the fifteen runs, roughly three peak between 35 and 40 animals and decline, roughly three go through a slow climb, and roughly five remain fairly level, usually below 20 animals. However, it is impressive that these fifteen runs seem to have found an equilibrium population size of 22 ± 5 llamas.

In Figure 7.2 we compare the curves for the average performance of all fourteen runs of the "Oliver Twist" model with the average of all fifteen runs of the "Santa Claus" model. On the average, "Santa Claus" herds reach their mean size of 22 animals within 12 years and remain close to that point. The average "Oliver Twist" herd, on the other hand, gradually declines toward zero.

Based on this simulation, we conclude that (1) the addition of a single llama of the appropriate age and sex to a herd that has shrunk to its minimum reproductive core will usually bring about a rebound, and that (2) herds can be kept going for 100 model years or more if such occasional inputs of new animals are possible. Indeed, such gifts can raise the average equilibrium population size from 0 to 22 ± 5. This would mean long-term stability for herds of 17 to 27 animals, even in the face of annual losses to pumas, rustlers, and mange like the ones observed in the Yanahuaccra-Toqtoqasa region. In addition, "Santa Claus" herds grow from 6 to 22 animals in fewer years than do "Oliver Twist" herds.

There is, of course, one major problem with the "Santa Claus" model: it is unrealistic. In the real world (sorry, Virginia) there is no Santa Claus.

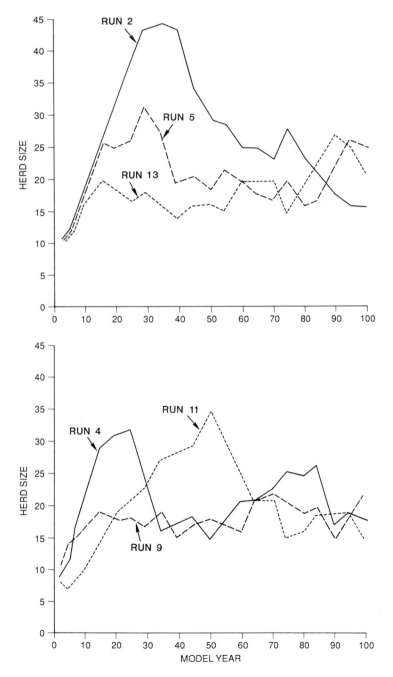

Figure 7.1 Outcomes of Runs 2, 5, and 13 and of Runs 4, 9, and 11 of the "Santa Claus" model.

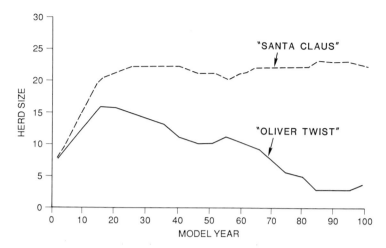

Figure 7.2 Average performance for all herds during all runs of the "Oliver Twist" and the "Santa Claus" models.

We have shown that occasional gifts of young animals can make a significant improvement in herd dynamics, but in the real world those gifts would have to come from other herders.

And, as a matter of fact, such gifts do take place. In every herding community known in the Ayacucho region, in the context of the important llama-decorating ceremonies of August, there are gifts known as *suñay*. In *suñay*, the owner of a sufficiently large herd gives away a llama to someone—even a nonrelative—who has demonstrated by his ritual participation that he is *kuyaq*, "one who loves me." Those ceremonies are described in the chapter that follows.

Eight

Chupa and *Waytakuy*

Once a year, in August, the herders of Ayacucho take time out to let the *wamani* know how much they appreciate their herds and how well they have taken care of them. It is a ceremony very widespread in the Andes and certainly ancient, although exactly how ancient will probably never be known. In some parts of Peru the llamas are forced to drink chicha along with their herders, while others are dressed up as if they were human members of the *ayllu*, gaily decorated so that they will be pleasing to the eyes of the *Tayta Urqu*. Two terms have survived from the ancient ceremonies held by speakers of Ayacucho Quechua: *waytakuy*, which literally means "to decorate with flowers," and *chupa*, which means "tail." One refers to the decoration of llamas and ritual paraphernalia, the other to the snipping off of the tips of the animals' tails as offerings to the *wamani*.

After the Spaniards arrived with their horses and cattle, the Indians quickly assimilated the custom of branding as a way of "decorating" those Old World animals. One result is that the Spanish term *herranza*, or "branding," has now become widely used for the traditional animal-decorating ceremony—even when the animals are llamas and no branding is involved. The distinction between branding cattle for ownership, notching llamas' ears for identification, and sewing ribbons into their ears for decoration has become somewhat blurred.

All over the Peruvian departments of Ayacucho, Huancavelica, and Junín, annual *herranzas* were held in the early 1970s (and are still held where guerrilla activity has not disrupted them). In some areas, such as the Río Pampas south of the city of Ayacucho, the ceremony could be extremely lavish, lasting four days. In other areas, including some *estancias* north of the city of Ayacucho, grinding poverty has limited the *herranza*

143

to one day. Almost certainly the ancient ceremony was an elaborate affair occupying several days.

Two acculturating influences on the *herranza* are (1) Spanish Catholicism and (2) the presence of Old World species such as sheep, cattle, horses, and donkeys. For example, some towns now have a communal *herranza* for the *cofradía*, the herds belonging to the church; this can be contrasted with the *herranza familiar*, or decorating ceremony for the herds of individual families. In many towns, llamas and alpacas are now so marginal a part of the economy that virtually the entire *herranza* is devoted to animals introduced by the Spaniards. In almost every community, such recent items as cigarettes, votive candles, and distilled alcohol have taken their place alongside aboriginal offerings like coca and chicha.

In spite of the effects of acculturation and local variation among communities, there are a sufficient number of shared features throughout Ayacucho so that one could describe a generic *herranza familiar* for the department as a whole. Although there are *wamanis* living on important mountain peaks at all four of the world's cardinal directions, each household has a particular peak whose *wamani* controls the fate of its herd. Each household also has a ceremonial bundle containing all the paraphernalia necessary to perform the *herranza*, and a supply of mineral powder called *llampu*, which symbolizes the snow of the sacred mountaintops and is used for ritual purification. Both the bundle and the *llampu* are stored all year until needed. On the evening prior to the *herranza*, both are readied.

A great deal of the ritual is carried out, not by the owner of the herd, but by a crew of his relatives and affines. His sons, sons-in-law, and daughters-in-law have important roles, and acculturation has now added to that list his *compadres*, or ritual coparents. The crew of participants must be wined and dined for their services. In addition, non-kin guests who contribute offerings for the *wamani* become *kuyaq* and are treated as temporary members of the owner's *ayllu*.

After a ceremonial table has been laid out in a corral set aside for the *herranza*, prayers and offerings are made to the *wamani*. Accompanied by songs and dances, the Old World animals are branded, and llamas have colored ribbons or yarn sewn into their ears. Small pieces of ears and tail are cut off the animals and, on the day following the *herranza*, these are taken up to a cave or crevice on the *cerro wamani* which is specific to the owner's household. There they are buried along with more prayers and offerings to the *Tayta Urqu*.

Most important for the purposes of our study is the custom of *suñay*, or gift giving, which takes place at the moment when the animals are decorated. The owner, when sufficiently drunk and pleased by the offerings some of his guests have brought, may give away an animal to one of them. The recipient of *suñay* need not be a relative, or even a member of the owner's *ayllu*; indeed, in some cases, intermediaries may already have informed the owner that a non-kin visitor, badly in need of a fertile young animal, has decided to make a handsome contribution to the offerings. Here, then, is a possible way in which someone whose herd is shrinking to the 4-female, 2-male minimum described in Chapter 7 can get a small input from someone whose herd is doing well.

Piña Killa: The Timing of the *Herranza*

August is the traditional month for the *waytakuy* of llamas. At many small communities, sheep are decorated and cattle and horses branded during this same ceremony. However, at other communities—especially larger ones—the *herranza* for Old World animals such as sheep, cattle, and horses takes place during *Carnaval*, a pre-Lenten festival in February. In these larger towns, appropriately enough, indigenous camelids are associated with the indigenous August *waytakuy*, while animals introduced by the Spaniards are associated with a traditional Spanish festival.

For example, consider the late 1960s ritual calendar for Sarhua, a community in the Río Pampas district which owned both *kichwa* and *sallqa* lands (Palomino Flores 1970; Earls 1973). We begin the cycle with September, when the first rains of the Andean spring begin. During this month, the irrigation canals of the *kichwa* were cleaned as part of a ritual called *Yarqa Aspiy*. Following this, in October, maize was planted in the *kichwa*, and *chuñu* potatoes in the *sallqa*. Cultivation continued during November and December, with *maswa*, wheat, and barley all planted by Christmas. In January, with the hard rains of the Andean summer beginning, common potatoes were planted in the *kichwa*, and the suspension bridge linking Sarhua with neighboring villages north of the river was given its annual repair.

February was one of the two most dangerous times of the year—a *piña killa*, or "angry month." Strong winds and heavy rains lashed the mountains and swelled the rivers; the hills opened and the *wamanis* emerged to walk the earth, hungry, needing offerings. At Sarhua, the marking ceremony for sheep and goats was held on the puna during the February *Carnaval*.

In March the rains began to slacken, finally ending in April. The harvest of *chuñu* potatoes began in the *sallqa* and continued into May; the harvest of maize and common potatoes in the *kichwa* began in May and continued into June. By June, the first frosts of the Andean winter had reached the *kichwa*, and the harvest of wheat and barley had begun. With the harvest now in full swing, there was abundant maize for the fermenting of chicha, and ritual surpluses of hominy, potatoes, faba beans, and other products had accumulated. The most important ceremony in June was a five-hour pilgrimage to the shrine of Yuraq Yaku ("White Water"), which lies at 4000 m on the high puna above Sarhua. There, offerings were made to the *wamanis* in all four cardinal directions, and the boundaries between Sarhua's lands and those of neighboring communities were reaffirmed. Harvests of wheat and barley continued into July, the peak of the Andean winter.

Then came August, another *piña killa*, a second time of great danger. All agricultural activity had ended, and the weather turned violent again, with strong winds and lightning. Once again the mountains opened and the *wamanis* emerged to walk the land, hungry and restless. They could, as one villager told Palomino Flores, "eat the hearts of men who dared to walk alone in the hills." It was now, during this period of temporarily unstable relations between the *wamanis* and their human herders, that the *waytakuy* for llamas was traditionally held in the *sallqa*; at Sarhua, cattle were also branded at this time. For villages located in the *kichwa* zone, the *herranza* was preceded by a long climb to the *estancia* on the puna where the animals were kept. At regular intervals along the route were boulder shrines at which the travelers prayed, drank, and made offerings, thereby assuring the *wamanis* of their good intentions as they ascended closer and closer to the dangerous *urqu* zone where the latter lived.

There were therefore three main reasons why the ceremony of llama decorating was traditionally held in August. First, the weather patterns made this month one in which the Indians were keenly aware of the displeasure of the *wamani*, in the form of storms, wind, and thunder from the puna brava. Second, August was a month without agricultural activity, so a great deal of time could be devoted to animals. Finally, the harvests of May, June, and July had provided each community with a generous supply of food and fermented beverages with which to underwrite the ceremony.

Studies of the Ayacucho *Herranza*

In the late 1960s, R. Tom Zuidema spent several years at the University of Huamanga in Ayacucho directing the research of a group of students from Peru and the University of Illinois. Some of the Peruvian students were natives of Ayacucho, bilingual in Quechua and Spanish, and had grown up in indigenous communities themselves.

Zuidema's project focused on the Río Pampas district, more than 100 km south of the city of Ayacucho—a region of isolated Quechua-speaking villages, many of which could only be reached by suspension bridges over classic Andean mountain gorges. One young Peruvian, Ulpiano Quispe, wrote a bachelor's thesis on the *herranza* at Choque Huarcaya and Huancasancos (Quispe 1969). Another, Salvador Palomino Flores, wrote a thesis on the village of Sarhua which includes data on the *herranza* (Palomino Flores 1970). One of the North Americans, Billie Jean Isbell, turned her doctoral dissertation into an important monograph on the community of Chuschi (Isbell 1978). An Australian student, John Earls (1973), also completed an Illinois degree and taught for a few years at the University of Michigan before overwhelming nostalgia for the Río Pampas lured him back to Ayacucho.

Unfortunately, this burst of ethnography was largely over by the time of MacNeish's archaeological project in Ayacucho. Our study of the *herranzas* at Pallqa and Toqtoqasa, presented in this volume, was done in the context of research on zooarchaeology and llama herd dynamics, not as part of a cadre of enthusiastic fellow ethnologists. We owe our preparation for the task to our colleague Ramiro Matos, a native of Huancavelica, for whom the *herranza* was part of his Quechua heritage.

In this chapter, we first present our descriptions of the *herranzas* at Pallqa and Toqtoqasa in 1971; we follow with an eyewitness account of the *herranza* at Niñobamba in the 1940s. Next, we briefly summarize the *herranzas* of the Río Pampas district which were witnessed in the late 1960s by Quispe and Isbell. Since there are many similarities in these descriptions, we give at the end of this chapter a glossary of terms which draws on all the authors mentioned. However, we should also point out some of the major differences.

All the communities studied in the Río Pampas district had lands in both *kichwa* and *sallqa*, but the main village was located in the agricultural lands of the *kichwa*. Those villages were also ones in which Old World species like cattle and sheep were far more important than llamas. The perspective of the observer, therefore, was that of a townsperson looking up at a ritual in the distant *sallqa*, a ritual which often did not involve camelids.

Hatun Rumi, Pallqa, and Toqtoqasa, on the other hand, were tiny *estancias* on the puna above Huamanguilla and Quinua. The perspective of the observer was that of a llama herder whose *kancha* lay virtually at the doorstep of the *wamani*—one of the *sallqaruna*, who felt out of place in the streets of the town below.

An equally significant difference is the fact that the theoretical framework used by Zuidema and his students was largely structuralist. There was a conscious search for dual categories and structural oppositions, with rituals seen as using symbolic means to reflect and reinforce the structure. Our framework included a conscious search for the adaptive consequences of human and camelid behavior; we were curious to see whether anything in the ritual could actually be shown to increase the long-term size and stability of the herds. To a significant degree, therefore, our data and those from the Río Pampas are complementary, in both theoretical approach and observer perspective. Taken together, they probably provide a broader view of the *herranza* and its variations than either body of data taken in isolation.

Herranza at Toqtoqasa: Pastor W.

In the *kancha* of Pastor W. at Toqtoqasa, August 21 was the date chosen for the *herranza familiar*. It was attended by all the usual residents of Pastor's household (see Chapter 4), as well as all his *masakuna* (sons-in-law) from as far away as Pallqa and El Balcón. Other guests included Pastor's sister; several cousins, aunts, and uncles from neighboring *estancias*; and Flannery and Vásquez, who contributed seven or eight dollars worth of locally produced supplies and a bottle of Jack Daniel's Black Label bourbon. This having been a poor year economically, Pastor stated that Flannery and Vásquez's contributions had made the difference between his being able to hold the *herranza* and not holding it.

This *herranza* was somewhat less elaborate than the one held by Félix

Figure 8.1 Framed by the mountain pass of Toqtoqasa, Pastor W. prepares to blow his *ccewayllo* and signal the start of his *herranza*. One hundred meters behind him, his llama herd stands assembled in the ceremonial corral.

M. at Pallqa (discussed below) owing to the more humble economic situation of the family involved. Preparations on the evening of the 20th were minimal, consisting mainly of the grinding of *llampu* and the assembling of foodstuffs. The ceremony of the 21st was divided into three segments of two hours each, with a half-hour break between segments to allow for drinking and coca chewing. Pastor opened and closed each segment by blowing an instrument known as a *ccewayllo* (Fig. 8.1). This ceremonial alpenhorn—nowadays made from the inflorescence of an introduced plant, the *Agave*—consisted of a 2.5-m tube with a cane or wood mouthpiece. The single bass note made by blowing it echoes for miles across the mountains, leaving no doubt in the minds of any neighboring herders that the *herranza* is about to take place. This is a de facto invitation to anyone who would like to arrive with contributed offerings in the hope of receiving a llama through *suñay*.

Figure 8.2 Their faces smeared with white *llampu*, female relatives sit along the wall of Pastor's ceremonial corral.

The scene was a specially cleaned ritual corral some distance from the main *kancha*. In this corral, Pastor and his five assistants—all sons, god-sons, or sons-in-law—had assembled 130 llamas representing the combined herds of at least four owners. Pastor's own animals, those of his son Manuel W., his adopted son Nestor G., and his son-in-law Manuel H. all jostled each other nervously as the *ccewayllo* was blown. Pastor's *masa* from El Balcón had come to assist but had not attempted to bring his own llamas from such a distance.

All the dogs had been shut up in one of the cottages; they were not allowed to enter the ceremonial corral because on this day they symbolized the Andean fox (*Dusicyon culpaeus*), a predator that had been a continual threat to the newborn *uñas*. Among the other symbols of life in the *sallqa* was an abundance of fine white cornmeal, ground specially by the women for this ceremony and mixed with the white mineral called *llampu*. This powder symbolized the purifying snow which fell on the puna, "and from which nothing escapes, man or woman, rich or poor, *chuklla* or *cerro wamani*." The women and young girls took great pleasure in smearing this powder on the faces of all the guests and participants (Fig. 8.2), reserving their most vigorous efforts for their own husbands and for visiting anthropologists. Indeed it often seemed that the more intimidating a man might have been under normal conditions, the greater the delight the women took in smearing away under the special conditions of the ritual.

Then, while the women sang songs of the *waytakuy*, Pastor and his *masa* from El Balcón began to lay out the *mesa*, the ceremonial table, in one corner of the corral (Fig. 8.3). In preparation, both men put on their traditional Andean *chullus*, knitted caps with earflaps, and laid aside their Spanish-style hats, which were not appropriate for the sacred task of laying the *mesa*. Over a blanket they laid the embroidered bib worn by the *delantero* of Pastor's herd, then bundles of *ichu* grass crisscrossing each other until a grid of eight squares had been constructed. Into each square went the offerings for the *wamani*—coca leaves, shot glasses of *cañazo*, cigarettes, votive candles, red carnations, and finally the bundles of colored yarn that would be sewn into the llamas' ears. Red was *kusi*, a "happy" color, one that pleased the *Tayta Urqu*. He was to receive the red flowers, and the llamas would ultimately sport pink or red tassels. Yellow would never be used—it was a "weak" color which indicated opposition, the kind of color a *pistako* might wear.

Pastor's wife Martina, his married daughter Teófila, and his daughter-in-law Vicenta provided most of the singing; his daughter Olimpia, still a

Figure 8.3 Wearing his traditional Andean *chullu*, Pastor places offerings of coca leaves in the spaces between *ichu* bundles on his *mesa ceremonial*.

Figure 8.4 Pastor (center) and his *masa* from El Balcón (left) take a "coca break" during the *herranza*. Pastor wore his Spanish-style hat over his *chullu* during this interlude.

teenager, was just learning the words. As the ceremonial *mesa* neared completion, the singing ended and the women began serving everyone shot glasses of *cañazo* and pottery cups filled with chicha. Women sat to one side of the *mesa*, men to the other. Cheeks were filled with coca leaves, quids were chewed, glasses continued to pass from hand to hand (Figs. 8.4 and 8.5). The major problem with twenty people drinking and chewing coca at the same time is that the tiny veins from the leaves begin

Figure 8.5 During a break in Pastor's *herranza*, women chew coca leaves selected from the piles in their laps.

to build up on the rim of the glass, making each drink offered just that much less attractive.

Pastor rose quietly and stood facing the rockiest peak overlooking Toqtoqasa. He knew that this was where the *wamani* identified with his *estancia* lived, and the numerous caves and crevices in the summit provided entry and exit for the *señor de los animales*. A cup of chicha was raised to that peak, its contents dashed to the floor of the corral, the cup refilled. This time, Pastor dipped his fingers into the chicha and sprinkled drops in the direction of the peak (Fig. 8.6). He then turned slowly and repeated this sprinkling to all four cardinal points—east, south, west, north—the four world directions that were so all pervasively important to the Indians of nuclear America (Marcus 1970, 1976, 1983). Finally, we offered the *Tayta Urqu* a shot of Jack Daniel's—undoubtedly his first. One can only assume, from the fact that no animals died that day, that the *Tayta Urqu*

Figure 8.6   The first cups of chicha are offered to the *wamani*. Left, Pastor dashes the contents of the first cup to the floor of his corral so that the earth can receive it. Right, he dips his fingers into the second cup and sprinkles drops to the *cerros wamanis* at the cardinal directions.

liked it. Unfortunately, it was not as big a hit with the herders themselves, who grumbled that *gringo aguardiente* was not very strong. Trust us: after you have been drinking *cañazo* for an hour, bourbon seems like Perrier water.

During the second and third segments of the *herranza*, Pastor and his helpers succeeded in decorating more than 100 animals. Most of these were decorated during the second segment, since the crew had been drinking for four hours by the time the third segment rolled around, and Pastor could barely blow his *ccewayllo*. The first llama decorated was, of course, the *delantero* of Pastor's herd, who was dressed in his *pechera* and given a pink yarn tassel at each ear tip, a red yarn tassel on the side of each ear, and a ribbon at the base of the ear (Figs. 8.7 and 8.8). Next to be marked

Figure 8.7   Pastor holds his *delantero* llama by its left ear while his *masa* sews yarn tassels into its right ear.

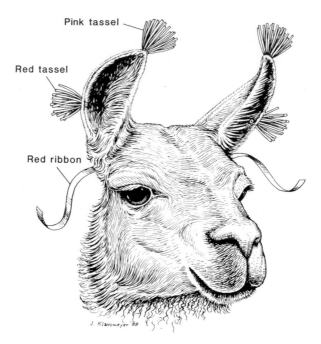

Pink tassel

Red tassel

Red ribbon

J. Klausmeyer '88

Figure 8.8   Decorations sewn into the *delantero* llama's ears.

were the *carga llamas* who served in the pack trains; each was held firmly
by one herder while another sewed the red and pink yarn into the animal's
ears with a sailmaker's needle. These burden carriers amounted to fewer
than half the animals in the corral, and their decoration was followed by
that of the adult females. *Uñas* and *maltas*—who made up only about
20% of the group—were left until the third segment of the *herranza*, and
some were never decorated at all. As the tassels were sewn, Pastor and his
helpers cut little snippets from the llamas' ears and tails; these would be
taken up to the *cerro wamani* on the following day and left in a crevice,
accompanied by offerings (Fig. 8.9).

While the decoration applied to each llama was relatively uniform, the
burden carrier judged to be the most troublesome ("*malcriado y desobe-
diente*") was singled out for special treatment. In addition to the yarn in

Figure 8.9 In this crevice below a boulder on the *cerro wamani* specific to his *kancha*, Pastor left ritual offerings and snippets of llama ears and tails on the day following his *herranza*.

his ears, he had a painful tassel sewn into the soft skin just above his nose, apparently to remind him of his misdeeds (Fig. 8.10). This punishment, however, was mild compared to that meted out in Cuzco. There Miller (1977) reports that the most disobedient llama is sometimes the one cho-sen to be eaten, a custom which should speed up the process of selection for docility.

Because of their extensive contributions to his *herranza*, Pastor offered to make Flannery and Vásquez the gift of a *malta* through *suñay*. They thanked him but explained that it would not be allowed on the airplane which returned Flannery to the states. He would keep it for them in his herd, Pastor suggested, and whenever they wanted to come back for it, they could simply repay him for the tender loving care it would have received. This seemed to be an acceptable alternative, and the handsomely decorated little *malta* selected by Flannery was left behind at Toqtoqasa so the *Tayta Urqu* could continue to admire her.

Figure 8.10 Pastor's most disobedient llama, punished by having a painful tassel sewn just above its nose (arrow).

Herranza at Pallqa: Félix M.

At the *kancha* of Félix and Agustina M. in the *estancia* of Pallqa, August 16 was the traditional date for the *herranza familiar*. In contrast to the more humble ceremony of Pastor W. at Toqtoqasa, Félix's *herranza* serves as an example of the kind held by one of the region's more economically secure families. Félix had a large group of *compadres* in attendance, and when these were combined with his extended family, his *masa*, and his other in-laws, the number of adults alone was greater than twenty. The flock of llamas was also substantial, since both Félix and Agustina had inherited animals at their fathers' deaths, and the combined herds totaled between 50 and 60 head (Fig. 8.11).

In terms of expense, the major outlay for the *herranza* consisted of the food prepared for all participants. We estimated the total value of expendable ritual paraphernalia—yarn, ribbons, candles, and so on—to be no more than $11.00 U.S. We were also not surprised that this slightly wealthier family put on a more acculturated version of the ceremony. Although many of the activities paralleled those of Pastor W., there was no sounding of the *ccewayllo*, and the duties of the *masa* (an aboriginal role) had been partly taken over by the *compadre* (a hispanic role considered more important in today's civic-religious system). In addition, the whole morning was devoted to animal species introduced by the Spaniards.

At 8 A.M., perhaps a dozen head of cattle were branded. Then came a one-hour break, beginning around 9 A.M., during which the twenty or so participants took a coca-chewing break and were invited to drink, in order, a cup of chicha, a glass of alcohol distilled from sugar cane (*cañazo*), a glass of alcohol distilled from cereal grain (*aguardiente*), and a cup of chicha sprinkled with seeds of *cañiwa* (*Chenopodium pallidicaule*). Interestingly, Ayacucho herders use the Quechua verb *upyay* when referring to the drinking of indigenous alcoholic beverages such as chicha, and *tomay* (a loan word from the Spanish *tomar*) when referring to the drinking of nonindigenous beverages such as *cañazo*. During this hour of refreshment, three young married women, all relatives or in-laws of Félix's, danced with bundles of *ichu* grass while an older woman played the *tinya* or drum (Fig. 8.12); they also sang songs of praise in Quechua to the *Tayta Urqu*. Toward the end of the hour, the faces of the participants were painted with white cornmeal and *llampu*, much as had taken place in Toqtoqasa. Significantly, however, Vásquez and Flannery were left unpainted this time. Because of their financial support of Pastor W.'s *herranza*, they had been considered *kuyaq*, non-kin contributors; at Félix M.'s they were merely visitors.

At 10 A.M. activities resumed, with a group of eight horses and donkeys brought in for branding; this was done leisurely, so that it occupied a full hour. At roughly 11 A.M., all participants took a break similar to the one at nine o'clock and repeated the same succession of drinks: chicha, *cañazo*, *aguardiente*, and chicha with *cañiwa*, all accompanied by a quid of coca. Again the young married women sang and danced with bundles of *ichu* while two older women played the drum. Many of the remaining older women—now considerably happier following this second round of drinks—sat along one wall of the corral, some singing along, others humming, still others keeping time in whichever way required the least effort.

While the singing continued, Félix M. began to eat his lunch. This was the signal for most participants to unwrap the bundles of food they had brought with them from their own *kanchas* and start in on their own lunch. Those who had brought nothing with them were served small bowls of boiled faba beans, potatoes, and *oca* (*Oxalis tuberosum*), accompanied by the now-familiar invitation, "This is our life; please do us the honor of eating it without disparaging us."

Figure 8.11   Part of the llama herd belonging to Félix and Agustina M. of Pallqa.

Figure 8.12   Félix's *llumchuys* dance with bundles of *ichu* grass during an early stage of his *herranza*.

While the participants ate, Félix took off his Spanish-style hat, put on his Andean *chullu*, and began to prepare the ceremonial bundle that would eventually become the core of the *mesa* for the llama-decorating ceremony. He unrolled a blanket on the ground to reveal the large bundle of *ichu* which would later form the second layer of the *mesa*; to this he added the coils of ribbon and balls of yarn that would be used in the actual marking. At 11:30, Félix prayed briefly over the blanket, rolled it up again with the ribbons and *ichu* inside, and carried it back inside his *chuklla*.

By 12:30 P.M. the *waytakuy* for llamas was about to begin. Félix did not have a special ritual corral like Pastor's, but for today's purposes one of his corrals had been cleaned and set aside especially for the llamas. While his *compadres* herded the animals into that corral, everyone else moved to the boulder wall and waited expectantly. Finally, Félix emerged from the house

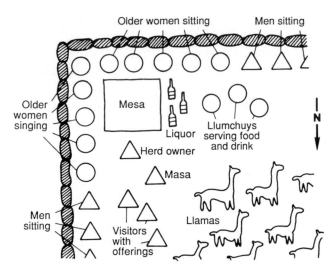

Figure 8.13 Diagram of the southeast corner of Félix's ceremonial corral, showing the *mesa ceremonial* and the arrangement of guests and participants at the *herranza*.

with the ceremonial bundle carried on his back and made his way to the corral.

Accompanied by his *compadres*, Félix went to the southeast corner of the corral, which because of the slope of the land happened to be the highest corner. Still wearing his *chullu*, he unrolled the blanket and placed it on the ground to provide the first layer of the *mesa*. The older women arranged themselves along the south and east walls of the corral near the blanket and continued to sing and beat the drum during all but the most solemn parts of the ceremony (Fig. 8.13). The men sat farther away, extending the lines of seated participants farther toward the north and west; they were served drinks from time to time by the *llumchuys*.

Over the blanket Félix laid the bib, or *pechera*, of his *delantero* llama. It was embroidered with dozens of small Andean motifs as well as the date "Año 1954," the year of its manufacture. Since that time it had been in continuous use by a succession of *delanteros* for almost two decades. Over the bib went the scissors, knives, and sailmaker's needles to be used in the decorating ceremony; beside the bib, but still on top of the blanket, Félix arranged the balls of yarn and ribbon in careful north–south rows (Fig. 8.14-1). The first layer of the *mesa* was now complete (Fig. 8.15).

Next came the weaving of a "bed" from bundles of *ichu* grass. The goal was to produce something resembling a giant checkerboard, with the lines between open squares consisting of *ichu* bundles as thick as a man's wrist (Fig. 8.16). Where east–west bundles crossed north–south bundles, they passed over the first, under the second, over the third, just as if Félix had been weaving a mat or coarse textile. The open squares then became places where offerings could be set: handfuls of coca leaves, bottles of *aguardiente*, shot glasses of *cañazo*, and packets of cigarettes (Fig. 8.14-2). Once Félix had placed his offerings of liquor, his *compadres* stepped forward one by one to present the bottles of *cañazo* they had brought, and those were added to the *mesa* as well. Finally, Félix added a layer of unlit votive candles and loose cigarettes—some arranged in rows along the bundles of *ichu*—and the ceremonial *mesa* was complete.

Now came the most solemn part of the ritual, and all drumming and singing stopped. Félix prayed *sotto voce* to the *Tayta Urqu*—asking him, in effect, to accept the offerings, to bless all the artifacts to be used in the llama decorating, to look with favor on the decorated animals, and to allow

Figure 8.14 Diagram of Félix's *mesa ceremonial*, Pallqa: 1, lower level, with most of the equipment needed for llama decorating; 2, upper level, with offerings placed in the open spaces of a lattice of *ichu* bundles.

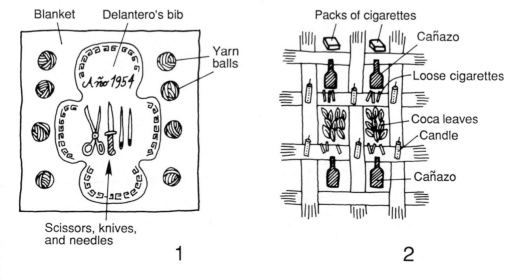

Félix to continue his successful shepherding of the *wamani's* flocks. The silence in the corral was so deep, so penetrating that one could even hear a lone vesper mouse (*Calomys lepidus*) scurrying through the boulder wall.

Félix took a cup of chicha poured by his *masa*, and with his fingers sprinkled droplets of chicha into the air as he turned slowly, 360 degrees. These droplets satisfied the *cerros wamanis* guarding each of the cardinal points. Félix next turned to face the *cerro wamani* specific to his *kancha*, offered it drops from the still largely full cup, took a sip himself, and dashed the remainder over the ground and the participants sitting nearby. After everyone had been served a drink, Félix went through the whole process again with *cañazo*: droplets to each of the world directions, a cup

Figure 8.15 While older women sing and play the drum, Félix (wearing his traditional *chullu*) arranges paraphernalia on the lower level of his *mesa ceremonial*. To the right, one of his *compadres* holds the bundle of *ichu* grass from which the upper level of the *mesa* will be woven. To the left, one of his *masas* stands ready to pour the first cup of chicha for the *wamani*.

Figure 8.16   Félix removes coca leaves from a plastic bag, preparing to place them in the open squares between *ichu* bundles in the upper level of his *mesa ceremonial*. Bottles of *cañazo* and packages of cigarettes have already been set in place, and Félix's *masa* is pouring the first cup of chicha.

shared with the *Tayta Urqu*, the rest cast to the earth. Not to have offered the first drops to the *wamani* would have been an unforgivable insult; the drops belonged to him, just as the first drops of blood from a butchered llama belonged to him.

At this crucial part of the ceremony, the only people allowed in the corral were Félix, his relatives and in-laws, and those *compadres* who had contributed liquor and gifts. All Félix and Agustina's llamas were assembled for everyone to see; all the gifts from *compadres* or *kuyaq* were on display. Félix embraced his *compadres*, calling them *sullkakuna*, "hermanitos." It was the moment appropriate for *suñay*, and he had already been informed through a series of intermediaries that one young man in the group wanted a female *malta* very badly. The youth in question had contributed several bottles of *cañazo*; calling him *sullkay*, "my brother," Félix gave him an alcoholic *abrazo* and told him to pick the animal he wanted.

Figure 8.17 While a woman in the background plays the *tinya*, a traditional drum, a *llumchuy* fills a cup with *cañazo*.

By 2 P.M.—after the ritual of the *mesa*, the presentation of gifts, the giving away of a *malta* through *suñay*, and the resumption of singing and drum beating—the actual decoration of llamas began. This was not done by Félix himself but by his *compadres* and *masakuna*; Félix served the decorating crew a generous number of drinks while they worked, and several women accompanied their efforts with song (Figs. 8.17 and 8.18). Each llama was held by one man with a stranglehold on its neck, or a tight grip on the base of the ears. Simultaneously, two other men seized one ear each and began sewing red yarn into its margin with a sailmaker's needle. Some llamas tolerated this with genuine stoicism; others squealed like pigs through the whole procedure.

Just as at Toqtoqasa, the first llama to be decorated was the *delantero* of the pack train (Fig. 8.19). In addition to the embroidered bib which had been ritually blessed as part of the ceremonial *mesa*, the *delantero* received an embroidered bridle and a bell to wear around his neck. Next came the *carga llamas* from the heart of the pack train, all of whom were decorated before the females; *maltas* and *uñas* were left until last. Each animal was supposed to have a ribbon or tassel in its ear tip and a series of yarns along the ear margin, but by now not every *compadre's* sewing hand was steady enough to accomplish that. As the hour grew later and the workers more and more inebriated on *cañazo*, there were blind staggers, lunges and heavy falls to the corral floor, clouds of dust, clumsy efforts to bulldog

Figure 8.18   His Spanish-style hat now worn over his *chullu*, Félix pours drinks for the women who sang and played the drum during his *herranza*.

reluctant llamas, and a great deal of off-key singing. By half past three, the *waytakuy* was essentially over.

Now there was another round of food for everyone who could still sit up straight; bowls of boiled potatoes, *oca*, and faba beans were passed around, while Félix wrapped up a bundle containing small snippets from the ears and tails of his llamas. These would be taken up to the *cerro wamani* specific to Félix's *kancha* on the morning following the *herranza* and hidden in a small cave along with offerings of liquor, cigarettes, and votive candles (Fig. 8.20). Only time would tell whether the *wamani* had been pleased by the ceremony, and if so, how pleased; his mood would be read in the health and fertility of the herd.

With the hard work and most solemn parts of the ceremony over, the rest of the day could now be devoted to serious drinking. Singing, dancing, *abrazos*, and slurred conversations would go on until the small hours of the morning. Some married men were now face down on the puna. Some of their wives, from the safety of the kitchen, were gazing and giggling at men they hardly knew. While the visiting anthropologist and his collabo-

Figure 8.19   While women sing, Félix's *compadres* sew yarn tassels into his *delantero* llama's ears.

Figure 8.20   In this cavelike opening between the boulders of a *cerro wamani* at Pallqa, Félix buried snippets of llama ears and tail, votive candles, and liquor on the day following his *herranza*.

rator were welcome to stay as long as they liked, it was a strategic time for them to leave. Tonight the herders of Pallqa were drunk enough to forget that two people must be four generations removed before they could sleep together. "*Kayna tutam, chay tutalla kascca, ccarccachakunapas wawata ruwachkanku.*" "Tonight," said Vásquez with a wink, "is the kind of night when *ccarccachas* are conceived."

Herranza at Niñobamba: The Good Old Days

"Silva" was born in 1913 at Niñobamba, a village in the mountains above the Pisco-Ayacucho road. His father owned llamas and alpacas and raised potatoes, maize, and *quinoa*. In the early 1970s Silva, then working in Ayacucho, looked back with sorrow and nostalgia on the passing of the old customs and the gradual deterioration of his native environment. He remembered the *herranza* carried out in the 1930s and 1940s by his community, which owned both *kichwa* and *sallqa* lands.

All the families at Niñobamba performed *herranza* together on a fixed day in August, with each family decorating its own animals. All believed that the *patrón wamani*—true owner of their flocks—lived inside a high mountain above town, surrounded by piles of gold and silver, with corrals of all kinds. At vespers on the day before the *herranza*, when Venus had appeared as the Evening Star, the people took offerings of alcohol, coca, oranges, grapes, and other delicacies up to a special place on the *cerro wamani*, where they hid it in a cave or crevice. If one were lucky at that moment, the whole mountain would open *"iglisia hinam kan"* ("just like a church") and one could walk inside and bring out more animals. *"Mana imamanta ricuricc"* ("It was a miracle").

On the day of the *herranza*, two calves were "married" in the manner described by Quispe (1969) for Choque Huarcaya (see below); the animals were dusted with *llampu*, and their ears were notched and beribboned to the accompaniment of music. Participants also staged a mock rustling—the theatrical version of one of the events the community feared most. All believed that if the ceremony was performed correctly, the herds could increase drastically, even miraculously, during the coming year. One could simply not afford to run out of anything used in the ritual, especially food and drink; it would be unheard of. If the feasting and drinking went well, the sounds could be heard far away.

After the *waytakuy*, the owner of the herd dispensed to his visitors chicha, *cañazo*, coca, cigarettes, and a meal, in that order. In preparation for the meal, the owner had provided a quantity of meat ranging from one sheep (for a small crowd) to a sheep, a llama, and an alpaca (for a large crowd).

After the owner had looked over the crowd, and they had looked over his llamas, and everyone had had quite a bit to drink, he might *suñay*, giving away animals to several participants. Although this was supposed to be done spontaneously and without prearrangement, it was not uncommon for intermediaries to have suggested the name of a needy herd owner in the crowd: a *compadre*, a younger man, even a widow in some cases. The assembly of llamas for the *herranza* had allowed all the participants to see whether the owner's herd was large enough to afford *suñay*.

Herranza Familiar at Choque Huarcaya

Quispe (1969) has described the *herranza familiar* during the 1960s at Choque Huarcaya, a village in the Río Pampas district. Choque Huarcaya was a community of the *kichwa* zone, and the *herranza* there focused strongly on cattle.

One or two weeks before the ceremony, herd owners went to the market to buy alcoholic beverages, coca, ribbons, sugar, bread, fruits, and a whole series of tropical delicacies from the *selva* or *montaña* zones east of Ayacucho. A few days prior to the *herranza* they ordered massive quantities of chicha, timing it so that the beverage would still be fresh. Finally, one day before the ceremony, they went to their *estancias* outside the village to cut up the decorative ribbons and grind the *llampu*.

This preparation of ribbons and *llampu* was accompanied by music. Major participants in the activity were the sons and sons-in-law of each herd owner, who engaged in careful preparation of the small boulder shrines along the route between village and *estancia*. The cutting of the ribbons (*cinta kuchuy*) was a very important activity, with both knives and scissors ritually dusted with *llampu* and *chakin* powder before being stored in the ceremonial bundle.

For the *herranza* on the following day, the herd owner was designated "*patrón*" and the participants "*peones*." These two terms were clearly borrowed from the Spaniards, and it is not clear what Quechua terms (if any) they may have replaced.

The *herranza* began with the "marriage" of a male and female calf on a bed of reeds which had been arranged by the owner's *masa*. The "bride and groom" were sprinkled with a cornmeal and *llampu* mixture, as well as metallic powder created by scraping *chawa quri* and *chawa qullqi* together. *Masakuna* and *llumchuykuna* performed ritual acts and prayers together with the *patrón* during this phase, suggesting that the ritual marriage of calves did more than symbolize a desire for herd increase—it provided a chance to remind everyone that a bride and groom were also son-in-law and daughter-in-law, ritually obligated to their affines.

Branding of cattle followed the bovine wedding. Then came the *chiku chiku*, or "winding down" of the ceremony. The ritual equipment was hidden again, bit by bit; the gate to the corral was opened, and, as each animal left, it was sprinkled with *llampu*. Finally, after all the ritual supplies had been used up, drunk, offered to the *wamani*, or rehidden, there was music and celebration. As in so many Native American rituals, the sequence of acts leading up to the branding was repeated in reverse order during the "winding down" phase, so that the ritual ended virtually as it had begun. The next day, pieces of the animals' ears which had been cut off during the *herranza* were buried at a special place where the *wamani* would be sure to find them.

Through this ceremony the herders had placated the *wamani* during August, one of the angry months in which he walked the earth. If all had gone well, their herds would thrive. At the same time, they had reinforced a number of ties between fathers-in-law and their *masas* and *llumchuys*, between kinsmen, and between *compadres*. They had stabilized relations between man and *wamani*—and, Quispe believes, between man and the *Pacha Mama*, "Mother Earth." For our part, we found the Pacha Mama relatively underemphasized in the Yanahuaccra-Toqtoqasa rituals, coming to center stage only when the first cup of chicha was dashed to the corral so the earth could receive it.

Herranza Familiar in Huancasancos

Huancasancos is another community of the Río Pampas district whose *herranza* was studied by Quispe (1969) in the 1960s. Like other villages of sufficient size, it had two types of marking ceremony: a communal *herranza* for the herds that belonged to the church, and a *herranza familiar* for each private herd owner. As with Choque Huarcaya, the decorating ceremony at Huancasancos involved mainly Old World species such as cattle and sheep.

Huancasancos had a strong emphasis on herding. During the rainy Andean summer, the animals were kept on the lower puna. After the harvest—which began in May and ended in July—they were taken down to graze in the *kichwa* zone, since by then there was no longer any danger of their eating the crops. During the dry Andean winter, they were taken up to the *estancias* of the higher puna.

Some of these *estancias* were a day-and-a-half journey from Huancasancos, and all along the route, spaced 6–10 km apart, were shrines made of boulder cairns with *ichu* crosses atop them. During the trip from Huancasancos to attend the *herranza* at an *estancia*, it was customary to have a drink at each of these *altares*.[1] In addition to the boulder cairns along the route, there were similar shrines next to each *chuklla*, on the boundaries between *estancias*, on the mountains where offerings were made to the *wamani*, and at the places where cut-off pieces of the animals' ears were buried. There was also a boulder shrine in the *herrana*—a special corral, better made than most—which each *estancia* used only for the decorating ritual. It is clear that many of these shrines served two purposes. In addi-

---

1. Similar boulder shrines were spaced along the trail from Huamanguilla to Yanahuaccra, suggesting that this custom may once have been followed there—probably in the days before don Claudio P.'s *hacienda*.

tion to their obvious role as indicators of sacred places, many also served as permanent boundary markers between *kanchas* and *estancias*—boundary markers that could not be moved because of their religious significance.

Perhaps because of its strong emphasis on herding, Huancasancos held a four-day ceremony in which the animal decorating occupied only the second or third day. Guests arrived at the *estancia* a day or two before the *herranza* in order to contribute *ayni* in the form of voluntary assistance. At vespers on the night before the animal decorating, the family owning each herd made an offering to the *wamani* at its own hilltop shrine. This boulder-and-*ichu* feature was found on top of, or on the slope of, a *cerro wamani* and was inherited patrilineally. Although every herd owner knew how to perform the ritual, it was usually carried out by a relative who had been designated a *mayordomo*, or ritual specialist, for the purposes of the *herranza*. Sprinkling drops of alcoholic beverages in each major world direction, the *mayordomo* made a series of offerings, and the participants joined in a song whose theme was "forgive the sins of your ungenerous shepherds." As at Pallqa and Toqtoqasa, each *estancia* had one *cerro patrón* whose *wamani* was particularly closely related to it.

Still in vespers of the night before the *herranza*, the group returned from the hilltop shrine to the boulder altar at the herd owner's *chuklla*. Using *llampu* to soften any rough relations with the *wamani*, they consecrated the ribbons and yarns which would eventually go in the animals' ears. The *mayordomo* then named the persons who would have important roles to carry out on the following day. Inevitably, one of these would be the owner's *masa*, and others would be sons and *compadres*. As we have seen, the assigned roles included felling the animals so that they could be decorated, cutting the ribbons to their appropriate length (*cinta kuchuy*), cutting small notches out of the animals' ears (*señalar*), and cutting small pieces off the animals' tails (*chupa kuchuy*). Later in the evening, the group decorated the ritual corral with branches and sang and prayed at the boulder shrine.

On the day of the *herranza*, all the animals were assembled in the ritual corral. After everyone had downed a few drinks, the *mayordomo* and his assistants carried the ceremonial bundle (containing the *llampu*, *ñawin*, *chakin*, ribbons, knives, and other paraphernalia) to the altar in the ritual corral. The *masa* prepared a bed of *chiriwar blanco* (*Calamagrostis* sp.), a puna grass, on which two calves were "married"; at Huancasancos, there were usually three such marriages. The bride and groom were the first animals marked, and the blood obtained by notching their ears was mixed with *aguardiente* for all to drink.

After a period of dancing in which the *llumchuys* and other women participated, all the other animals were decorated. Each was sprinkled with *llampu* as it was released; when the last of the animals had gone, all traces of activity in the ritual corral were cleaned up by the participants. The owners and their ritual assistants, now robustly inebriated, imitated cattle drinking and mating while they continued to imbibe. As the ceremony wound down, ritual paraphernalia were returned to the ceremonial bundle and hidden again for another year. Meanwhile, just as at Niñobamba, some of the guests staged mock robberies and murders, with their theatrics rewarded by the herd owner.

On the day following the *herranza*, the *mayordomo* and other participants climbed the *cerro wamani* to bury the tiny fragments of ears and tails at the boulder shrine there. Once again there were prayers, sprinkling of *aguardiente* over the ground, and shot-glass offerings of *cañazo*. The *señales*, or animal parts, concealed in an *ichu* grass basket, were hidden at the shrine amid great sprinkling of *llampu* and liquor. Nearly every object involved was decorated with flowers (*waytakuy*)—almost certainly a survival from an earlier time when there were no Spanish branding irons with which to decorate animals.

Finally, on the fourth day of the ceremony came the *despedida*, or "farewell." The owner of the herd presented his *mayordomo*, his *masa*, all his *compadres*, the three musicians who accompanied the songs and dances, and even some of the *kuyaq* who had participated with a *kanka*—a sheep with its throat cut, ready for skinning, roasting, and eating. Given the fact that this act would be repeated by every owner at every *estancia* in the region, a considerable redistribution of meat took place during the month of August.

Herranza Familiar in Chuschi

Still another Río Pampas community with an *herranza* in August was Chuschi, studied in the late 1960s by Isbell (1978). Isbell attended only the branding of cattle, not the decoration of llamas, but she provides data and insights not seen in other accounts. In addition to recording the hierarchy of *wamanis*, Isbell witnessed the use of *illas*—small stone effigies of animals—which had their origins in prehispanic times. However, since Isbell's monograph is widely available for consultation, our summary of the *herranza* she attended is brief.

Comañawi, a 4750-m peak south of the Río Pampas, was the most powerful *cerro wamani* of the region. One tier lower in the supernatural hierarchy was the *wamani* who lived in Lake Yanaqocha near Chuschi; in what can only be described as a classic case of syncretism, the local church sponsored an annual payment to this *wamani* for his protection of the *cofradía* herds. Finally, still lower in the hierarchy came the local *wamanis* worshiped by individual families in Chuschi; those beings lived in places like Lake Tapaqocha and Cerro Ontoqarqa, where certain families had established places for payment to them. Isbell suggests that specific *wamanis* might have been inherited—along with their place of payment, a ceremonial bundle, and the house in which the latter was kept—by the agnatic line of a kindred (perhaps, by analogy with Huancasancos, a patriline).

The *herranza* witnessed by Isbell had the same three-day format seen elsewhere: preparations at vespers of the first day, branding on the second day, payment to the *wamani* on the third. On the evening of the first day, participants left the village of Chuschi for the two-hour trip to the herd owner's hut and corral on the puna; they took with them the ceremonial bundle, a branding iron, coca, and *trago* (the Chuschi version of *cañazo*). On their arrival at the hut, there were songs and drinks. The ceremonial bundle was untied, revealing white and red *llampu*, *chakin*, *ñawin chicha*, *trago*, small stone *illas* of a cow, sheep, and bird, coca, and a whole series of tropical plants, including one species often used for hallucinogenic snuff.

Isbell also witnessed *llampu kutay*, the grinding together of *llampu* and cornmeal to produce the purifying white powder used at all the *herranzas* so far described. The *llampu* was ground between previously unused stones; the corn ears had to be chosen in pairs, selected both for their large-grained whiteness and for their lack of missing kernels. The *wamani* was offered a drink before starting, and then all kernels were carefully removed and ground. As a woman sang and played the drum, the *llampu* and cornmeal were ground, together with a few added seeds, flowers, and "raw gold and silver" from the *chakin*.

At dawn on the second day, the herd owner—bearing his ceremonial bundle in a way "denoting subordinate status"—walked to a nearby lake to pour offerings of liquor into the waters where his *wamani* lived. Other drinks were poured at the opening where the *wamani* would later be offered pieces of the animals' ears and tail. This was called *llallipay*, "to gain an advantage" by making a preliminary payment.

Later that day, the *masa* and *compadres* arrived, along with other persons chosen to be ritual or branding specialists. Isbell was told that under ideal conditions there should be two *masas* and two *llumchuys* present, with the daughters-in-law preparing the morning meal.

The owner and his ritual specialists then proceeded to set the ceremonial table in the corral, using a poncho as the basal layer. Features of the *mesa* included the branding iron, a reed cross, red *llampu* with *illa* figurines set up in it, a marine shell filled with white *llampu*, and other items from the ceremonial bundle. Three lines of *llampu* were laid on the table, and coca leaves were scattered along them. A knife dipped in *llampu* was placed on the center line; lumps of "raw gold and silver" were placed on the other lines. First the *masa* and the branding specialist knelt, crossed themselves, and prayed, then the *patrón* and his mother followed suit.

After the branding crew had prepared themselves with several rounds of *trago* and chicha, the actual branding began. Both the corral and the cattle were purified with *llampu*; after the iron was applied, the *masa* poured chicha on the wound, while other participants fastened ribbons to the animals' ears and tied necklaces of bread and fruit to their horns. More *llampu* was sprinkled on the cattle as they left the corral, and then (as we have seen in every *herranza*) the drinking, singing, and coca chewing went on late into the night. Isbell was told that the "marriage" of two calves (which Quispe recorded for Huancasancos) would only be performed if there were at least one male and one female calf present who had never been through the *herranza*.

On the third day, much as at Choque Huarcaya, bits of the cattle's ears and tails were left at the *caja*, or opening, where the *wamani* was thought to receive his payment. The approach to this place of offering was considered so dangerous that women were not allowed to participate. Such was the participants' anxiety about the powers of the *wamani* that several more rounds of ritual drinking and *llampu* sprinkling were required to get the men through the whole procedure.

In the Chuschi *herranza*, continuity with the past was maintained by digging up two bottles of liquor which had been buried at the *caja* during the previous year's ceremony. Drinks were served from these bottles, whereupon they were refilled and buried for another year. This custom was also followed at the small offering caves above the *estancias* we studied at Yanahuaccra, Pallqa, and Toqtoqasa. Unfortunately, mestizo hunters from Ayacucho knew about it and occasionally helped themselves to a sacrilegious nip of this buried liquor while stalking viscachas in the chilly fog of a *cerro wamani*.

Interpreting the *Herranza*: A Roster of Possibilities

Having looked in varying degrees of detail at a half-dozen *herranzas*, let us now reflect on what the function and meaning of the ritual might be. It is immediately clear that the answer depends on one's theoretical perspective.

In the cosmology of the Indians themselves, August is a dangerous month. The mountains open and the *wamani*, real owner of the llamas, walks abroad on the earth. Relations between man and the supernatural are at their shakiest point. Correct performance of the *waytakuy*, with its countless prayers and offerings, can restore those relations. The decoration of the llamas, accomplished with tools purified by snowlike *llampu*, can convince the *wamani* that his flocks have been well taken care of. If he is pleased, the herds will thrive during the coming year.

Of course, we as Western scientists do not see it that way. We are confident that such a ceremony cannot really make herds increase; among other things, in the coming year, most new llamas will be born in Feburary, which means that they had already been conceived in March—six months before the *herranza*. We are also sure that mock marriages of calves are just theatrics, and that *llampu* is only an inert powder. So we search for other ways to explain the ritual.

For many structuralists working in Peru in the 1960s and 1970s, one obvious role of the ceremony was the mediation of oppositions. Dual organization was a major theme of that era (Lévi-Strauss 1956, 1967), and the *herranza* was seen as an important showcase for opposing categories such as "townsman" versus "herder," *kichwa* versus *sallqa*, Father Mountain versus Mother Earth (Palomino Flores 1970, 1984). Other, more functionally inclined investigators have suggested that the ritual publicly reinforces the ownership of the animals and tightens bonds between relatives, in-laws, and *compadres*. For at least some investigators, any further search for an adaptive function underlying the *herranza* would probably be misguided. The structure of Ayacucho Quechua culture should be understood in terms of its own logic, and since the ceremony reflects that structure and is logically consistent with it, why search for a "cause" in the logic of Western science?

For those with ecological sympathies, on the other hand, such causes were also pursued in the 1960s and 1970s. Especially in the case of man's relationship with domestic animals, adaptation was considered by many an appropriate perspective (Leeds and Vayda 1965; Rappaport 1968). Animals, lacking culture, were assumed to be acting more in accord with genetically programmed behavior than with anything resembling the mental structures of human society. Uncertain what was happening at the interface between the two, a number of anthropologists felt more comfortable analyzing both animals and man by the same adaptive framework. Some concentrated more heavily on food getting, on exchanges of matter and energy. Others, perhaps glimpsing a bridge between ecology and structuralism, concentrated more heavily on exchanges of information.

Scholars interested in matter and energy exchanges could point to the fact that the *herranza* forces residents of the *sallqa* to import products of the *kichwa* (maize, chicha, *cañiwa*) and the *montaña* (coca, tropical fruits) for feeding guests and making offerings to the *wamani*; in turn, this reinforces the symbiosis between environmental zones in the Andes, the kind of "vertical economy" of which Murra (1972) has written. The sacrifice of sheep, llamas, and alpacas to feed guests, as well as the gifts of *kanka* to participants, could be seen as the redistribution of high-quality protein—an especially important process for *kichwa* villagers, whose diet is normally low in meat.

For those interested in exchanges of information, the whole ceremony of the *herranza* is exceptionally rich. The obligatory visits to shrines on the boundaries between neighboring *kanchas, estancias*, and communities can be seen as a public resurvey of property and territorial boundaries. The decorating ceremony itself, with the sound of the *ccewayllo* summoning visitors to the owner's corral, amounts to an "epideictic display" (Wynne-Edwards 1962:16) which lets everyone know exactly how many llamas the owner has. For its part, this information lets relatives and *kuyaq* alike decide whether the owner can afford to give away an animal through *suñay*. And that brings us to our particular perspective on the ceremony.

Suñay

We have seen that most herders inherit llamas from their father, or receive llamas from their father and father-in-law when they marry. Llamas are supposed to be inherited patrilineally and kept within the *ayllu*. Under normal circumstances, there is no way that a needy herder could expect to be given a llama, across *ayllu* lines, from someone unrelated to him.

What is needed is a context in which the normal rules of animal transfer are suspended, and here is where the *herranza* comes in. It is a deeply religious event at which everyone who assists the herd owner, or enriches his offerings to the *wamani*, is treated as a member of the owner's *ayllu* and can potentially receive a gift, whether or not he is an actual relative. Even the visiting gringo who makes a substantial contribution becomes *kuyaq*— "one who loves me"—and can receive *suñay* during the peak of alcoholic euphoria.

While *suñay* may be an outgrowth of *ayni*, it is more than reciprocity. A fertile llama worth 500 soles is given to a stranger who has contributed 40 soles worth of liquor, with no expectation that the gift will ever be equaled or reciprocated. No effort is made to protect a prime animal; the recipient is allowed to pick the one he wants, which is almost always a young female. It is a situation in which the normal criteria for kinship are suspended in the face of a serious need to placate the *wamani* with offerings. *Suñay*, therefore, could be the mechanism we were searching for in Chapter 7, a mechanism to move llamas from large herds to struggling ones at crucial times.

It would be easy to say simply that the latent function of *suñay* is to redistribute llamas periodically so that no herd becomes extinct. But to leave it at that would be simply to dump one more plausible story into the literature. The 1960s produced so many unsupported assertions of that type that they provoked an antifunctionalist backlash from many anthropologists. And we could expect equal skepticism from evolutionary biologists, who might well ask what possible advantage could accrue to a herd owner who bailed out the herd of someone to whom he was not genetically related—and with no expectation of reciprocation.

In Chapter 9, therefore, we go back to our original simulation and add the institution of *suñay*. Our goal is to see whether a gift-giving program more realistic than our "Santa Claus" model can still make the difference between success and failure for individual herds. Beyond that, we try to see whether the long-term effects of such gift giving could be beneficial to the whole network of herds participating in it.

A Glossary of Terms Used in the *Herranza*

ayni: Voluntary, private, delayed reciprocal assistance (Quechua).

atado ceremonial: A ceremonial bundle (Spanish). At Toqtoqasa it could include *ichu* bundles, ribbons, yarn, *llampu*, scissors, etc. In the Río Pampas area it often included *ñawin*, *llampu*, *chakin*, etc.

caja: "Strongbox" (Spanish). A term used in the Río Pampas area for the opening where payments to the *wamani* are made—sometimes a crevice in the mountain.

Carnaval: A Spanish festival preceding Lent. In some districts of Ayacucho, livestock of Old World origin (cattle, horses) were branded at this time rather than at the August *herranza*.

ccewayllo: A ceremonial trumpet, consisting of a 2.5-m tube with a cane or wood mouthpiece, used in the *herranza* at Toqtoqasa (Quechua).

chakin: A kit composed of *chawa quri* and *chawa qullqi*, kept in a mollusc shell in the ceremonial bundle in the Río Pampas area. At the moment of branding, the *quri* and *qullqi* were scraped together so that a metallic powder fell on the animals (Quechua).

chawa qullqi: "Raw silver" (Quechua). At Choque Huarcaya, an old white coin with a hole drilled in the center and ribbons attached, kept in the *chakin*.

chawa quri: "Raw gold" (Quechua). A black-colored piece of metal kept in the *chakin*.

chiku chiku: At Choque Huarcaya, the stage of the *herranza* ceremony which followed branding and included the burying of the ritual equipment (Quechua).

chupa: "Tail" (Quechua). A term for the *herranza* which refers to the cutting off of the tips of the animals' tails as offerings to be buried.

cinta kuchuy: The ritual cutting of the ribbons to be put in the animals' ears; from Spanish *cinta* ("ribbon") and Quechua *kuchuy* ("to cut"; a loan word from Spanish *cuchillo*, "knife").

herrana: A special corral used only for the decorating ceremony at places such as Toqtoqasa and Huancasancos.

herranza: An annual ceremony carried out in August by the owner of livestock for the purpose of ensuring the reproduction and good health of the animals by placating the ire of the *wamani*; literally, "branding" (Spanish).

illa: Small stone effigy of an animal, thought to belong to the *wamani*, and used ritually during the *herranza*; its use began in prehispanic times and continues today (Quechua).

kanka: "Roasted" (Quechua). In Huancasancos, a sheep with its throat cut, given to the crew of helpers in the *herranza* by the owner; later roasted and eaten.

kuyaq: "Those who love [me]" or "those who care [about me]" (Quechua). For Quispe—and in our studies of Pallqa and Toqtoqasa—the term applied to guests who helped or contributed but were not members of the owner's kin, affines, or *ayllu*. For Isbell, it included all those who attended and helped in the *herranza*, including the owner's relatives and affines.

llallipay: "To gain advantage" (Quechua), as by making a preliminary offering to a *wamani*.

llampu: "Soft to the touch" (Quechua). A clay mineral, ground to a powder and mixed with white cornmeal, used to allay the adversity caused by breaking relations with the *wamani*; at Pallqa and Toqtoqasa, it symbolized the snows of the puna, which fell on humans and *cerros wamanis* alike.

llampuchay: "To soften" (Quechua).

llampu kutay: To grind *llampu* and cornmeal together (Quechua).

llampu putu: The gourd vessels in which *llampu* is often kept (Quechua).

llampu qipi: A term sometimes used for the ceremonial bundle in the Río Pampas district (Quechua).

puka llampu: Red *llampu* (Quechua).

yuraq llampu: White *llampu* (Quechua).

llumchuy: Daughter-in-law (Quechua); she has ritual obligations to her in-laws, including the cooking of certain meals during the *herranza*.

marcar: To brand, as in the case of cattle (Spanish).

masa: Son-in-law (Quechua); he has certain ritual obligations to his in-laws, such as playing a prominent role in the *herranza*.

mayordomo: A ritual specialist, almost always a relative of the herd owner, to whom much of the responsibility of directing the *herranza* was delegated in those communities where the ceremony was most elaborate (Spanish; has probably replaced a Quechua term).

mesa ceremonial: A multilayered ritual table (actually more like a series of superimposed mats) in the corral, on which much of the ritual of *herranza* was carried out (Spanish).

ñawin: "Vegetable broth" (Quechua). In this context, "special" or "ceremonial." A container with the alcoholic beverages used in the *herranza*, such as *ñawin trago* (ceremonial *cañazo*), *ñawin aqa* (ceremonial *chicha*), or *ñawin vino* (ceremonial wine).

Pacha Mama: Mother Earth (Quechua). Term of address for a powerful supernatural.

señalar: To decorate the ears of llamas by notching them with a special knife and/or sewing ribbons into them (Spanish).

señal pampay: To bury the cut-off pieces of llama ear after the *herranza*, in the Río Pampas district; from Spanish *señal* ("marking") and Quechua *pampay* ("to bury").

suñay: To give a live animal as a gift during the course of the *herranza* ritual (Quechua).

Tayta Urqu: Father Mountain (Quechua). Term of address for a powerful supernatural.

tinya: A drum played by women during rituals (Quechua).

wamanero: A ritual specialist who knows how to placate the *wamani* (a Quechua word with a hispanicized suffix).

wamani: One of many supernaturals living in mountain peaks or puna lakes; the real owner of all animals and livestock (Quechua).

cerro wamani: One of the mountain peaks inhabited by a *wamani*; from Spanish *cerro* ("mountain").

Nine

Herd Dynamics III:
The "Surf City" Model

In Chapter 7 we learned that our simulated llama herds could attain an average equilibrium population size of 22 ± 5 animals, provided that an additional llama was available at certain crucial times. However, we also acknowledged that it was unrealistic to provide those herds with a "Santa Claus" whose supply of llamas was unlimited. In Chapter 8 we discovered the way that additional llamas are, in fact, provided to needy herds in the real world of the Ayacucho herder: at specific annual rituals, a llama from one herd can be given to another through *suñay*. This mechanism for gift giving provides us with the basis for a simulation more realistic than the "Santa Claus" model.

What we have done in this new model is to create a regional system consisting of four herds. Each of these herds is subject to the same rates of fertility and mortality (from pumas, rustlers, mange, and natural causes) as the herds in our original "Oliver Twist" model. Each can request an additional llama of the appropriate age and sex whenever it falls below our minimum reproductive core of 4 young females and 2 fertile males. In contrast to the "Santa Claus" model, however, the needy herd must receive the additional animal from one of the three other herds in the regional system. Animals can be donated only once during each time step or model year, and only if the donor has enough young llamas to do so, making the conditions approximate those of *suñay*.

One of the factors making this four-herd model more realistic is that not all requests for an additional llama can be satisfied. Over time, any herd's environment can impose limitations on its ability to supply animals, as in the following situations: (1) if the number of requested llamas cannot be provided without endangering the minimum reproductive core of the donor herd (i.e., lowering it below 4 young females and 2 fertile males);

(2) if the donor herd has sufficient numbers of fertile llamas to fill the request, but only with llamas that are not maximally productive (e.g., the females have already had some offspring). In model years when these limitations apply, needy herds may have to settle for a less-productive llama, or for no llama at all.

To be sure, in Andean ideology *suñay* is considered a spontaneous act of generosity, not the response to a request. However, we know from experience that such may be only its superficial appearance. Young men with small herds did make ritual contributions to the *herranzas* of older men with large herds, and intermediaries made sure that the older men knew about it in advance. The massing of a large herd in its ritual corral was an epideictic display that left no doubt whether or not the owner could afford *suñay*, and the ethic of generosity to "those who love me" was so pervasive as to be virtually inescapable.

In Chapter 10 we consider what the consequences might be if this were not so—if *suñay* were extended only to close relatives, for example, or were optional. What would happen if the herd owner had sufficient numbers of llamas to handle a request, but refused to do so, or gave only older and less productive animals? These would represent cultural, not environmental, limits on the granting of a request, and their discussion is deferred until later. In this chapter we assume that all requests will be granted if the donor herd is large enough.

Because one goal of this model is to ensure that every herd in the system has at least 4 young females and 2 fertile males at all times, our shorthand reference to it is the "Surf City" model. Some readers will perhaps remember that in that idyllic city, immortalized in the 1960s song by Jan and Dean, there was a similar ratio of "two girls to every boy."

Modifying the Algorithm

In the "Surf City" model, the REQUEST function remains the same as in the "Santa Claus" model; however, the DONOR function is modified. Given a request for a number of females m and a number of males n, the DONOR function is as follows:

    if (NO._FERTILE_FEMALES minus 4) $\geq m$
      then GIVE_BEST (m, "females")

    else if (NO_FERTILE_FEMALES minus 4) > 0
      then GIVE_BEST (NO._FERTILE_FEMALES minus 4, "females")

    else CANNOT_GIVE

The same function is applied to determine how many males can be given, except that a "2" is substituted for the "4" in the commands above.

The GIVE_BEST function selects the llamas to be given. The goal is first to give as many 3-year-olds as possible. If there are fewer 3-year-olds than requested, preference is given to the youngest llamas over 3 years of age. For females, if two llamas are of the same age, preference is given to the llama with the lowest NO._OF_OFFSPRING and a BIRTH_FACTOR = 0 (i.e., no offspring the previous year).

To the community of four herds already mentioned we have added a coordination process called MATCHMAKER, which matches requests from needy herds with possible donor herds. At the end of each model year, each request for llamas is processed by MATCHMAKER. MATCHMAKER finds the one herd in the system with the greatest number of fertile llamas of the sex requested and gives the request to that herd. The donor herd then processes the request, and if it can respond, the donated llama(s) are removed from the donor herd and added to the herd making the request. Their progress is then monitored through time, just as every other llama in every herd is monitored.

Results

Two versions of the "Surf City" model were run. In one version, the system began with one large "established" herd (of 25 llamas or so) and three small "new" herds (of under 10 animals). In the second version, the system began with two large established herds and two small new herds. We felt that both versions approximated the situation on the Ayacucho puna, where we had observed a mix of established flocks owned by senior herders and small herds owned by younger men. Many of the latter were herds resulting from the division of a deceased father's animals among his sons.

We performed ten runs of the 1-large/3-small herd system; Runs 1 and 2 are illustrated as Figure 9.1. All herds survived to 100 model years and most consisted of 12 to 27 animals at that point. In Run 1, Herd 1 was the

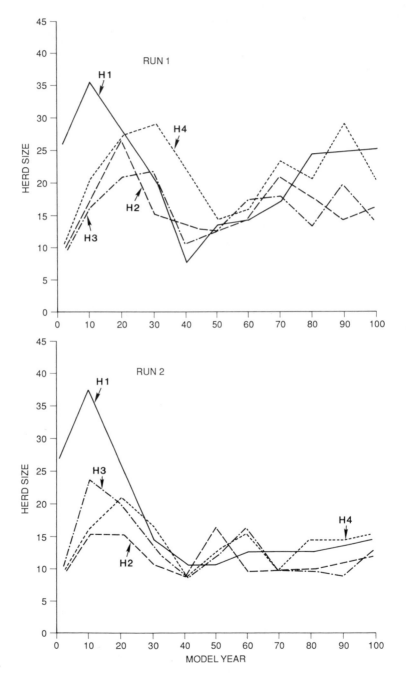

Figure 9.1   Outcomes of Run 1 and Run 2 of a "Surf City" simulation which began with one large herd (H1) and three small herds (H2, H3, H4).

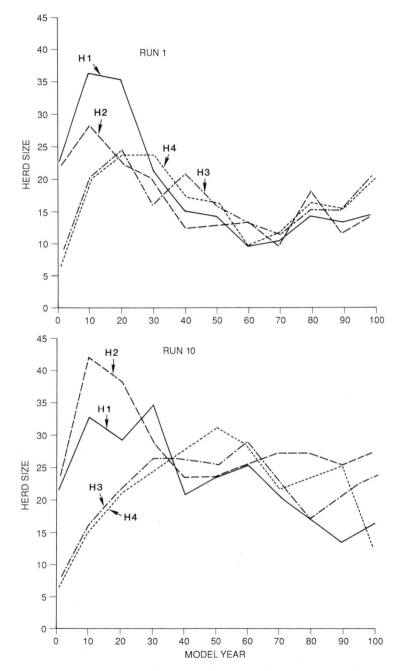

Figure 9.2 Outcomes of Run 1 and Run 10 of a "Surf City" simulation which began with two large herds (H1, H2) and two small herds (H3, H4).

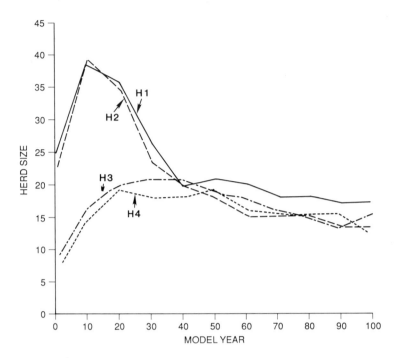

Figure 9.3 Average behavior of Herds 1–4 over all ten runs of the "Surf City" model which began with two large herds (H1, H2) and two small herds (H3, H4).

large herd at the start, climbed to over 30 animals briefly, and had become the second largest herd (ca. 25 llamas) by year 90; briefly, around year 40, it became the smallest herd (6 animals). Herd 4, the smallest herd at the start, became the largest (28 animals) around year 90. In Run 2, all herds grew between years 1 and 20, then declined; after (roughly) year 40, all converged in size and remained quite stable between 10 and 15 animals.

We also performed ten runs of the 2-large/2-small herd system; Runs 1 and 10 are illustrated as Figure 9.2. Once again, all herds survived to 100 model years and, in fact, this version seems to have produced great stability over time. Individual herds never got as large as in earlier simulations (usually peaking below 40 animals), but their oscillations were reduced as well. This set of runs, which required the gift of a llama somewhere in the system roughly every two years, probably came the closest to simulating the herds we saw in the field in the early 1970s.

A graph which shows the average behavior of Herds 1–4 over all ten runs of this second version (Fig. 9.3) shows the two large established herds (#1 and #2) peaking around 36 animals at year 11 and declining to around 20 animals by year 40. The two small new herds (#3 and #4) grew to about 20 animals by year 20. After year 40, all four herds remained stable at 12 to 18 animals through year 100 and appeared ready to go on forever that way.

Figure 9.4 compares the average performance of all runs of the "Oliver Twist" and "Santa Claus" models with that of Herd 3 in the 2-large/ 2-small herd "Surf City" model. The "Surf City" model is almost as successful as "Santa Claus" and has the advantage of being more realistic than the latter.

Actually, we can offer two different measures of success for the "Surf City" model—herd size and herd uniformity. Figure 9.5 shows the differences in mean herd size among the "Oliver Twist," "Santa Claus," and 2-large/2-small herd "Surf City" models. "Surf City" herds averaged 2.27 animals more than "Oliver Twist" herds, and the difference was statistically significant at the .05 confidence level. Perhaps even more

Figure 9.4   Average performance of all herds during all runs of the "Oliver Twist" and "Santa Claus" models compared to the average performance of Herd 3 in all runs of the 2-large/2-small herd "Surf City" model.

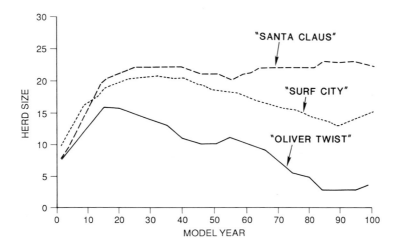

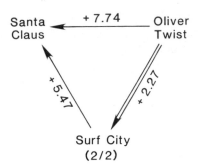

Figure 9.5 Differences in mean herd size among the "Oliver Twist," "Santa Claus," and 2-large/2-small herd "Surf City" models (average of all runs). Arrows point in the direction of herd size increase. Thick arrow indicates that the difference is statistically significant at the .05 level; thin arrows indicate that the differences are not significant at the .05 level because of the variability among runs.

noteworthy, however, is Figure 9.6, which shows the differences in standard deviation among the same three models. "Surf City" herds had a standard deviation in herd size 1.0 animal less than the "Santa Claus" model and 2.4 animals less than the "Oliver Twist" model; both differences were significant at the .05 level. Thus the "Surf City" model produced the greatest uniformity in herd size over time.

Figure 9.6 Differences in standard deviation in herd size among the "Oliver Twist," "Santa Claus," and 2-large/2-small herd "Surf City" models. Arrows point in the direction of increases in standard deviation. Thick arrows indicate that all differences are statistically significant at the .05 level. Note that the "Surf City" herds had the lowest standard deviation of any model.

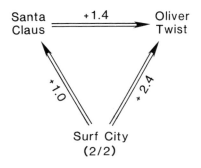

We conclude that a four-herd system in which one or two of the herds are established and two or three of the herds are new—and in which *suñay* takes place whenever one of the herds falls to the minimum reproductive core—can reach stability in 40 years and probably go on indefinitely without any of the herds becoming extinct. All it requires is a gift somewhere in the system about once every two years, a frequency not at all out of line with our observations in Ayacucho. If we now state that *suñay* can make a significant difference in herd size and uniformity over time, we are no longer simply making a plausible assertion; its significance has now been statistically demonstrated.

Ten

Herd Dynamics IV:
Suñay and Adaptation

In previous chapters we examined the way *suñay* worked among Ayacucho herders of the early 1970s and showed that, when that type of gift giving is added to our model of herd dynamics, it makes a statistically significant improvement in herd size and uniformity. But *suñay*, as practiced in Ayacucho, violates some of the expectations of sociobiological theory. In this chapter we consider what compensatory benefits it might provide.

One of the most widespread ideological tenets in the Andes is that of delayed mutual aid. *Ayni*, or symmetrical reciprocity, is extended between *ayllu* members; *minka*, or asymmetrical reciprocity, is extended between humans and *wamanis*. The *wamanis* can cause herds to flourish, but only if the herder propitiates them with offerings chosen and presented properly. Among *ayllu* members, mutual aid is given freely because adherence to the principle of *ayni* is too universal for cheating to occur. *Suñay*, gift giving without the expectation of reciprocation, may have grown out of *ayni*.

We have seen that under normal conditions animals are given to one's children, siblings, or conceivably even more distant *ayllu* members. Under the special ritual conditions of the *herranza*, however, certain non-kin can become *kuyaq* and receive *suñay*. These *kuyaq* can even include North American anthropologists, whose genetic relationship to the Andean herders could not be demonstrated by even the most mathematically sophisticated sociobiologist.

From the perspective of individual or inclusive fitness, it makes no sense to give animals to such genetically unrelated individuals. One should seek to support—and increase the herds of—one's children, other close relatives, and perhaps more distantly related *ayllu* members. To support and increase the herds of non-kin whose descendants may one day outnumber yours, and who may one day compete for the same puna meadows, seems evolutionarily foolish. One should cooperate with one's relatives and ignore everyone else.

We decided, therefore, to modify our original "Surf City" model to test the importance of full cooperation in *suñay*. In Chapter 9, our donors had responded to every request for a llama that did not threaten their own herd's minimum reproductive core. In addition, they always responded by giving the best llama available—for example, a 3-year-old female who had not given birth during the previous year. This is the kind of behavior one might expect among close relatives; and after 100 model years, the resultant herds were larger and much more uniform than those of our original "Oliver Twist" model.

We wondered, however, what would happen if donors were not required to cooperate all the time. Suppose, for example, that they were only expected to cooperate fully with close relatives. What would the implications be? To find out, we changed our model to allow for two new possibilities:

1. Donors always give, but they do not always give the best animal available; they may, for example, give a 12-year-old female whose best years are behind her. This we call the "cheating" model.
2. Donors can choose whether or not to give at all; this we call the "non-cooperation" model. In it, donors can be programmed to cooperate 25% of the time, 50% of the time, or 75% of the time. When they do cooperate, however, they give the best animal available.

The "Cheating" Model

This is basically a new version of the "Surf City" model in which the DONOR function is modified so that no constraints are placed on the nature of the donated llama other than that it must be of the sex requested. This modified DONOR function is as follows:

if (NO._FERTILE_FEMALE minus 4) $\geq m$ then GIVE (m, "females")

else if (NO._FERTILE_FEMALES minus 4) > 0
    then GIVE (NO._FERTILE_FEMALES minus 4, "females")

else CANNOT_GIVE (m, "females")

The GIVE_BEST function described in the original "Surf City" model is replaced by the GIVE function. The GIVE function selects at random a llama of the sex requested. During the initial stages of the simulation, this procedure has less impact, since most animals are still young and fertile (for example, the small, "new" herds are all starting out with 3-year-olds). However, as the herds mature, such blindfolded selection of gifts can result in the donation of older and less productive llamas.

We performed five runs of the four-herd system with unconstrained random donations. Each run began with one large established herd and three small new herds, as described in Chapter 9. After model year 40 of the simulation (a point by which all herds had effectively matured), the average number of llamas exchanged per run was 113. This means that during the last 60 years of the simulation, an average of nearly two llamas per year were given—more than double the number donated in the original "Surf City" model.

Figs. 10.1 and 10.2 illustrate this escalation in gifts. Figure 10.1 shows the animals given by Herd 4 during Run 1, and Figure 10.2 shows the animals received by Herd 2 during the same run. Note, in particular, the large number of donations from Herd 4 to Herd 2 between model years 50 and 75. The number is high because the donated llamas—chosen at random—were usually too old and unproductive to solve Herd 2's problem, which was a shortage of fertile young females. This led to repeated requests for more. Thus one aspect of the "cheating" model is that donor herds are subject to twice as many requests, since their inferior gifts do not fully meet the recipient herd's needs. A second aspect, to be discussed next, emerges from a study of the model's results.

By giving less than the best animals available, Herd 4 is able to keep more fertile llamas for itself than would be the case under scrupulous adherence to *suñay*. Herd 2, on the other hand, is never able to achieve success and stability. The four herds in the system are soon divided into "haves" and "have-nots," which oscillate around different population means. Herd 4 (one of the "haves") fluctuates around a mean of 27; Herd 2 (one of the "have-nots") fluctuates around a mean of 17.

Superficially, one could interpret these results as evidence for successful herd management by Herd 4 through cheating at *suñay*; such is not the case, however. In the situation just described, problems arise when one or more of the large herds is hit by a random cluster of mortality factors which produce the familiar imbalance in the sex ratio. When that happens, it is unlikely that the small herds in the system will be in a position to donate

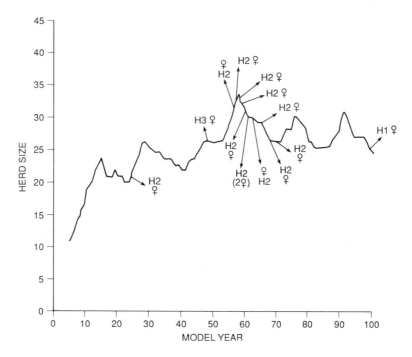

Figure 10.1 The history of animal giving by Herd 4 during Run 1 of the "cheating" model. The heavy line follows fluctuations in the size of Herd 4. The small arrows leading away indicate the year in which an animal was given, the sex of the animal, and the herd to which it was given.

fertile llamas, precisely because they themselves have been denied them in the past. Instead, the whole four-herd system may eventually dwindle. This is precisely what happened in several runs of the "cheating" model; the original donor herd did not give enough good llamas to the other three, and when it was hit by a catastrophe, they could not help it.

The main outcomes of "cheating" in gift giving are to increase the variability in herd size within a four-herd system and to make it more difficult for needy herds to maintain their minimum reproductive core. Because those herds cannot help their neighbors, this is also a more fragile system than the one displaying universal *suñay*. In our original "Surf City" model, no herds ever failed. In the cheating model, 20% of the herds failed, and some of those that survived did not do too well; indeed, the number of gifts required to keep them going was often excessive.

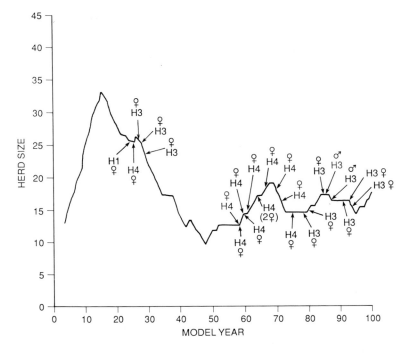

Figure 10.2   The history of animal receiving by Herd 2 during Run 1 of the "cheating" model. The heavy line follows fluctuations in the size of Herd 2. The small arrows indicate the year in which an animal was received, the sex of the animal, and the herd from which it was received.

Significantly, in the real world of the Ayacucho herder, cheating is impossible because it is standard practice for the owner to invite the recipient to pick the llama he wants.

The "Non-Cooperation" Model

The "non-cooperation" model is still another modified version of "Surf City." Here it is assumed that all llamas given as gifts are the best animals possible, but also that a potential donor is able to decline the opportunity to give. The likelihood that a particular herd will cooperate is expressed in probabilistic terms.

In this model, each herd is assigned the same COOPERATION_PROB value, between 0 (no cooperation) and 1 (total cooperation). We then modify the DONOR function in the following way:

GENERATE_RANDOM_NUMBER, R.
if R<COOPERATION_PROB then

if (NO._FERTILE_FEMALES minus 4) $\geq m$
   then GIVE_BEST (m, "females")

else if (NO._FERTILE_FEMALES minus 4) > 0
   then GIVE_BEST (NO._FERTILE_FEMALES minus 4, "females")

 else CANNOT_GIVE

We performed five runs of the four-herd system at a COOPERATION_PROB of .25, five more at .50, and five more at .75. Each four-herd system began with one large established herd and three small new herds, as in

Figure 10.3   Average performance of Herd 1 (large) and Herd 4 (small) at a cooperation level of 25%.

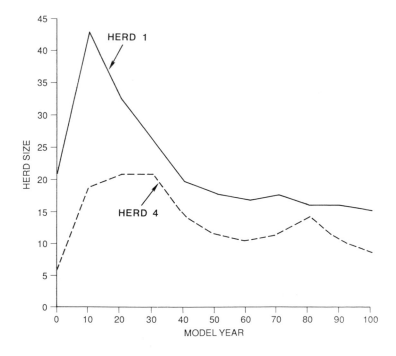

some "Surf City" models. It was not necessary to produce new runs with COOPERATION_PROBS of 0.0 and 1.0, since our "Oliver Twist" model had no gift giving (i.e., 0.0% cooperation) and our original "Surf City" model had 100% cooperation. These two previous models could therefore be combined with the "non-cooperation" model to produce a spectrum of five possible levels of cooperation.

Figure 10.3 shows the average performance of Herd 1 (a large herd) and Herd 4 (a typical small herd) over all five runs in which cooperation was only 25%. Initially, Herd 1 did well (peaking above 40 llamas) because it gave up so little of its breeding stock. After model year 20, however, it usually began to decline steeply and was unable to rebound because there were no other large herds it could reliably count on for animals. Herd 4, after the usual early spurt caused by its initial youth, went into a cycle of decline. By year 100, on the average, both herds were in the 10–15 animal range.

Figure 10.4 Average performance of Herd 1 (large) and Herd 3 (small) at a cooperation level of 50%.

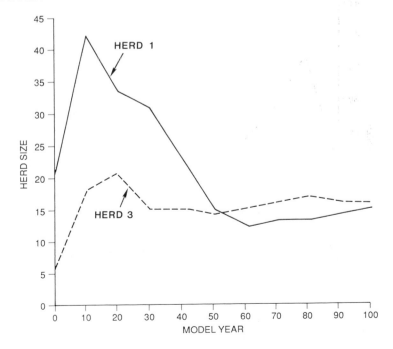

Figure 10.4 gives the five-run averages for Herd 1 (large) and Herd 3 (small) at a cooperation level of 50%. The pattern is similar to that of the previous figure, with Herd 1 undergoing an initial burst of growth followed by precipitous decline. The average curves for both herds flatten out around 15 animals, below the average for the "Surf City" model.

Finally, Figure 10.5 gives comparable five-run averages for Herd 1 (large) and Herd 3 (small) at the level of 75% cooperation. Once again, Herd 1 does well for 20 model years and then goes into a decline which flattens out below 15 animals; Herd 3 never gets over the 20-llama hump and appears to be still declining at year 100. Because of the high random mortality which characterizes these five runs, the average herd in this model did poorly even relative to the 25% and 50% models.

Figure 10.5   Average performance of Herd 1 (large) and Herd 3 (small) at a cooperation level of 75%.

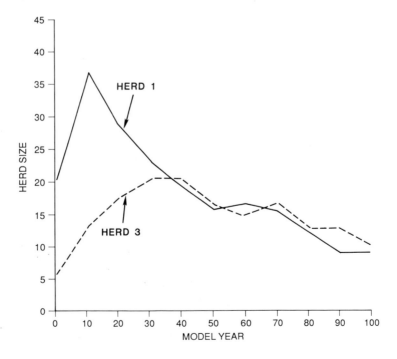

Herd Survival

One measure of the effect of a given COOPERATION_PROB is the percentage of herds that survive to 100 model years over all the runs at that particular probability. We consider a herd to have survived if after 100 years it still contains the minimum reproductive core of 4 young females and 2 fertile males.

Figure 10.6 gives the percentage of surviving herds at cooperation probabilities of zero (the "Oliver Twist" model); .25, .50, and .75 (the "non-cooperation" model); and 1.0 (the original "Surf City" model). Under conditions of zero cooperation, almost no herds survive. The survival percentage rises to 40% at .25 cooperation, but the curve then flattens out between .25 and .50 cooperation. With .75 cooperation, the curve rises again, to 60% survival. The move to total cooperation (1.0) produces a steep rise to 100% survival of all herds.

Figure 10.6 The greater the probability of cooperation in *suñay*, the greater the percentage of herds whose minimum reproductive core is still intact after 100 years.

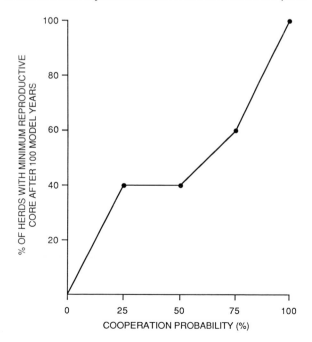

This graph makes clear the impact that different cooperation probabilities have on the survival rates of herds within a four-herd system. The effects are particularly strong at the extremes of the system; the steepest improvements in herd survival take place between zero and .25 and between .75 and 1.0. We can state these results simply: the more universally and generously *suñay* is adhered to, the better it is for every herd in the system.

Implications

Our experiences with the "cheating" and "non-cooperation" models suggest to us that the advantages of widespread generosity in *suñay* outweigh the advantages of cheating or ignoring those who are not one's kin. Indeed, we can see how the custom of *suñay*, once adopted, might have been strongly selected for at the group level. In our models, four-herd systems that practice it have larger and far more stable herds after 100 years than systems without it. In other words, universal adherence to *suñay*—even if it includes giving good breeding stock to non-kin—can make it possible for one's children to pass on more animals to one's grandchildren. It does that by ensuring that there will be lots of other herds around from which the children and grandchildren can get *suñay* when they need it.

Our largest system included only four herds. It is likely that systems of eight herds, or sixteen herds, or more would be even more stable; and, of course, those are the kinds of systems one sees in the real world of the Ayacucho herder. However, even as such larger systems increase the likelihood of getting an animal when one needs it, they also increase the likelihood that not everyone in the system is genetically related.

This situation is anticipated by the dual inheritance theory of Boyd and Richerson (1985). It is simply a case where one's genetic descendants stand a better chance of having thriving herds if one does *not* try to drive the herds of unrelated competitors to extinction. In such cases, Boyd and Richerson suggest, a "group selection" of culturally programmed behavior wins out over the individual selection of genetically programmed behavior.

> Group selection occurs whenever the fitness of an individual depends on the behaviors of other individuals in a local group. . . . If the incremental benefit of investing in the public good exceeds its incremental cost . . . then groups with more than the average number of cooperators have higher average fitness. Such groups contribute disproportionately to the next generation, and thus selection among groups increases the frequency of

cooperation. However, because cooperators have lower fitness than other members of their own group, selection within groups decreases the frequency of cooperators within each group. Cooperation will increase in the whole population only if selection among groups is a stronger force than selection within groups. (Boyd and Richerson 1985:230).

Among the herders we studied, cooperation in *suñay* was close to 100%.

Boyd and Richerson's model of "indirect bias" also suggests how *suñay*, once established, could spread rapidly. For example, if we assume that *suñay* originally took place only among biological kin (as sociobiological theory would predict), a four-herd system composed of related individuals would have a high success rate over 100 years. Such groups should be widely imitated by their neighbors, who would assume that the great success and stability of their herds was the result of proper behavior in the eyes of the *wamani*. Such imitation (or "indirect bias"), on the other hand, would be more difficult for larger groups which included unrelated families. Only if kinship could be extended to non-kin could they also maximize the effects of *suñay*.

The adaptive benefits of such an arbitrary extension of kinship should be clear from Figure 10.6. For example, a four-herd system in which only three of the herd owners were related might see requests for *suñay* honored only about 75% of the time; in such a system, only 60% of all herds would survive to 100 years. If there were some way to extend kinship to all four herds, *suñay* and herd survival could reach 100%. Groups practicing universal *suñay* should therefore thrive economically, relative to groups who practiced it more selectively.

This is where the concept of *kuyaq* comes in: in the context of a ritual, it converts non-kin into kin and makes possible the universal extension of *suñay*. Here is a significant difference between culture and biology. Because lower animals may behave in altruistic ways toward their kin, a great deal of recent writing in evolutionary biology has been concerned with the ways animals recognize their kin. Humans, however, can use culture to create fictive kin toward whom they behave altruistically, and the models in this chapter suggest that there may be situations in which such extensions of kinship would be selected for. Note that we do not argue that such extensions result from shrewd decisions based on practical reason; rather, we suggest that, once made, they may be selected for—which is not the same thing. Any behavior that benefits one's offspring might be selected for, even if it arose arbitrarily out of a previous cultural pattern that was adaptively neutral.

Eleven

Suñay and Dual Inheritance Theory

In Chapter 10 we showed why selection should have favored groups of herders whose gifts of llamas were extended even to non-kin. We suggested, however, that the long-term advantages of treating supportive strangers like kin would not have been apparent to the herders themselves. The beneficial effects of universal *suñay* only become evident after herd dynamics are simulated for up to 100 model years.

We must assume that a few herders had always extended *suñay* to non-kin, if only to provide selection with something to work on. Such cooperators may not have been numerous, but, as we learned in Chapter 10, one of the most dramatic increases in herd survival occurs when cooperation in *suñay* goes from zero to 25%. In this chapter we consider ways in which the frequency of cooperation with non-kin could show an initial increase, even if slight, without assuming that herders had any insight into its long-term benefits.

To do this, we place the problem in the context of Boyd and Richerson's dual inheritance theory. We have referred to the Boyd–Richerson theory from time to time throughout this study, but without tying our results to any of their specific models. Later in this chapter, we finally link our work directly to one of their models for "frequency-dependent bias and the evolution of cooperation" (Boyd and Richerson 1985:204–240).

Kuyaq and *Suñay* in Historical Perspective

There can be little doubt that *ayni* and *minka* were present in some form in prehispanic Andean culture. In Chapter 5 we mentioned the way sixteenth-century *ayllu* members assisted each other in managing the communal herds (an example of *ayni*), and the way farmers serving the *curaca* could be paid in llamas (an example of *minka*). Whether the concepts of *kuyaq* and *suñay* go back as far as *ayni* is unknown. Since all three are indigenous Quechua words, it seems likely that they all preceded the Spanish introduction of *compadrazgo*, for which a loan word is used. However, we are uncertain exactly when they took on the meanings they have today.

What does seem certain is that the collapse of the prehispanic state after A.D. 1532 greatly changed the environment for llama herding. Prior to that date, there had been a whole series of mechanisms for pooling small flocks into large flocks. The state had used its manpower to maintain immense government herds, which were relatively immune to the sex-ratio imbalances of smaller ones. Some of these herds may have provided reserves of animals almost as inexhaustible as those of Chapter 7's "Santa Claus." While *suñay* may already have existed among the prehispanic commoners who tended *waqchallama*, it could not have been as crucial to herd survival then as it is today. The prehispanic system was simply less vulnerable to the demographic problems of small herds, and there were more potential sources from which extra llamas could be obtained. We suspect that the collapse of the prehispanic state established an environment in which there was more pressure to perform *suñay*—one of the few remaining mechanisms for obtaining new breeding stock when needed.

An increase in *suñay*, therefore, might have followed the transition from a prehispanic culture (in which there were immense reserves of llamas, and gift giving took place mainly between blood relatives) to a post-conquest culture (in which there were only small, individually owned herds, and *suñay* was extended to everyone). In Boyd and Richerson's terms, we treat this transition as a change in cultural transmission from one generation to the next.

Cultural Inheritance

Boyd and Richerson propose a series of models for "cultural inheritance" (the learning of those behaviors specific to a particular culture), most of them analogous to current models of genetic inheritance. Genetic inheritance results from natural selection acting on a pool of phenotypes; the latter are selected for or against, based on their fitness within a particular environment. Such a process should emphasize phenotypes that support fitness-maximizing behaviors by individuals. However, Boyd and Richerson (like Williams 1966, before them) argue that individual humans often demonstrate behaviors which appear to benefit their group more than themselves. Such behaviors seem at odds with the traditional model of genetic inheritance through natural selection.

Boyd and Richerson go on to develop a theory of cultural inheritance (often expressed in algebraic equations analogous to those of population genetics) to account for individual behaviors that favor groups—even groups including unrelated individuals. The theory assumes that behavioral traits transmitted from one individual to another are relatively stable structures and can be transmitted through a variety of processes. We mention a few of those here, though in much less detail than in Boyd and Richerson's original exposition.

In *guided variation*, "naive individuals" (young persons who are still incompletely acculturated) acquire their initial behavioral phenotypes by imitating their "cultural parents" (their true parents, plus the other adult role models who influence them). Gradually, however, as a result of experiencing their environment, they assimilate enough information to modify their behavioral phenotype according to some criteria.

In *biased transmission*, naive individuals are called upon to select from a set of behavioral alternatives found in their culture, with at least three possible sources of bias (Boyd and Richerson 1985:135):

1. *Direct bias* occurs when one cultural variant is simply more attractive than the others; it can be a slow process, involving information collection and rational decision making on the part of the naive individual.
2. *Indirect bias* results from imitating the behavior of a highly successful role model; it is a more rapid process, but one which does not necessarily lead to the behavior most adaptive for the naive individual.
3. *Frequency-dependent bias* results from selection of the behavior used most frequently in the culture, or by the majority of one's role models. It, too, is less time consuming than direct bias, but not as adaptive as the latter unless the most common variant also happens to be the best one for the naive individual.

In a novel situation, the naive individual may be subjected to some combination of the above biases, and his or her ultimate choice of behavior may reflect one, two, or all three.

Cultural Variation

In the specific case before us, we are curious about the way gift giving to unrelated individuals who are ritually supportive might have arisen out of a preexisting pattern of cooperating largely with one's kin. Can we suggest some combination of the transmission processes described above which could increase the extension of fictive kinship to appropriate strangers?

Let us answer this question by formally linking up with the algebra of dual inheritance theory. Be assured that we intend to do so in the simplest way possible. The Boyd–Richerson theory is long and complex, and we do not want our ethnographic engine to be shunted onto an algebraic siding. With a little work, however, we can connect our study to an important body of theory.

We use only one of the Boyd–Richerson transmission processes—biased transmission—and one of the simplest forms of bias at that. Both indirect bias and frequency-dependent bias are easier to implement than direct bias, because of the latter's drawn-out learning procedures. Indirect bias by itself, however, does not seem likely to have supported the development of universal *sunay*; our "non-cooperation" model suggests that, at least initially, some of the most successful role models would have been non-cooperating herders. We must therefore develop a scenario in which frequency-dependent bias is sufficient, over time, to produce an increase in gift giving to non-kin.

Let us imagine an early post-Conquest environment in which *sunay* is regularly granted to one's kin, but in which the extension of *kuyaq* status and *sunay* to non-kin is rare. In this environment, we have two variants of cultural behavior: one may either cooperate (C) in making gifts to non-kin or choose not to cooperate (NC). Although C is the less frequent of the two behaviors, there were some prehispanic precedents for it—for example, the gifts of llamas that destitute individuals sometimes received from local *curacas* or *sapsi* herds.

Naive herders used older individuals in their communities as role models for behaviors to be acquired. While there would probably have been many such models among an individual's cultural parents, for the sake of parsimony we assign each naive individual only three role models. This situation is shown in Table 11.1. Here a naive individual is provided with three cultural parents, whose commitments to NC (*sunay* only with kinsmen) or C (*sunay* with everyone) vary. All possible combinations of behavioral

Table 11.1
Calculating the probability that a naive individual will acquire Variant C or Variant NC as the result of exposure to three role models

Variant of Model 1	Variant of Model 2	Variant of Model 3	Probability that offspring acquires cultural variant[a]	
			C	NC
C	C	C	1	0
C	C	NC		
C	NC	C	$\frac{2}{3} + \frac{D}{3}$	$\frac{1}{3} - \frac{D}{3}$
NC	C	C		
NC	NC	C		
NC	C	NC	$\frac{1}{3} - \frac{D}{3}$	$\frac{2}{3} + \frac{D}{3}$
C	NC	NC		
NC	NC	NC	0	1

[a] D = the impact of frequency-dependent bias on the selection process.

variants are shown, as well as the mathematical likelihood that the naive individual will acquire Variant C or Variant NC.

In Table 11.1, D corresponds to the impact that frequency-dependent bias has on the selection process. If we set D to zero, the frequency of acquired variants is unchanged after transmission. If D is not zero, however, the frequencies associated with the two variants change in successive generations. If $D > 0$, the probability of the more common variant is increased and that of the alternative variant decreased. If $D < 0$, the frequency for the less common variant is increased at the expense of the more common.

Now let us imagine a set of n independent communities in Ayacucho at the time of the Spanish Conquest. Let us assume that, after the breakdown of the indigenous prehispanic state, D can vary randomly among these communities. Let us suppose that the probability of gift giving with non-kin by individuals in the ith community is $p(i)$ at the time of the conquest. For the sake of argument, let us also suppose that $p(i)$ is less than .5, meaning that fewer than half the herders extended *suñay* to non-kin.

Assuming that the set of models given in Table 11.1 constitutes a random sample of our naive individual's cultural parents, we can then derive a relationship between the new probability for cooperation with non-kin p′ as a function of its current probability p and the bias parameter D. Such a relationship is shown below for community i:

$$p'(i) = p(i) + Dp(i)(1 - p(i))(2\,p(i) - 1)$$

If the ith community is one where D is negative, it can be demonstrated that $p(i)$ increases in spite of the fact that C may not be as attractive to the individual herder as NC (see proof in Boyd and Richerson 1985:208). And since our simulations show that groups which achieve high frequencies of C have larger and more stable herds over the long run, individuals acculturated in those communities should be more successful at passing on thriving herds to their *piwi churi*, their other sons, and their *masas*. Both they and their indoctrinated sons and sons-in-law should serve as role models, affecting other communities not only by example but also through expansion or migration to new areas in search of pasture. Little by little, over the centuries, groups practicing universal *suñay* should become more numerous than groups which do not.

Twelve

Nature, Culture, and Practical Reason

In the 1951 motion picture *The African Queen*, Humphrey Bogart plays Charlie Alnut, the gin-swilling captain of a seedy riverboat. Katharine Hepburn plays Rose Sayer, the straight-laced sister of an Anglican missionary, whose goal is to save Alnut from his decadent ways. "What're you bein' so mean for, miss?" Alnut pleads during one classic confrontation. "A man takes a drop too much once in a while, it's only human nature."

"Nature, Mr. Alnut," replies Sayer, "is what we are put in this world to *rise above*."

From time to time, that scene on the *Queen* has struck us as an allegory for the ongoing debate between sociobiologists and symbolic anthropologists. Speaking on behalf of the sociobiologists, Alnut argues that people must do what they do because it is in their genes; it is "human nature." And Sayer, speaking for the symbolic anthropologists, reminds him that the arbitrary rules of human culture serve to keep such animal instincts in check. It is a scene appropriate for introducing a chapter on nature and culture.

Nature and Culture

On many occasions through the long evolutionary history of mammals, two species from different orders have found their destinies linked. No process has escalated this linkage, however, as strongly as domestication, a fact that long ago caught the attention of Darwin.

With the apparent blessing of the *wamani*, the prehispanic Indians of the Andes domesticated the guanaco. By so doing, they became members of a pair of linked species which illustrates the difference between a mammal with culture and a mammal without it.

In the wild, guanacos behave just as an evolutionary biologist would predict they should behave. Males compete for females, and in the process a small percentage of dominant alpha males emerge; subdominant males are driven off and form all-male groups on suboptimal forage. Alpha males locate and recognize areas of good forage, on which they establish territories; groups of 15 to 18 females are attracted to these territories and a family group forms. Intruders are warned away by threatening behavior and by communal dung piles left near territorial borders. Alpha males maximize their fitness by siring offspring with large numbers of females, whom they guard from subdominant males.

At times of environmental depletion, guanaco herds migrate long distances to better pasture. During these migrations large numbers of animals flock together, temporarily restraining their competitive behavior for the course of the trip; this behavior reemerges as soon as territories are again established by the alphas on their new ranges. It is presumed that virtually all these behaviors are genetically programmed.

The human herders of the llama, however, do not always behave as an evolutionary biologist would wish them to behave. Sociobiological theory does a good job of predicting the close ritual bond between a father-in-law and his *masa*, since the son-in-law's wife is carrying many of her father's genes. However, that same father's gift of a female llama to a young man unrelated by blood or marriage—a gift that could well enable the stranger's offspring to compete for pasture with the donor's own children one day— seems at odds with sociobiological theory. Despite this, our simulations suggest that the more widespread and universal the performance of these gifts, the better it is for everyone in the group practicing them. As we stated earlier, our rule of thumb has been, If it fits, acknowledge it; if it doesn't fit, don't force it. We therefore acknowledge evolutionary biology's power to explain the roles of *masa* and *llumchuy*, but we prefer Boyd and Richerson's dual inheritance theory for an explanation of *suñay*. In their words, there is no point in attacking neo-Darwinian theory *per se*; one need only "show how models that take culture into account actually generate more satisfactory hypotheses about human behavior without violating the assumption of natural origins" (Boyd and Richerson 1985:14).

We have no doubt that some hard-core sociobiologist could design a complex "Rube Goldberg" explanation suggesting that *suñay* maximizes individual fitness. One would only seek to do so, however, if one seriously believed that all human behavior, even the most arbitrary, was controlled by genes and strove to maximize genetic transmission. To anyone attracted to dual inheritance theory, such a position misses the whole point of culture.

While the *origins* of culture are clearly biological, it seems very unlikely that culture has continued to develop simply to do the things that biological instinct does in other species. If that is all it could do, there would seem to be little need for it, since thousands of other species do quite well without it. When something so clearly nonbiological appears, it seems more logical to assume that it evolved to do things biology cannot do— including, occasionally, to counteract some biological imperatives.

Two points made vehemently by biologists are that Lamarckian inheritance is impossible and that group selection is rare or absent. Here, then, are two things culture can do but which biology finds difficult or impossible. "The cultural information acquired by an individual may be affected by the events of his or her life, and, if so, the changes will be transmitted to an individual's cultural offspring. This property of cultural transmission makes for a kind of 'Lamarckian' evolution, in the sense that acquired variation is inherited" (Boyd and Richerson 1985:8). And as we saw in Chapter 10, group selection occurs when the incremental benefit of investing in the public good exceeds its incremental cost, causing groups with more than the average number of cooperators to contribute disproportionately to the next generation.

To us, these are the basic differences between a mammal with culture and a mammal without it. Wild camelids behave so as to maximize their fitness, undergo selection at the individual level, and display no Lamarckian inheritance. We presume that llama herders have undergone *biological* selection for high-altitude physical adaptation (Baker 1968; Frisancho 1975), but they also exhibit Lamarckian inheritance and group selection for *cultural* behaviors.

The Consequences of Domestication

In the course of domestication, the camelids' "selfish genes" met their match in "selfish man" (see Flannery 1986:15). Humans began to select for characters that had been selected against by natural selection, producing the domestic subspecies we know as the llama. Yet just as guanacos were being turned into llamas by genetic modification, hunters were being turned into farmers and herders by nongenetic means. Since not even the most fervent sociobiologist has argued that there are genes for being a hunter, farmer, or herder, we have to conclude that these supremely important changes were the product of culture. Ironically, when we look at the growth of human populations following the food-producing revolution, we also have to conclude that no previous genetic change had as great an impact on fitness as this cultural change did.

The Andean natives produced a race of camelid that went on to be more numerous, within its geographic range, than its guanaco ancestors; it even threatened that ancestor with local extinction. Since they could not counteract the genetically based competitive behavior inherited from guanaco ancestors, the Indians raising small herds presumably castrated all but a few males. This eliminated fighting and took the "male group" out of existence. Herds now consisted of 1–2 fertile males, 10–15 gelded males, and 10–15 females plus their young. No longer was the male herd sire a self-selected alpha; instead, he was chosen by the herders on the basis of their arbitrary cultural standards of conformation. Human selection for docility counteracted nature's selection for fighting ability. Coat color, which natural selection had kept in the tawny range, exploded into a variety of colors under human selection. Pure white would have been detrimental to survival in the wild, but herds of pure white llamas were raised for sacrifice by Quechua speakers for whom the color *yuraq* symbolized *riti*, or snow.

Once guanacos had migrated widely in search of forage; now llamas were kept in *kanchas*, where their communal dung piles became fertilizer for potato gardens rather than boundary markers for territories. To meet the constant need for fresh pasture, it was now the herders who had to migrate; they established a series of *estancias* in the lower and upper *sallqa*, between which they moved their herds on a seasonal basis. During the agricultural season, the animals had to be kept away from the *chakras* at lower elevations; that was accomplished by keeping llamas at higher elevations for longer periods than their guanaco ancestors would have liked. This in turn lowered their fertility, as it does that of nearly all domestic mammals kept in the *sallqa*.

During our 1970s fieldwork, we saw just how interlinked the two species are. The herder's subsistence base depends on the growth and stability of his herd, which he also hopes to pass on intact to the children who bear his genes. In turn, the llamas' fitness depends as much on the actions of the herders as on the actions of nature. As a result of the variables of fertility and mortality described in earlier chapters, each herd is an oscillating population of fewer than 50 creatures, doomed to reach equilibrium at zero unless a new animal or two can be added whenever its minimum reproductive core is threatened.

There are probably several ways such additional animals could be provided. We suspect that during the early stages of prehistoric domestication newly captured wild guanacos could have been added to domestic herds, as the Chukchi occasionally do with their reindeer. As time went by and guanaco populations dwindled, however, this option would have been increasingly less available. Under Inca rule, when the state had the power to reduce thieves and predators, keep large groups of males and females separate, and pool large numbers of small herds into one big regional population, llama herding entered its most productive era. At the community level, *sapsi* herds provided a reservoir of breeding stock which was counted in public twice a year. Like the *herranza*, such public counts were epideictic displays which let needy herders know the size of the community's reserve.

These labor-intensive herding institutions gradually withered away after the Spanish Conquest. At Yanahuaccra and Toqtoqasa in the 1970s, on the fringes of a society with little interest in llamas, few options remain. One is the custom of *suñay* which our earlier chapters have documented. Our simulations show that such gift giving can make a significant improvement in the size and stability of the local llama population, and that the more universally it is carried out, the better chance every herd has. This undoubtedly has a reinforcing effect on the continuance of the herders' cultural lifeway; certainly it increases their chances of passing on large, healthy herds to the children who bear their genes.

The Origins of *Suñay*

There are two aspects of *suñay* that should be stressed here. One point is that it is an arbitrary cultural practice, springing logically from an underlying and very ancient ideology rather than from a genetically based instinct. The second point is that its arbitrary origins in no way imply that it is adaptively neutral.

Suñay may be an outgrowth of the Andean custom of *ayni*, the symmetrical reciprocal aid usually practiced only with one's kinsmen. Some evolutionary biologists (e.g., Trivers 1971; Flinn and Alexander 1982) suggest that voluntary reciprocity in humans arose through repeated interactions among a large but finite group of rational, selfish individuals, while

Boyd and Richerson (1985:230) prefer to see it evolve through group selection. They point out that, while the theory of interaction of pairs of individuals has undergone recent breakthroughs (e.g., Axelrod 1984; Axelrod and Hamilton 1981), the theory of interaction in larger groups is still in its infancy. Whatever the case, *suñay* requires a different explanation, for it is not the same as *ayni*. *Ayni* carries the assumption of reciprocation in kind—herding for herding, housebuilding for housebuilding. *Suñay* is supposed to be spontaneous gift giving, with no expectation of reciprocation from the same person or his family, even at a later date.

It is probably no accident that *suñay* takes place in the context of a ritual which reestablishes relations between the herders and the *wamani*. Even if we grant the biologists' supposition that individual humans (like other mammals) are selfish, religious ritual provides a sacred context in which the arbitrary, unselfish ideologies of human culture are more likely to be adhered to scrupulously (Rappaport 1971). Wander into a herder's *kancha* in July to ask him for a llama, and you will be out of luck (and possibly even dead). Show up at his *herranza* in August with an *arroba* of coca and a liter of *cañazo*, and you may even become his *kuyaq*. Ritual cannot change anyone's genes, but it has its own way of changing a stranger into a relative.

Practical Reason

Finally, let us turn to the debate over practical reason. Have we merely invoked adaptation "to explain the properties, persistence, or, most weakly, the mode of functioning of a cultural form" (Sahlins 1976a:209)? Have we simply been predisposed to argue "the rationality of institutions with respect to their environments" or "the rationality of institutions with respect to other elements in the society, especially the economy" (Friedman 1974)? Or have we identified a cultural behavior that, however arbitrarily it may have arisen, should have been selected for at the level of the group practicing it?

It seems to us that the debate over practical reason has been kept alive by at least two problems. One of these is a lack of rigorous testing; the other is a lack of diachronic perspective.

The problem of testing reminds us of a similar debate in biology, namely, the argument over the extent to which community structure is shaped by competition between species. Some zoologists (e.g., Roughgarden 1983) argue forcefully for the importance of competition; others (e.g., Simberloff 1983) claim that the alternative "null hypothesis" has never been rejected. When Connell (1983) and Schoener (1983) reviewed field experiments which claimed to have demonstrated cases of interspecific competition, it became apparent just how difficult it is to demonstrate competition under real-life conditions.

When two yeasts are allowed to compete under perfect laboratory conditions, one drives the other to extinction just as the Lotka–Volterra equations would predict. In a real ecosystem, however, fluctuating environmental parameters or predation by other species may cloud the issue by preventing competitive exclusion (Paine 1966). Similar mitigating factors cloud the debate between biologists who believe that animals forage optimally and those who doubt that they do (Stephens and Krebs 1986:206–215).

Because human cultures must be studied in the real world, any attempt to demonstrate adaptation faces similar constraints. Indeed, most functionalists' claims of adaptation are mere assertions, which is why most symbolic anthropologists remain unmoved. Yet if function cannot be demonstrated simply by logical introspection, neither can it be rejected simply because it does not fit one's theoretical stance. Both positions require testing and demonstration, and so far we have had painfully little of that.

We do not believe that llama herders have genes for *ayni* or *suñay*. We agree, therefore, with the symbolic anthropologists who would see them as concepts arising arbitrarily out of Andean culture—only two out of the scores of possible concepts that could have arisen. The people of the puna did not create the *waytakuy* ceremony as a practical solution to the problem of small-herd demographics; they created it out of concern for the anger of a supernatural being called the *wamani*. They hold the ceremony in the month when they feel he is most angry, and they placate his anger by purifying *his* llamas with a powder that symbolizes snow. So important is this pacification of the *wamani* that, when a visitor's concern for the success of the ceremony leads him to make a substantial contribution, he becomes enough like kin to receive a llama as a gift.

Agreeing that *suñay* is created arbitrarily out of culture, however, does not mean agreeing that it is adaptively neutral. That also has to be demonstrated. For this purpose, we have run five separate models of the growth of llama herds over time, using birth and death rates taken from the real world. These models indicate that *suñay* can make such a difference in herd growth that, however arbitrary its origins, it ought to have been selected for as soon as the problem of small-herd demographics arose. In the long run, a group of herders who practiced *suñay* would have had considerable advantage over a group who did not.

Perhaps the key phrase here is "in the long run," which brings us to the problem of diachronic perspective. Evolution is a series of long historic transformations, characterized not only by universal processes but also by historical accidents. Only by taking a long-term approach can we see some of the processes, and the delayed effects of some of the accidents. After a mere 20 model years of our "Oliver Twist" simulation, it was still not clear that every llama herd would eventually reach equilibrium at zero. After a mere five years at Yanahuaccra, no anthropologist would really have conclusive evidence to show whether *suñay* was adaptive or not. His or her conclusions would therefore depend on whether he or she was a materialist or an idealist.

Further complicating the issue is the possibility that some cultural behaviors may have been adaptive at the time they arose—a century ago, two centuries ago—but cannot be shown to be more than neutral under today's altered conditions. Indeed, many human behaviors—debated by sociobiologists, symbolic anthropologists, and human ecologists alike— probably cannot be understood without a perspective that is several centuries long. We cannot resist pointing out how similar that perspective is to the archaeologist's.

Archaeologists turn often to ethnologists, even to symbolic anthropologists, for inspiration. The typical ethnologist, however, turns to an archaeologist only if he or she has something heavy to be carried upstairs. Yet there are problems in anthropology that require a diachronic, historic, evolutionary perspective, perhaps even accompanied by rigorous testing or mathematical modeling. From time to time we daydream about how exciting it would be if ethnologists, archaeologists, and evolutionary biologists could actually collaborate on attacking some of the fundamental issues in anthropology. Of course, after listening to an hour of debate at our next faculty meeting, we will once again realize how foolish a dream that is.

Perhaps, however, we can take hope from this: at the end of *The African Queen*, Rose Sayer and Charlie Alnut are married. She touches in him a core of culturally defined decency that no one had touched in years; he awakens in her a genetically based passion that she never suspected was there. Their marriage could be taken as a sign that, whenever there is enough mutual respect, there might even be hope for anthropology and evolutionary biology.

References

Acosta, José de

1940   *Historia Natural y Moral de las Indias . . .* [1590]. México, D.F.: Fondo de Cultura Económica.

Alberti, Giorgio, and Enrique Mayer

1974   *Reciprocidad e Intercambio en los Andes Peruanos.* Lima: Instituto de Estudios Peruanos.

Alexander, Richard D.

1979   *Darwinism and Human Affairs.* Seattle: University of Washington Press.

Allen [Wagner], Catherine J.

1978   *Coca, Chicha and Trago: Private and Communal Rituals in a Quechua Community.* Ph.D. dissertation, Department of Anthropology, University of Illinois, Urbana.

1982   Body and soul in Quechua thought. *Journal of Latin American Lore* 8 (2): 179–196.

Arriaga, Pablo José de

1968   *The Extirpation of Idolatry in Peru* (1621). Translated and edited by L. Clark Keating. Lexington: University of Kentucky Press.

Ávila, Francisco de

1966   *Dioses y Hombres de Huarochirí* [1598?]. Translated from the Quechua by José María Arguedas. Lima: Museo Nacional de Historia and Instituto de Estudios Peruanos.

1983   *Hijos de Pariya Qaqa: La Tradición Oral de Waru Chiri* [1598?]. Spanish translation from the Quechua by Jorge L. Urioste. Latin American Series no. 6. Maxwell School of Citizenship and Public Affairs, Syracuse University, Syracuse, New York.

Axelrod, Robert

1984   *The Evolution of Cooperation.* New York: Basic Books.

Axelrod, Robert, and William D. Hamilton
1981   The evolution of cooperation. *Science* 211:1390–1396.

Baker, Edward W., and G. W. Wharton
1952   *An Introduction to Acarology.* New York: MacMillan.

Baker, Paul T.
1968   *High Altitude Adaptation in a Peruvian Community.* Occasional Papers in
        Anthropology no. 1. Department of Anthropology, Pennsylvania State
        University. University Park.

Banks, Nathan
1915   *The Acarina or Mites.* U.S. Department of Agriculture, Report no. 108.

Barnett, Gene
1983   Comment on Bray and Dollery's "Coca chewing and high-altitude stress: A
        spurious correlation." *Current Anthropology* 24 (3):275.

Beals, Ralph L.
1970   Gifting, reciprocity, savings, and credit in peasant Oaxaca. *Southwestern Journal
        of Anthropology* 26 (3):231–241.

Belding, David L.
1942   *Textbook of Clinical Parasitology.* New York: Appleton-Century-Crofts.

Bolton, Ralph, and Enrique Mayer (editors)
1977   *Andean Kinship and Marriage.* Special publication of the American
        Anthropological Association no. 7. Washington, D.C.

Boyd, Robert, and Peter J. Richerson
1985   *Culture and the Evolutionary Process.* Chicago: University of Chicago Press.

Bray, Warwick, and Colin Dollery
1983   Coca chewing and high-altitude stress: A spurious correlation. *Current
        Anthropology* 24 (3):269–282.

Chagnon, Napoleon A., and William Irons (editors)
1979   *Evolutionary Biology and Human Behavior: An Anthropological Perspective.* North
        Scituate, Mass.: Duxbury Press.

Cieza de León, Pedro de
1862   *Primera Parte de la Crónica del Perú . . .* [1550]. Biblioteca de Autores Españoles
        2:349–458. Madrid.
1932   *Parte Primera de la Crónica del Perú.* Madrid: Edición Espasa-Calpe.
1943   *Segunda Parte de la Crónica del Perú . . .* [1550], edited by A. M. Salas. Buenos
        Aires: Ediciones Argentinas "Solar."

Clemente Perroud, Pedro, and Juan María Chouvenc

1970 *Diccionario Castellano-Kechwa, Kechwa-Castellano: Dialecto de Ayacucho*. Santa Clara, Perú: Seminario San Alfonso en Santa Clara (Ate), Padres Redentoristas.

Cobo, Bernabé

1890– *Historia del Nuevo Mundo* [1653], 4 volumes. Edited by Marcos Jiménez de la
1895 Espada. Sevilla: Sociedad de Bibliófilos Andaluces.

1956 *Historia del Nuevo Mundo* [1653]. Edited by Francisco Mateos, Biblioteca de Autores Españoles, Tomos 91–92. Madrid.

1979 *History of the Inca Empire . . .* [1653], translated by Roland Hamilton. Austin: University of Texas Press.

Cock C., Guillermo

1981 El ayllu en la sociedad Andina: Alcances y perspectivas. In *Etnohistoria y Antropología Andina: Segunda Jornada del Museo Nacional de Historia*, compiled by Amalia Castelli, Marcia Koth de Paredes, and Mariana Mould de Pease, pp. 231–253. Lima: Centro de Proyección Cristiana.

Connell, J. H.

1983 On the prevalence and relative importance of interspecific competition: Evidence from field experiments. *The American Naturalist* 122:661–696.

Cunow, Heinrich

1929 *El Sistema de Parentesco Peruano y las Comunidades Gentilicias de los Incas* [1890]. Translated from the German by María Woitscheck. Paris: Biblioteca de Antropología Peruana.

Díez de San Miguel, Garci

1964 *Visita hecha a la provincia de Chucuito . . .* [1567–1568]. Documentos Regionales para la Etnología y Etnohistoria Andinas no. 1. Lima: Casa de la Cultura del Perú.

Donnan, Christopher B.

1964 An early house from Chilca, Peru. *American Antiquity* 30:137–144.

Dunnell, Robert C.

1980 Evolutionary theory and archaeology. In *Advances in Archaeological Method and Theory*, vol. 3, edited by M. B. Schiffer, pp. 35–99. New York: Academic Press.

Durham, William H.

1979 Toward a coevolutionary theory of human biology and culture. In *Evolutionary Biology and Human Social Behavior: An Anthropological Perspective*, edited by Napoleon Chagnon and William Irons, pp. 39–59. North Scituate, Mass.: Duxbury Press.

1982 Interactions of genetic and cultural evolution: Models and examples. *Human Ecology* 10:289–323.

Duviols, Pierre

1976   La Capacocha. *Allpanchis Phuturinqa* IX: 11–57. Cusco, Perú: Instituto de
        Pastoral Andina.

Earls, John

1973   *Andean Continuum Cosmology*. Ph.D. dissertation, Department of Anthropology,
        University of Illinois, Urbana.

El Comercio

1980   En el Perú domesticaron camélidos hace 6 mil años. *El Comercio*, año 141,
        no. 76–353 (8 November 1980), p. 1. Lima.

Engel, Frédéric

1963   A preceramic settlement on the central coast of Peru: Asia, Unit I. *Transactions
        of the American Philosophical Society*, n.s. 53 (3):1–139.

Falcón, Francisco

1918   Representación hecha por el Licenciado Falcón en concilio provincial, sobre los
        daños y molestias que se hacen a los indios [1580?]. Edited by Horacio H.
        Urteaga and C. A. Romero. In *Colección de Libros y Documentos Referentes a la
        Historia del Perú*, 1st series, Vol. 2, pp. 133–176. Lima.

Fernández, Diego

1876   *Primera y Segunda parte de la historia del Perú . . .* [1571]. Documentos Literarios
        del Perú, Vols. 8 and 9. Lima.

Fernández Baca, Saúl, and César Novoa M.

1968   Primer ensayo de inseminación artificial de alpacas (*Lama pacos*) con semen de
        vicuña (*Vicugna vicugna*). *Revista de la Facultad de Medicina Veterinaria,
        Universidad Nacional Mayor de San Marcos* 22: 9–18. Lima.

Flannery, Kent V.

n.d.   Faunal remains from sites above 3000 meters. To appear in a future volume of
        Prehistory of the Ayacucho Basin, Peru, edited by Richard S. MacNeish. Ann
        Arbor: University of Michigan Press.

Flannery, Kent V. (editor)

1986   *Guilá Naquitz: Archaic Foraging and Early Agriculture in Oaxaca, Mexico*.
        Orlando, Florida: Academic Press.

Flannery, Kent V., and Elizabeth S. Wing

n.d.   Modern-day fauna of the Ayacucho Basin. To appear in a future volume of
        Prehistory of the Ayacucho Basin, Peru, edited by Richard S. MacNeish. Ann
        Arbor: University of Michigan Press.

Flinn, Mark V., and Richard D. Alexander

1982   Culture theory: The developing synthesis from biology. *Human Ecology*
        10:383–400.

Flores Ochoa, Jorge A.

1968   *Los Pastores de Paratía: Una Introducción a su Estudio.* Serie Antropología Social
        no. 10. México, D.F.: Instituto Indigenista Interamericano.

1979   *Pastoralists of the Andes: The Alpaca Herders of Paratía.* Philadelphia: Institute for
        the Study of Human Issues.

1986   The classification and naming of South American camelids. In *Anthropological
        History of Andean Polities*, edited by John V. Murra, Nathan Wachtel, and
        Jacques Revel, pp. 137–148. Cambridge: Cambridge University Press; Paris:
        Editions de la Maison des Sciences de l'Homme.

Flores Ochoa, Jorge A. (editor)

1977   *Pastores de Puna: Uywamichiq punarunakuna.* Instituto de Estudios Peruanos,
        Estudios de la Sociedad Rural no. 5. Lima.

Fonseca Martel, César

1974   Modalidades de la minka. In *Reciprocidad e Intercambio en los Andes Peruanos*,
        edited by Giorgio Alberti and Enrique Mayer, pp. 86–109. Lima: Instituto de
        Estudios Peruanos.

Franklin, William L.

1975   Guanacos in Peru. *Oryx* 13:191–202.

1983   Contrasting socioecologies of South America's wild camelids: The vicuña and
        the guanaco. In *Advances in the Study of Mammalian Behavior*, edited by J. F.
        Eisenberg and D. G. Kleiman, pp. 573–629. Special Publication 7, American
        Society of Mammologists.

Friedman, Jonathan

1974   Marxism, structuralism, and vulgar materialism. *Man*, n.s. 9:444–469.

Frisancho, A. Roberto

1975   Functional adaptation to high altitude hypoxia. *Science* 187:313–319.

Garcilaso de la Vega, "El Inca"

1960   *Comentarios reales de los Incas* [1604]. Biblioteca de Autores Españoles, Tomos
        133–135. Madrid.

1966   *Royal Commentaries of the Incas and General History of Peru* [1604]. Translated by
        H. V. Livermore. Austin: University of Texas Press.

González Holguín, Diego

1952   *Vocabulario de la Lengua General de Todo el Peru Llamada Qquichua e del Inca*
        [1608]. Lima: Universidad Nacional Mayor de San Marcos.

Gow, David

1976   *The Gods and Social Change in the High Andes.* Ph.D. dissertation, Department of
        Anthropology, University of Wisconsin, Madison.

Guaman Poma de Ayala [Waman Puma], Felipe

1980   *El Primer Nueva Corónica y Buen Gobierno* [ca. 1614]. Edited by John V. Murra and Rolena Adorno, with translations and textual analysis of the Quechua by Jorge L. Urioste. Mexico: Siglo Veintiuno.

Guardia Mayorga, César A.

1967   *Diccionario Kechwa-Castellano Castellano-Kechwa*, 3d ed. Lima: Ediciones los Andes.

Herre, Wolf

1952   Studien über die wilden und domestizierten Tylopoden Südamerikas. *Der Zoologische Garten*, n.f. 19:70–98.

1961   Tiergeographische Betrachtungen an vorkolumbianischen Haussäugetieren Südamerikas. *Schriften des Geographischen Instituts der Universität Kiel* 20:289–304.

Holdridge, Leslie R.

1967   *Life Zone Ecology*. San José de Costa Rica: Tropical Science Center.

Hole, Frank, Kent V. Flannery, and James A. Neely

1969   *Prehistory and Human Ecology of the Deh Luran Plain*. Memoirs of the Museum of Anthropology, University of Michigan, no. 1. Ann Arbor.

Holland, John H.

1975   *Adaptation in Natural and Artificial Systems*. Ann Arbor: University of Michigan Press.

Holland, John H., Keith J. Holyoak, Richard E. Nisbett, and Paul R. Thagard

1986   *Induction: Processes of Inference, Learning, and Discovery*. Cambridge, Mass.: MIT Press.

Isbell, Billie Jean

1977   "Those who love me": An analysis of Andean kinship and reciprocity within a ritual context. In *Andean Kinship and Marriage*, edited by Ralph Bolton and Enrique Mayer, pp. 81–105. Special Publication no. 7, American Anthropological Association. Washington, D.C.

1978   *To Defend Ourselves: Ecology and Ritual in an Andean Village*. Prospect Heights, Illinois: Waveland Press (second edition, 1985).

Kelly, Raymond C.

1985   *The Nuer Conquest: The Structure and Development of an Expansionist System*. Ann Arbor: University of Michigan Press.

Kitcher, Philip

1985   *Vaulting Ambition: Sociobiology and the Quest for Human Nature*. Cambridge, Mass: MIT Press.

Koford, Carl B.

1957   The vicuña and the puna. *Ecological Monographs* 27 (2):153–219.

Latcham, Ricardo E.

1922   *Los Animales Domésticos de la América Precolombina.* Publicaciones del Museo de Etnología y Antropología de Chile no. 3. Santiago, Chile.

Leeds, Anthony

1965   Reindeer herding and Chukchi social institutions. In *Man, Culture, and Animals,* edited by Anthony Leeds and Andrew P. Vayda, pp. 87–128. Publication 78, American Association for the Advancement of Science. Washington, D.C.

Leeds, Anthony, and Andrew P. Vayda (editors)

1965   *Man, Culture, and Animals.* Publication 78, American Association for the Advancement of Science. Washington, D.C.

Lévi-Strauss, Claude

1956   Les organisations dualistes existent-elles? In *Bijdragen tot de Taal, Land, en Volkenkunde* 112:99–128. Leiden.

1967   Do dual organizations exist? In *Structural Anthropology,* pp. 128–160. New York: Anchor Books, Doubleday.

Lewontin, Richard C., Steven Rose, and Leon J. Kamin

1984   *Not in Our Genes.* New York: Pantheon Books.

MacNeish, Richard S., Angel García Cook, Luis G. Lumbreras, Robert K. Vierra, and Antoinette Nelken-Terner

1981   *Prehistory of the Ayacucho Basin, Peru,* vol. 2. Ann Arbor: University of Michigan Press.

Marcus, Joyce

1970   *An Analysis of Color-Direction Symbolism among the Maya.* Manuscript in the Tozzer Library, Harvard University, Cambridge, Massachusetts.

1976   *Emblem and State in the Classic Maya Lowlands: An Epigraphic Approach to Territorial Organization.* Washington, D.C.: Dumbarton Oaks Research Library.

1983   A synthesis of the cultural evolution of the Zapotec and Mixtec. In *The Cloud People: Divergent Evolution of the Zapotec and Mixtec Civilizations,* edited by Kent V. Flannery and Joyce Marcus, pp. 355–362. New York: Academic Press.

1987a Prehistoric fishermen in the kingdom of Huarco. *American Scientist* 75 (4):393–401. New Haven, Connecticut.

1987b *Late Intermediate Occupation at Cerro Azul, Perú: A Preliminary Report.* Technical Report 20, Museum of Anthropology, University of Michigan, Ann Arbor.

Marcus, Joyce, Ramiro Matos Mendieta, and María Rostworowski de Diez Canseco

1983– Arquitectura Inca de Cerro Azul, Valle de Cañete. *Revista del Museo Nacional*
1985   47:125–138. Lima.

Martínez Ríos, Jorge

1964   Análisis funcional de la "Guelaguetza Agrícola." *Revista Mexicana de Sociología*
        26:79–126.

Mayer, Enrique

1977   Beyond the nuclear family. In *Andean Kinship and Marriage*, edited by Ralph
        Bolton and Enrique Mayer, pp. 60–80. Special Publication 7, American
        Anthropological Association. Washington, D.C.

Miller, George R.

1977   Sacrificio y beneficio de camélidos en el sur del Perú. In *Pastores de Puna:
        Uywamichiq Punarunakuna*, edited by Jorge Flores Ochoa, pp. 193–210. Lima:
        Instituto de Estudios Peruanos.

Moore, Katherine M.

n.d.   *Evolution of Specialized Animal Economies in Prehistoric Highland Peru*. Ph.D.
        dissertation, Department of Anthropology, University of Michigan, Ann Arbor.

Moro, Manuel

1968   Enfermedades de los Auquénidos. *Instituto Veterinario de Investigaciones Tropicales
        y de Altura (IVITA), Tercer Boletín Extraordinario*, pp. 61–74. Lima: Facultad de
        Medicina Veterinaria, Universidad Nacional Mayor de San Marcos.

Murra, John V.

1965   Herds and herders in the Inca state. In *Man, Culture, and Animals*, edited by
        Anthony Leeds and Andrew P. Vayda, pp. 185–215. Publication 78, American
        Association for the Advancement of Science. Washington, D.C.

1972   El "control vertical" de un máximo de pisos ecológicos en la economía de las
        sociedades andinas. In *Visita de la Provincia de León de Huánuco* [1562], by Iñigo
        Ortiz de Zúñiga, visitador, vol. 2, pp. 427–476. Huánuco, Perú: Universidad
        Hermilio Valdizán.

ONERN

1976   *Mapa Ecológico del Perú: Guía Explicativa*. Lima: Oficina Nacional de Evaluación
        de Recursos Hidraúlicos.

Orlove, Benjamin S.

1977   *Alpacas, Sheep, and Men: The Wool Export Economy and Regional Society in
        Southern Peru*. New York: Academic Press.

Ortiz de Zúñiga, Iñigo

1957   *Visita fecha por mandado de Su Majestad . . .* [1562]. Lima: Revista del Archivo
        Nacional del Perú.

1972   *Visita de la Provincia de León de Huánuco . . .* [1562]. Huánuco, Perú:
        Universidad Hermilio Valdizán.

Paine, R. T.

1966   Food web complexity and species diversity. *The American Naturalist* 100:65–75.

Palomino Flores, Salvador

1970   *El Sistema de Oposiciones en la Comunidad Sarhua.* Bachelor's thesis in Anthropology, Universidad Nacional de San Cristóbal de Huamanga, Ayacucho, Peru.

1971   La dualidad en la organización de algunos pueblos del area andina. *Revista del Museo Nacional* 37:231–260.

1984   *El Sistema de Oposiciones en la Comunidad de Sarhua.* Lima: Editorial "Pueblo Indio."

Parker, Gary J.

1963   Clasificación genética de los dialectos quechuas. *Revista del Museo Nacional* 32:241–252. Lima.

1969   *Ayacucho Quechua Grammar and Dictionary.* The Hague: Mouton.

Picón Reátegui, E.

1968   Effect of coca chewing on metabolic balance in Peruvian high altitude natives. In *High Altitude Adaptation in a Peruvian Community,* edited by Paul T. Baker, pp. 556–563. Occasional Papers in Anthropology no. 1, Department of Anthropology, Pennsylvania State University. University Park.

Polo de Ondegardo, Juan

1916a   Los errores y supersticiones de los indios, sacadas del tratado y averiguacion que hizo el Licenciado Polo . . . [1559]. Edited by Horacio H. Urteaga and C. A. Romero. *Colección de Libros y Documentos Referentes a la Historia del Perú,* primera serie, vol. 3, pp. 1–43. Lima.

1916b   Relación de los fundamentos acerca del notable daño que resulta de no guardar a los indios sus fueros . . . [1571]. *Colección de Libros y Documentos Referentes a la Historia del Perú,* primera serie, vol. 3, pp. 45–188. Lima.

Poole, Deborah Ann

1984   *Ritual-Economic Calendars in Paruro: The Structure of Representation in Andean Ethnography.* Ph.D. dissertation, Department of Anthropology, University of Illinois, Urbana.

Quispe M., Ulpiano

1969   *La Herranza en Choque Huarcaya y Huancasancos, Ayacucho.* Instituto Indigenista Peruano, Monografía no. 20. Lima: Ministerio de Trabajo.

Raedeke, Kenneth J.

1979   *Population Dynamics and Socioecology of the Guanaco (Lama guanicoe) of Magallanes, Chile.* Ph.D. dissertation, College of Forest Resources, University of Washington, Seattle.

Rappaport, Roy A.

1968   *Pigs for the Ancestors: Ritual in the Ecology of a New Guinea People.* New Haven:
        Yale University Press.

1971   The sacred in human evolution. *Annual Review of Ecology and Systematics*
        2:23–44.

1979   *Ecology, Meaning, and Religion.* Richmond, California: North Atlantic Books.

Redding, Richard W., Jr.

1981   *Decision-Making in Subsistence Herding of Sheep and Goats in the Middle East.*
        Ph.D. dissertation, Department of Anthropology, University of Michigan, Ann
        Arbor.

Relaciones Geográficas de Indias, Perú [1580s]

1965   Volumes edited by Marcos Jiménez de la Espada [1881–1897]. *Biblioteca de
        Autores Españoles*, vols. 183–185. Madrid: Ediciones Atlas.

Reynolds, Robert G.

1976   Linear settlement typology on the upper Grijalva River: The application of a
        Markovian model. In *The Early Mesoamerican Village*, edited by Kent V.
        Flannery, pp. 180–194. New York: Academic Press.

1986   An adaptive computer model for the evolution of plant collecting and early
        agriculture in the eastern Valley of Oaxaca. In *Guilá Naquitz: Archaic Foraging
        and Early Agriculture in Oaxaca, Mexico*, edited by Kent V. Flannery,
        pp. 439–500. Orlando, Florida: Academic Press.

Rick, John W.

1980   *Prehistoric Hunters of the High Andes.* New York: Academic Press.

Rindos, David

1986   The evolution of the capacity for culture: Sociobiology, structuralism, and
        cultural selectionism. *Current Anthropology* 27 (4):315–332.

Rostworowski de Diez Canseco, María

1981   La voz parcialidad en su contexto en los siglos XVI y XVII. In *Etnohistoria y
        Antropología Andina: Segunda Jornada del Museo Nacional de Historia*, compiled
        by Amalia Castelli, Marcia Koth de Paredes, and Mariana Mould de Pease,
        pp. 35–45. Lima: Centro de Proyección Cristiana.

1988   *Conflicts over Coca Fields in XVIth-Century Peru.* Studies in Latin American
        Ethnohistory & Archaeology, vol. 4, edited by Joyce Marcus. Memoirs of the
        Museum of Anthropology, University of Michigan, no. 21. Ann Arbor.

Roughgarden, Jonathan

1983   Competition and theory in community ecology. *The American Naturalist*
        122:583–601.

Rowe, John Howland

1946   Inca culture at the time of the Spanish Conquest. In *Handbook of South American Indians*, vol. 2, edited by Julian H. Steward, pp. 183–330. *Bureau of American Ethnology Bulletin* 143. Washington, D.C.: Smithsonian Institution.

Sahlins, Marshall D.

1976a   *Culture and Practical Reason*. Chicago: University of Chicago Press.

1976b   *The Use and Abuse of Biology*. Ann Arbor: University of Michigan Press.

Santa Cruz Pachacuti Yamqui Salcamaygua, Joan de

1879   Relación de antigüedades deste reyno del Pirú [1613]. *Tres Relaciones de Antigüedades Peruanas*, edited by Marcos Jiménez de la Espada, pp. 229–328. Madrid.

1963   Relación de antigüedades deste reyno del Perú [1613]. *Crónicas Peruanas de Interés Indígena*, Biblioteca de Autores Españoles, Tomo 209, pp. 281–319. Madrid.

Santo Tomás, Fray Domingo de

1951a   *Lexicón o Vocabulario de la Lengua General del Perú Llamada Quichua* [1560]. Edición facsimilar, con un prólogo por Raúl Porras Barrenechea. Lima: Universidad Nacional Mayor de San Marcos.

1951b   *Grammática o Arte de la Lengua General de los Indios de los Reynos del Perú* [1560]. Edición facsimilar, con un prólogo por Raúl Porras Barrenechea. Lima: Universidad Nacional Mayor de San Marcos.

Schoener, T. W.

1983   Field experiments on interspecific competition. *The American Naturalist* 122:240–285.

Simberloff, Daniel

1983   Competition theory, hypothesis testing, and other community ecological buzzwords. *The American Naturalist* 122:626–635.

Skar, Harald Olav

1982   *The Warm Valley People: Duality and Land Reform among the Quechua Indians of Highland Peru*. Oslo Studies in Social Anthropology no. 2, Ethnographic Museum, University of Oslo, Norway (distributed by Columbia University Press, New York).

Soto Ruiz, Clodoaldo

1976   *Diccionario Quechua: Ayacucho-Chanca*. Lima: Instituto de Estudios Peruanos.

Stephens, David W., and John R. Krebs

1986   *Foraging Theory*. Princeton, New Jersey: Princeton University Press.

Torero, Alfredo

1964   Los dialectos quechuas. *Anales Científicos de la Universidad Agraria* 2 (4):446–478.

Tosi, Joseph, Jr.

1960   *Zonas de Vida Natural en el Perú*. Lima: Instituto de Ciencias Agrícolas, Organización de Estados Americanos.

Trivers, R.

1971   The evolution of reciprocal altruism. *Quarterly Review of Biology* 46:35–57.

Tschopik, Harry, Jr.

1946   The Aymara. In *Handbook of South American Indians*, edited by Julian H. Steward, vol. 2, pp. 501–573. *Bureau of American Ethnology Bulletin* 143. Washington, D.C.: Smithsonian Institution.

Weberbauer, Augusto

1945   *El Mundo Vegetal de los Andes Peruanos: Estudio Fitogeográfico*. Lima: Ministerio de Agricultura (first edition 1911, under the title *Die Pflanzenwelt der Peruanischen Anden*. Leipzig: Wilhelm Engelmann).

Webster, Steven Sebastian

1972   *The Social Organization of a Native Andean Community*. Ph.D. dissertation, Department of Anthropology, University of Washington, Seattle.

1973   Native pastoralism in the south Andes. *Ethnology* 12:115–133.

1977   Kinship and affinity in a native Quechua community. In *Andean Kinship and Marriage*, edited by Ralph Bolton and Enrique Mayer, pp. 28–59. Special Publication no. 7, American Anthropological Association. Washington, D.C.

Williams, George C.

1966   *Adaptation and Natural Selection: A Critique of Some Current Evolutionary Thought*. Princeton: Princeton University Press.

Wilson, E. O.

1978   *On Human Nature*. Cambridge, Massachusetts: Harvard University Press.

Wilson, Paul, and William L. Franklin

1985   Male group dynamics and inter-male aggression of guanacos in southern Chile. *Zeitschrift für Tierpsychologie* 69:305–328.

Wing, Elizabeth S.

1977   Animal domestication in the Andes. In *The Origins of Agriculture*, edited by Charles A. Reed, pp. 837–859. The Hague: Mouton.

n.d.   Faunal remains from sites between 2000 and 3000 meters. To appear in a future volume of *Prehistory of the Ayacucho Basin, Peru*, edited by Richard S. MacNeish. Ann Arbor: University of Michigan Press.

Wynne-Edwards, V. C.

1962   *Animal Dispersion in Relation to Social Behavior*. New York: Hafner.

Zárate, Agustín de

1853   *Historia del Descubrimiento y Conquista de la provincia del Perú* . . . [1555]. Madrid.

1947   *Historia del Descubrimiento y Conquista de la Provinica del Perú* . . . [1555]. Biblioteca de Autores Españoles 26:459–574. Madrid.

Zeder, Melinda A.

1985   *Urbanism and Animal Exploitation in Southwest Highland Iran, 3400–1500 B.C.* Ph.D. dissertation, Department of Anthropology, University of Michigan.

Zeigler, Bernard P.

1976   *Theory of Modeling and Simulation*. New York: Wiley.

Zuidema, R. Tom

1977   The Inca kinship system: A new theoretical view. In *Andean Kinship and Marriage*, edited by Ralph Bolton and Enrique Mayer, pp. 240–281. Special Publication no. 7, American Anthropological Association. Washington, D.C.

Zuidema, R. Tom, and Ulpiano Quispe

1967   Un viaje a dios en la comunidad de Warkaya. *Wamani*, Órgano de la Asociación Peruana de Antropólogos, Filia-Ayacucho, Año II (2):109–116. Ayacucho.

Index